THE BEST
SHORT
PLAYS

*By* MARGARET MAYORGA

# THE
# BEST SHORT PLAYS
## OF 1953-1954

Edited by
MARGARET MAYORGA

DODD, MEAD & COMPANY
NEW YORK                    1954

PRINTED IN THE UNITED STATES OF AMERICA
BY THE VAIL-BALLOU PRESS, INC., BINGHAMTON, N. Y.

# PREFACE

American theatre enterprises, in the 1953–1954 season, have shown a burgeoning of activity not unlike that of the grasses that bloom in the spring. Everywhere, in summer festivals, in round theatres, in radio's introduction of trans-Atlantic music and plays, in television's experiments, and even within the traditional four stage walls, there are signs of great forces at work. In this country, we are used to experiencing great forces at work, but to discover them—at last—in the theatre is cheering.

This editor would need to be a many-legged, mosaic-eyed and tireless creature just to view the total and complicated scene that now emerges; but more than thirty years of study of dramatic arts leave me with the feeling that the climate is changing. To conservatives who are happy only within gracious drawing-rooms, the climate may seem to be worsening, now that living, dining, cooking, and a seat at the theatre all try to occupy the same place, and frequently, at the same time. But let's face forward: only the Yankee Stadium and Madison Square Garden could accommodate a small television audience. Many people think that the fireside armchair is an improvement on the seats in the arenas and in the theatres.

But changes are apparent, also, in habits other than seating arrangements. In fact, the audience is demonstrating that it can get up and go great distances when something unusual and attractive is offered by the theatre, such as a historical pageant, a dance theatre, a tent opera. From California, Colorado, Virginia, the Carolinas, and northeasterly to Connecticut and Massachusetts, dramatic festivals of many kinds are coming alive.

In June, for instance, Brandeis University at Waltham, Massachusetts, offered something new, a festival of creative arts in the comic spirit. It would have been attraction enough to offer

v

dramatic comedy and tap dance on the same stage, but Brandeis' humor developed from early opera of Pergolesi, through Saul Steinberg's art and Al Capp's comic strips and Fred Allen's deadpan wit, to the modern dramatic reading, and the Lemonade Opera Company. The weather itself was prankish. The temperature called for fur coats and winter underwear; but while two thousand people in the amphitheatre shivered and sighed for a non-existent hot coffee, they shook with laughter at everything from Fred Allen's description of how he majored in adolescence at a Boston college to the Lemonade Opera's American version of Francis Poulenc's comic opera, *Les Mamelles de Tiresias,* superbly executed musically under Leonard Bernstein, charmingly set by Raoul Pene du Bois, with Max Leavitt giving a masterful direction of the whole. In fact, not since the production of *The Man Who Married a Dumb Wife* (about the time of the first World War) have New Yorkers been privileged to see, within their environs, as scintillating and expert a play in the vein of French comedy. *Les Mamelles de Tiresias* was rated, by those who saw it more than once, a milestone along the way of dramatic festivals.

There were more festivals, later, to point the way forward, notably the dance at Connecticut College for Women, and at Jacob's Pillow, Massachusetts, when the Mormon children came East.

About that time, the summer temperature not only began to catch up with expectations, but even to surpass them, and it made good business for the rural theatres with air-conditioning units. It must have been those days which rendered writers and producers too inert to move a muscle which stirred their dreams and ambitions for the 1953–1954 season, because by October, radio and television almost burst its buttons with a flock of good works.

As my readers know, I am no Pollyanna about theatre business; there are many aspects of it that I consider unnecessary evils. But neither can I subscribe to the currently popular society of the ever-loaded sock, because I believe in giving credit when it is due. Truly, there was more than one Sunday in October when it would have been a dour customer who could not arrange a day's profitable entertainment and nurture for himself, simply by moving a few dials in a chosen direction. If I had not kept an accurate check on it, I might now have a tendency to think it had been too good to be true. But here, item by item, dialing back and forth from TV to FM to AM, was the way one member of the audience spent a very satisfying day, stretched out on a lounge, in the modern American theatre.

Noon  FM,  WNYC—Music Festival from France

12.30         WNBC—"The Eternal Light" drama

1 PM        WNYC—"The Ways of Mankind" drama, followed by British Weekly and U.S. News Reports

2 PM          —(a brief respite for some food)

2.30  FM,  WCBS—N.Y. Philharmonic Symphony, for a while

3 PM        WNYC—Theatre Seminar

4 PM  FM,  WQXR—Sunday Symphony, for a while

5 PM  TV, 2     —"Omnibus," staying for the entire show

6.30         WNBC—"Star Playhouse"

7.30 to 9 PM    —(time out for preparation of something once called Sunday night tea, but now with background music from FM, WNYC)

9 PM TV, 2 and 4—Taking 15 minutes each, and staying with the winner until 9.30

9.30         WNBC—"Theatre Royal"

10 PM FM, WQXR—High Fidelity Music

11 PM       —News

11.15       WNBC—U.N. Story

(And to bed! Wakened after midnight by a field mouse digging for a winter home in my wall, I turned the radio on loud to scare him off, and found myself in the middle of a musical piece new to me, FM, WNYC. It lasted for two hours,

while I was torn between curiosity and slumber, and a growing fascination for the composition. About 3 AM, I learned
that it was Mahler's Ninth Symphony; by that time I had
become a Mahler fan, thanks to a field mouse which did
not like music, and a program, "While the City Sleeps,"
directed to those who do.)

I cite this personal day to show that the American theatre, in
certain areas, exhibits strength and to spare, at least sometimes. Not all Sundays equal that one in October.

It is wise, therefore, for audiences to check the newspaper
regularly for comparative statistics: including who is married
to whom, and who is still circulating in the flesh. The miracle
of television recently delivered the astounding feat of present-
ing Charles Coburn in three different roles within a single
hour, while Mr. Coburn was no doubt seated with me in the
audience dialing madly back and forth among his various spir-
its. This kind of video can be really confusing, even to the
young viewers who may know all about the status of television's couples.

For the majority, American theatre is just beginning. If it
wrenches the eyes of old-timers to have to look at the theatre
on the stereographic plane, is the strain worse than it was
from the old peanut gallery? Granting that some of us hold
many nostalgic memories going back to the days of the carriage
trade, and that there never will be any substitute for the thrill
of the live actor before a live audience in a play that sparks, it
seems to me that the time has come to rebuild our edifices and
our audiences, to give everybody in America time to catch up
with the kind of drama that those born near Broadway have
known all their lives.

We are fortunate to have the Ford Foundation helping to
set standards at this time, for the Foundation has estimated
the audience intelligence as higher than fourteen years. In
their second year of theatrical enterprise, the Ford apprentices
have shown that they can out-gouge Shakespeare's *Lear,* and

undo the carefully tied bows about the bed-time stories of the bees and the flowers. Some of their ballet presentations have been especially creative, adding real new dimensions to the theatre. In their methods in general, they have demonstrated that there are things that can be done effectively on television that could not be done the same way in any other medium. They accomplish all this and more within the framework of a program slanted to the quiet family Sunday evening, but shyly looking forward to broad horizons for everybody.

Are some of my readers thinking, "What about the kind of plays that are being done on television? Can something good be said about them, too?" The answer is again a matter of perspective, for the plots that are old to old-timers will fortunately soon look stale to the bright new generation, as well. I doubt that the youngsters will tamely accept as much pulp on television as their parents did on radio. Some sponsors have already canceled "them papers." In the meantime, many a crumbly television concoction is being held together for the length of the program by the superb acting of a veteran actor or actress, bringing to the new medium the skill and command that everybody applauds in any kind of theatre.

But obviously, a performer can do more with a good play than with a shoddy one. And writers might well ponder the words of Eva LeGallienne, speaking before an audience of students this year, saying that it took her more than two decades of study to become an actress. Young playwrights, do you think you can learn to be dramatists in any shorter time?

Along with the privileges and social responsibilities, and the necessity of conveying knowledge through action—all of which must be learned—a good playwright must also study the American language. Language has frequently been tossed about on stage as irreverently as so much garbage in masticating machines; but an earnest writer will try to find his way through the many controversies which now enmesh our language, so that when he speaks his piece, it will be his alone. This is usually the most elusive skill for a playwright to acquire, and frequently it is decisive. Certainly, it has become a deciding factor in the choices of plays that have gone annually into THE BEST ONE-ACT PLAYS, and now: THE BEST SHORT PLAYS.

Margaret Mayorga

Long Island,
January, 1954.

# CONTENTS

# THE LITTLE FLAW OF ERNESTO LIPPI

By

## LEE SCHAEFER

*(Published here for the first time)*

# THE LITTLE FLAW OF ERNESTO LIPPI

## CAST

### (In Order of Their Appearance)

ERNESTO LIPPI
LENA
ANTONIO
JOSEPH
ROSE
MARIA
MRS. FIORI
MRS. CAPASSE
MRS. SANTANELLI

TIME: The present.
PLACE: Brooklyn, N.Y.

# LEE SCHAEFER

Lee Schaefer, who was born in Frederic, Maryland, and raised in Norfolk, Virginia, is a first-year student at the Yale Drama School, and *The Little Flaw of Ernesto Lippi* is her first short play.

She is not without experience, however. She is married to a writer, whom she met while working as a reporter on a Virginia newspaper, and she has three daughters. For several years, they lived on a Virginia farm, breeding black angus cattle, then moved to Connecticut so that the children might be closer to schools.

Her previously published works include two children's short stories and about eight poems to "Child Life," as well as several articles which appeared in a Connecticut magazine.

# THE LITTLE FLAW OF ERNESTO LIPPI

## SCENE 1

*This is a tiny living room of a front apartment in Brooklyn. It is an Italian home. Italian music, played upon a mandolin, is heard faintly off stage, as if down the street. It is in the early morning hours. The apartment is lit only by flashing neon signs reflected into the apartment from business establishments across the street. There is a sofa, a round table, straight chair, and a rocker.*

*The room appears empty. There is someone sleeping on the couch, but this is not apparent. As the music fades,* ERNESTO LIPPI *enters the room from the bedroom, beyond. He is a short, chubby and endearing Italian of about fifty-five, with grey hair and a full black mustache, and he is dressed in pajamas and is barefoot. He approaches the couch and peers, and the sleeper there is noticeable.*

ERNESTO. [*In a loud whisper.*] Mama? [*He puts out a hand, but brings it back without touching her.*] Mama! [*He shakes her gently.*] Mama! Wake up!

LENA. [*Coming awake with a start.*] What do you want?

ERNESTO. [*Extending a hand in a pleading gesture.*] Mama . . .

LENA. [*Angrily.*] Go back to bed. You will catch cold. [*She settles down again.*]

ERNESTO. [*Anguished.*] Mama! It is the middle of June! [*He stands there desolate.*] I am cold nowhere but in my heart.

LENA. [*Heaving over and turning her back to him.*] Don't talk foolishness, Papa. Go back to bed. [*She tugs at the covers, trying to cover her rear portion. Her feet are exposed.*]

ERNESTO. [*Tenderly covering her.*] I don't want to go back to

5

bed. [*He fidgits, then reaches out and shakes her again, gently.*] Mama! *You* go back to bed, Mama. If you don't want to share the bed with me, *you* go back to bed. I will use the sofa.

LENA. [*Rising majestically and dragging the bedclothes close around her. She is a small, gray-haired woman, with a nervous charm. She is dressed in a high-necked white flannel nightgown, and her hair hangs down.*] I will get up. If you do not want me to rest, I will get up.

[*When* LENA *becomes agitated she always begins pinning up her hair, and whenever she becomes overwrought it comes tumbling loose.*]

ERNESTO. [*Dropping triumphantly upon the sofa.*] Tonight *I* sleep on the sofa!

LENA. [*Stumbling among the bedclothes.*] Then *I* sleep in the rocking chair.

[*She sits in the rocker.*]

ERNESTO. [*Wailing.*] Mama! Why can't you go to sleep in the bed?

LENA. Because I do not desire to sleep in the bed.

[*She rocks brusquely. All is quiet for a bit. The music comes again and fades again.*]

ERNESTO. When the children were at home, there was not this empty quiet.

LENA. [*Scornfully.*] It is the middle of the night. And why shouldn't it be quiet?

ERNESTO. It is too quiet in the daytime, too. [*Rising and pacing.*] Maria should bring the babies more often. [LENA *rocks.*] Is it for nothing we are their grandparents? [LENA *rocks.*] Maria should bring *our* grandchildren more often. [LENA *rocks.*] *Why doesn't she bring them more often?*

LENA. [*Stops rocking.*] What *is* the matter with you? She brings them every Sunday . . .

ERNESTO. That is not what I mean.

LENA. . . . And that great big husband of hers, who only knows how to eat a great deal and go to sleep afterward. [*Rocks again vigorously.*] Aie! He sleeps after *every* meal!

ERNESTO. He does not sleep every time, Mama. He does not

sleep at noontime when he is working on building houses. He would lose his job over that.

LENA. Hah! Men! They are impossible!

[*Pause. Only the sound of rocking.*]

ERNESTO. Perhaps if you were not so angry with our Salvador for marrying the little widow, *they* might visit us sometime.

LENA. Hah!

[*She throws aside the bedclothes and stands in her nightgown; then she bends and picks up the bedclothes and folds them and lays them somewhere. The music is there again, faintly, and then it fades.*]

ERNESTO. [*Softly, plaintively.*] Why are you so angry with me, Mama? Why do you not sleep in the bed? I have asked you *over* and *over*.

LENA. Hah!

ERNESTO. [*With great dignity.*] Please do not "Hah" me. I ask you simply a question and you *never* give me an answer. . . . Is it because Antonio does not live at home any longer? [*Pacing.*] Did *I* send him away? No! He is a young man and wants to live his own way. . . . If he wants to get married, can I help it? [*More quietly.*] Or is it now that all the children are grown you have time to look at me, and find you do not like me after all? [*He stops short at the thought.*] I forbid it! [*He shakes his fist at her back.*] Mama! *You should talk to me!*

LENA. [*Swinging to him, her hands on her hips.*] Hah! Listen to him now. He yells now! Listen to him. [*Lowering her voice to a hiss.*] But does he yell in the mornings? No! No more he doesn't. And why? Why is the little Papa so good before his breakfast now? Is it maybe something else he is up to? Yes?

ERNESTO. [*Eagerly, coming to her.*] Aie! That is what I mean, Mama. Tell me what it is you hate me for! At night I cannot sleep, and I dream. And I go to confession, but not even with Father Domingo helping can I uncover my sin against you.

LENA. [*In terrible derision.*] Sst! When a man changes his ways after so long a time, he is up to something. [*Practically spitting.*] Do I look so stupid?

ERNESTO. [*Still trying.*] No, no, no, Mama. Of course not. But *what* am I up to?

LENA. [*Cutting him with a deadly look.*] Hah!
[*Drawing herself up in high distain and holding her nightgown away from possible contamination, she marches regally into the bedroom, and slams the door. Music.* ERNESTO *walks slowly to the windows and looks out, as the neon lights fade and the stage is left in darkness.*]


## SCENE 2

*The music picks up the tempo of hammering a steady beat. Light comes up on a shoe repair shop. There is a sign reading,* LIPPI BROS. SHOE REPAIRS. JOSEPH, *a wiry, medium-sized Italian, about sixty, rather dour and short tempered, is seated on a long bench surrounded by shoes, and is hammering on one.*
ANTONIO *is a young Italian, big and good-looking. He is draped dolefully over the counter. The music fades.*


ANTONIO. Damn the female of the species! Damn their processes of thinking! Their thinking be damned . . . their thinking, hah! Women can't think. They're all just a bundle of instincts, and the most predominant instinct is fear, fear, fear.

JOSEPH. [*Not looking up.*] You learn some big words since you put on long pants. But where is your Papa this morning?

ANTONIO. From the day they are first laid in the cradle, they yell. And what for? Because they are afraid. Afraid they won't get fed, afraid they won't be loved, or rocked, or dressed, or some other damn fool thing. They're afraid the cradle will fall, that the roof will cave in, that the sun will come pinballing out of the sky . . .

JOSEPH. Baby boys cry, too—sometime. And I ask, where again this morning is your Papa?

ANTONIO. But *they* learn, Uncle Joe; they learn. But girls! What do they do? They just turn into bigger bundles of fear, that's all. Afraid of ants and cockroaches, anything with spidery legs. They scream at a mouse and shiver at ordinary frogs and lizards carried by curious little boys. They have nightmares full of tigers and little green men . . .

JOSEPH. When I was a little boy I dreamed about a *big* green man. He frightened *me*. And I am going to frighten your Papa when he comes.

ANTONIO. And when they get bigger, their fears get bigger. Then they fear old men with money, and little boys with rocks, and they are afraid all the men in between will ask them—or won't ask them. They are afraid of not finding love, and afraid of love *when* they find it. They have ways—ahh, they have ways of reasoning about love that would drive a man to distraction. That *can* drive a man to distraction! When a woman attempts to reason, it becomes a twisting of the simple into the complex . . .

JOSEPH. I could follow you better on the *little* words.

ANTONIO. This—this female—*wrangler* with her so-called logical approach *and* her sacred intuition, is the most frightening thing God has ever created. It's the God's truth. He created them; maybe he can understand them, but I, a mere humble, a simple and uncomplicated man who yearns for love in a simple uncomplicated fashion, and who longs to give love, in a simple and uncomplicated fashion . . . I say, take them away from me! *Take them away!*

JOSEPH. I see no one after you. You are safe enough. Be calm. [ERNESTO *enters the shop in a sorrowful way. He practically limps over to the coat-rack and takes off his little black coat and puts on a leather apron.*]

A-a-h! Aha! You finally decide it is time to fix shoes again? It is a wonder that you have come at all. Each day it is getting worse and worse. Am I to do all the work by myself? How can we keep the business if you always are so late? What is the matter with you? Did we not decide that we would have a business together? That we would work side by side . . .

ERNESTO. [*Sadly.*] Good morning, everybody.

ANTONIO. Hello, Papa.

JOSEPH. Good morning? It is good night, more like it!

ERNESTO. It may rain. [*The day is very sunny.*] I think we

maybe might have a bad storm this day. [*He sighs heavily.*]
Perhaps the lightning may even strike.
[*He stands looking drearily out of the window.*]

JOSEPH. Hah! You and your son are both suffering some sort
of illness, it seems. While I must sit and do all the work!

ERNESTO. [*Absently.*] Tonio? You are ill? What is it that makes
you feel sick, Tonio?

ANTONIO. Women!

ERNESTO. [*Preoccupied.*] Yes—yes. I think it maybe will rain—
and thunder very much.

JOSEPH. It could not be more gloomy outside than it is in here.

ANTONIO. [*Rising on his feet.*] She says that I'm always doing
this or that—that I have this fault or that fault—that I did not
love her yesterday the same as I loved her the day before—
that I love her more today, so that what about yesterday? Why
didn't I love her the same yesterday? She asks me will I love
her tomorrow the same as today, and if I say, "Of course," she
answers me back, "Why can't your love grow?" But if I say
that I will love her even better tomorrow, then she will want to
know just *what* did my love amount to today. [*With an extreme
and wild gesture.*] I'll yell at her. I'll tell her how she reasons in
a circle—that she is illogical—that she is splitting hairs—that
she magnifies the unimportant and ignores the basic facts—that
she is narrow and fanatical and confined within the limitations
of fear. Goddam! I'll tell her a lot more.
[*He exits.*]

ERNESTO. [*Sits. He does not seem to have heard* ANTONIO *or
be aware that he has left.*] It is a terrible thing.

JOSEPH. That Antonio is ill? Or that you are so late coming?

ERNESTO. It is a very terrible thing to have a woman like my
Lena angry. She will say *nothing* to me.

JOSEPH. Well—well—is that bad? For a woman *not* to talk?
Why do you sit and brood like a miserable wet hen?

ERNESTO. [*Morosely.*] I cannot expect you to understand. A
man who lives alone is different from a man who lives with a
woman.

JOSEPH. So?

ERNESTO. When they do not talk to you it is worse, much worse, than when they talk too much.

JOSEPH. Hah! They fix you either way.

[*He strides up and down.*]

ERNESTO. And then she will not sleep in the bed. [JOSEPH *stops dead. He does not look at* ERNESTO, *but stares transfixed into the audience.*] I have told her over and over she must use the bed—that I will sleep on the sofa. I have even got to the sofa first, but she will only sit on the chair by the window. [*His voice rises.*] I cannot sleep then on the sofa, if she will not use the bed! [*Defeated.*] And she will not. Then I go back to the bed, so that at least she may rest on the sofa. [*Now growing slightly hysterical and beginning to rock back and forth.*] But then, if I go back to the bed, I am so miserable that *I* cannot sleep and must sit in the rocking chair all night.

[*He ends on a high wail.*]

JOSEPH. [*Softly.*] My God!

ERNESTO. [*Almost sobbing.*] There I am, rocking all night . . .

JOSEPH. [*Still awestruck.*] It is terrible. Soon you will both go mad.

ERNESTO. [*Looking up at him wildly.*] What do you think? Look at me! I am afraid I am mad, already. I dream—terrible dreams. Voices come at me. And in between such dreamings, I sit in the rocking chair—or on the sofa—and long to shake my Lena, to make her say what is wrong. [*His voice rises again.*] She must not treat me this way! [*Shaking his fist at* JOSEPH.] I forbid it!

JOSEPH. [*Soothing him.*] It is nothing, nothing at all. [*Sitting and patting* ERNESTO.] Now, we got to figure this out systematic. [ERNESTO *wipes his eyes and nods and snuffs.*] Umm, you say you have been to confession?

ERNESTO. Yes, Joseph.

JOSEPH. Hmm! You say after this nothing has changed?

ERNESTO. No, Joseph.

JOSEPH. Ahh, you say you cannot think of any par-tic-u-lar-ly *large* sin you have made against Lena?

ERNESTO. No, no, no, Joseph!

[*He sinks his head, in despair, between his hands.*]

JOSEPH. [*Snapping his fingers.*] Come now! Sit up! To business! And you say that she will not tell you of any? [*He holds up his hand to stop* ERNESTO *from answering.*] And you say this has been going on long enough? Now. Ah-hem.

ERNESTO. [*Timidly.*] Yes, Joseph?

JOSEPH. [*Waving at him, irritably.*] We must have one clue. At least one. How is a man to know how to begin? [*He goes behind the counter.*] Maybe a little wine will help us to think more clearly. [*He pours out two glasses; they sip.*] Now. You say she was talking to you once and it was something about a shouting?

ERNESTO. Yes. And once I came home and she was talking to a friend, and I heard the friend ask, "And how is dear Ernesto?" And my Lena said, very quiet and like she hated me, "Oh, he is well enough, but he does not shout in the mornings any more." And the friend made a little noise in her throat and said, "Oh." You would think it was my funeral they spoke of— or that I had caused a murder. It is terrible. I can understand none of it.

JOSEPH. [*Moodily.*] And things will be no better when you go home drunk from the wine tonight. [ERNESTO *nods drearily. They drink again.*] I cannot understand about the shouting. What has it all to do with the shouting?

ERNESTO. I do not know. Besides, I never did really shout so much.

JOSEPH. [*At the breaking point.*] This shouting! It mixes me up. I do not understand anything about this shouting.

ERNESTO. [*Obstinately.*] It was never very true, anyway. My Lena made it up all out of her head. The women say when they visit together [*He rises and speaks in an extreme falsetto.*] "My husband does not clean off his shoes when he enters the house." [*He pretends to be scandalized.*] "No! Well, *my* husband is a fool about women!" [*Disparaging them both with a hands-out gesture and a shrug.*] "Oh, that is *nothing.* My husband spends all his money on himself." [*Bitterly.*] All of them talking, talking, and never a good word for any husband. Only faults. And then my Lena says, [*Mimicking* LENA.] My husband is very bad-tempered in the mornings. He is always shouting." [*He sits in despair.*]

JOSEPH. [*Staring.*] I do not understand.

ERNESTO. [*Snippishly.*] You needn't look at me so! You do not know what it is like to live with a woman.

JOSEPH. That is right. That is very right.

ERNESTO. And then I did do some little shouting for her before breakfast. Sometimes I could do very well with it, so that Lena would have something to tell to her friends at their next getting-together. [*Appealing to* JOSEPH.] But I am really a peace loving man, Joseph, and I have not exhausted myself in that manner for a long time. [*Wistfully.*] Lena is only noticing because the children are all grown-up and the place is so quiet.

JOSEPH. [*Raising his hand as though bestowing a benediction.*] Ernesto, my brother . . .

[ANTONIO *enters swiftly. He stalks into the shop and confronts the two men in an aggressive stance.*]

ANTONIO. Hellsfire and damnation! Do you know what it is? I have suffered through a hassle with her and do you know what it is? What's the matter with all women?

JOSEPH. Yes. You have already told us.

ANTONIO. [*Relaxing. Going to them and speaking intimately.*] They *have* to find something wrong. They are afraid to love all the way, so they save aside something . . . They find something wrong with us and that gives them an edge. You get me?

ERNESTO. [*Irritably.*] We don't understand what you are talking about, Tonio.

JOSEPH. We could all get drunk.

ANTONIO. Oh, my God! Look, it's like this: you take a man. When he loves, he just loves and that's that; but a woman? My God, it's the truth, they just have to get it all involved. It's a crime what they do to something so elemental, so simple. They have a million ways of testing and examining love, and when they do finally decide to take a chance on it, they want a certain guarantee of safety. There must be that quota of safety—

an escape hatch, sort of. So they find something wrong with the guy. They hold it up and polish it and keep it always in sight, so that they won't have to love him all the way. Y'see? They're afraid *all* the time!

JOSEPH. [*Dully.*] If I were fool enough to love a woman, I would certainly not want something *wrong* with her.

ANTONIO. But that's the point! It doesn't work that way for men!

ERNESTO. [*Standing as though seeing a vision.*] My Lena *wants* me to shout?

ANTONIO. The fools! The fools! They exist in a world of cowardliness. [*To* ERNESTO.] Papa, I will never be fool enough to get married. You can tell Mama I remain a bachelor.
[*He exits with great dignity.*]

ERNESTO. [*Unaware of his words or his departure.*] Joseph, my Lena *wants* me to shout!

JOSEPH. Well, shout—then! It is that simple, simpleton. Hokum pokus. Magic. Just like that—your Lena will be yours again. Yah! Women!

ERNESTO. [*In despair again.*] But I don't understand.

JOSEPH. [*Throwing his arms to heaven.*] Why does everybody have to understand everybody? [*More quietly.*] Look—don't use your head! With women maybe it works better. Here. [*Holding up his glass of wine.*] Drink to the shouting! [ERNESTO *smiles weakly and holds up his glass.*] Skoal! [*They drink, and* JOSEPH *whirls and throws his glass against the floor and counter, breaking it.*] There! Just like they do in the movie pi'tures.
[ERNESTO *beams. He throws his glass after* JOSEPH's. *The lights black out.*]


SCENE 3

*The lights come up on the apartment, the same afternoon. The crashing of glass in the previous scene is used as a bridge to this scene. Four women are seated at a card table. They are* MARIA, MRS. FIORI, MRS. CAPASSE, MRS. SANTANELLI. *All are rather heavy-set matrons, except that* MARIA *is a bit younger than the others.*

ROSE *is combing her hair before a mirror. She is a young girl, about eighteen, very pretty, with long black hair.* LENA *is caught in mid-stride, coming from the kitchen. She has just dropped a glass dish of candy, and the dish has broken with a crash.*

MARIA. [*Jumping up.*] Oh, Mama! Your best piece of cut glass!

LENA. [*Swooping to gather up the pieces.*] Oo, Maria, my best piece of glass that Papa gave me!

THE WOMEN.

What happened?

Did something get dropped?

My, my, Lena, was it your pretty glass piece?

Now, ain't that a shame?

ROSE. Mama Lippi, use this dish! [*Picking up a dish from the table before her.*] Here, put the candy here!

LENA. [*Getting up stiffly.*] I been so nervous all today because I got no sleep last night. My Ernesto was prowling half the night without his slippers. . . . Oh, my pretty dish! . . . I been so upset—and I didn't sleep.

MARIA. [*Sitting again.*] Never mind, Mama.

LENA. [*Bustling off.*] I go make the coffee.

MRS. SANTANELLI. [*Aggressively.*] Well, is anybody going to play cards?

[*They start to play. It is quiet except for the slap of cards.* ROSE *still combs her hair.*]

MRS. FIORI. I hear you get married, Rosie—to Mrs. Lippi's Antonio.

ROSE. [*Tossing her head.*] Today, I'm not so sure—after the way he acted this morning. He'll have to change his ways.

[LENA *appears at kitchen doorway.*]

LENA. My Antonio's got nice ways, Rosie.

ROSE. I know, Mama Lippi, but . . .

LENA. My Antonio is okay.

[*She huffs out of sight again.*]

MRS. SANTANELLI. Pay attention!

[*The card game resumes. It is quiet except for the slap of cards.*]

MRS. FIORI. [*Softly.*] Are you *really* wanting to get married, Rosie?

ROSE. Oh I suppose so, but . . .

MRS. SANTANELLI. I bid four.

MRS. FIORI. Why do you, Rosie?

ROSE. Well, because—because . . .

MRS. SANTANELLI. Because she's in love, you idiot! I bid . . .

MRS. CAPASSE. [*Sighing.*] Aie, we were all like that once upon a time.

MRS. FIORI. Yes, yes. But it is a snare and a delusion. [*Gazing sadly at* ROSE.] A snare and a delusion.

MARIA. That's right. Just wait until you have four noisy kids like mine. Then you won't be in such a hurry to get married.

MRS. SANTANELLI. She'd better.

[LENA *enters with the coffee things. She sets them down.*]

ROSE. But, Maria, I thought you liked being married.

MRS. SANTANELLI. Is anyone going to play cards?

MARIA. I suppose, but let me warn you, Rosie, no man is what he seems before he gets you to go and get married.

LENA. Except my Antonio.

MARIA. Oh, Mama, he's no better than all the rest.

MRS. FIORI. That's right.

LENA. [*Rearing.*] Mrs. Fiori, you do not know my Antonio. I know my Antonio. What do you know about my Antonio?

MRS. SANTANELLI. [*Very loudly.*] Isn't anybody going to play cards?

MRS. FIORI. [*Almost in tears.*] It's not your Antonio I mean, Mrs. Lippi. No! It is just men that I mean. All men! My husband, I mean. My husband *reads* all the time. He used always to pay attention—but now he only reads. [*She snuffles into her handkerchief.*] He reads all the time—all the time.

[*There follows a slight silence, which* MARIA *breaks.*]

MARIA. Hah, that is nothing. At least he *sits* there. *My* husband [*She throws back her head and laughs roughly.*] my husband *sleeps!*

MRS. SANTANELLI. Cards, anybody?

MARIA. He sleeps and he sleeps and he sleeps.

LENA. Now, Maria, he is a good husband to you. [*Considering.*] But he does sleep too much. [*Warming up.*] Too much he sleeps. [*Warmer.*] Why, he sleeps after every meal! But now, you take my Ernesto . . .

MARIA. [*Loudly claiming the floor.*] I have never seen a man before so fond of bed!

MRS. SANTANELLI. Considering four children, it would seem so. [*A slight silence.*]

MRS. CAPASSE. Ah-hem! What do you think *my* husband does?

THE WOMEN. [*Staring at her in fascination.*] Wh-h-a-t?

MRS. CAPASSE. [*Enjoying the attention.*] Guess.

THE WOMEN. Oh, we can never! What does he do, Mrs. Capasse?

MRS. CAPASSE. [*Gleaming evilly.*] He belches!

THE WOMEN. [*Withdrawing in confusion.*] Oh-h!

MRS. CAPASSE. [*Proudly.*] He does. It's a filthy habit, don't you think?

MRS. FIORI. Well, my sister's husband [*She hesitates, then leans forward and whispers.*] swears!

MARIA. [*With a big laugh.*] Well, you girls are lucky! There's a big ape lives next door t'me and his wife says he won't clean off his feet for nobody when he comes inside. Not for God hi'self! [*She laughs again.*] He tracks mud all over the place, right after she's just finished cleaning up, too. That's awful, I think.

LENA. Oh, I don't know. Now, you take my Ernesto . . .

MRS. CAPASSE. [*Over-riding them all.*] Yes, sir—belches. Morning, noon and night, that's all he does. It's disgusting.

MRS. FIORI. [*To* ROSE.] You see, dearie? A snare and a delusion!

ROSE. [*Frantically.*] But—but—but . . .

LENA. [*Shrilly, above them all.*[ My ERNESTO SHOUTS!

THE WOMEN. [*Looking at her, entranced.*] Shouts?

LENA. [*Weakly, now.*] Yes. [*She sits.*] He shouts.

MARIA. Why, Mama, what do you mean? Papa used to be a little loud maybe, but it was only to wake himself up.

LENA. Well, whatever his reason, he does not do it any more.

And that is the trouble . . .

MRS. CAPASSE. Hmpf! I can't say that's up to belching.

MRS. FIORI. Nor swearing.

MRS. SANTANELLI. Oh, la, la, la.

MRS. CAPASSE. [*Aggressively.*] What do you mean, "La, la, la"?
I suppose your husband does something worse?

MRS. SANTANELLI. [*Mildly.*] He's dead and out of the way—
like the cards.

THE WOMEN.
Well, then!
It isn't fair for you to judge.
If you don't have one to live with . . .

MRS. SANTANELLI. I expect he had as many faults as yours—
living.

ROSE. [*Gently.*] Was there anything special, Mrs. Santanelli,
that he did?

MRS. SANTANELLI. Oh, it wasn't much. He used to grind his
teeth. That's all.

THE WOMEN. *Grind his teeth?*

MRS. SANTANELLI. [*Smiling to herself, remembering.*] When
he slept sound, he did. Whenever he worked real hard, he always
slept real sound. Then he'd grind his teeth. [*They all stare.
Loneliness touches her.*] Well, that's as bad as any of yours!
[*Glaring.*] It used to be terrible. Sounded like shucking corn.
[*Waving her hands with fervor.*] I tell you I used to wake up
and shake him out of the bed, so he would stop it.
[*They are impressed. They cluck with sympathy. She unob-
trusively takes a small handkerchief out of her dress and wipes
her eyes.*]

MRS. FIORI. [*Softly.*] A snare and a delusion.

LENA. [*Excitedly.*] Yes, but all of your husbands keep *doing*
these things?

THE WOMEN. Of course. It is terrible.

LENA. [*Beginning to sob into her handkerchief.*] But my
Ernesto does not.

MARIA. [*Alarmed.*] Mama!

LENA. [*Trying to control her weeping.*] The little Papa—the little Papa [*She throws up her head and faces them all bravely.*] he does not shout any more in the mornings. After twenty years he has *stopped* his shouting.

THE WOMEN. [*Like the air going out of a tire.*] Ah-h-h!

[LENA *collapses in a chair and puts her arms on the table and her head down on her arms, her shoulders shaking with small sobs. The ladies slowly rise and each one goes gently to* LENA *and touches her on the hair and files out of the apartment, down the steps and exits, while* MARIA *stands at her mother's side like a stern faced sentinel.*]

MRS. CAPASSE. [*Forebodingly, in the silence.*] When a man changes his ways after twenty years—he is up to something.

MRS. FIORI. [*In a ghostly voice.*] A snare and a delusion.

[*The lights gently dim. Faint music is heard. Then the lights go out altogether and the stage is dark.*]


## SCENE 4

*The music increases both in strength and tempo, until it is gay. A soft spotlight finds* ERNESTO *stage left, down front. He is whistling the tune of the background music. He executes a few little hops, supposed to be dance steps. The music fades.*

ERNESTO. [*Calling out.*] Wish me luck, Joseph! Tonight I try the shouting.

[*He skips and hops and whistles on, out of the spotlight, and disappears into darkness. Lights come up on the apartment, as* ERNESTO *appears in the apartment doorway. He calls.*]

Lena! Where is my dinner? [*He clears his throat, straightens himself and bellows.*] Do you hear? Where is my dinner?

[*He pounds on the card table, which holds several soiled cups and saucers.*] I am waiting!

[LENA *appears in the doorway to the kitchen, staring at him. He sees her and deliberately picks up a cup, holds it high and lets it crash to the floor, and turns to her with a smile.*]

I will break more, if you do not bring in my dinner!

[*He prowls up and down, stomping.*]

Look at me! I am the man here! I can kick things like this
[*He kicks at a chair.*] if I like to. I can yell for my dinner, too.
Do you hear me?
[LENA *approaches, and stalks him like a cat. He stands still. She
walks around him and regards him from all sides, and he watches
her proudly, standing arrogantly, but also curiously.*]
Do you like me? I am *shouting* now. Do you have my dinner
ready, Mama?

LENA. Hah! [*She pauses and speaks again into his face.*] Hah!
[*Closer, as though trying to knock him down with it.*] Hah!

ERNESTO. And why this "Hah"?

LENA. [*Circling him.*] So!

ERNESTO. *I am waiting!*

LENA. [*Half crouched, arms akimbo, head forward like a
snake.*] So now the little Papa is yelling again? He is returning
to us?

ERNESTO. [*Eagerly.*] I will bang around, too, in the mornings,
Mama. More even than this little bit I am now doing. You will
see. From this minute, I will shout so that you will like me again
and [*Waving his arms wide.*] all this miserable quiet will be
gone!

LENA. [*Still prowling.*] And he is all finished with the other
little something he was up to? And now he comes back to the
shouting? [*He nods eagerly.*] Maybe. [*Very sweetly.*] Maybe I
was not really certain before. Maybe I was just worried.
[*He watches her happily, but then she screams violently.*]
BUT NOW I AM CERTAIN!

ERNESTO. [*In absolute confusion.*] Mama, Mama . . .
[*She whirls and rushes to a corner, drags out an old beaten-up
suitcase, drags it back into the center of the room and throws
it on a chair; yanks it open.*]
Mama, I don't understand.

LENA. [*Hissing at him, as he gets in her way.*] Get out of my
way, *ladies boy!*
[*She flounces through to the bedroom. He follows to the door
and leans against the door jamb.*]

ERNESTO. But, Mama . . .

[*She returns with an arm-load of clothes, almost knocking him down, and begins throwing them into the suitcase.*]

LENA. Do not stand and look at me!

ERNESTO. [*Almost in a whisper.*] But Mama, where you are going?

LENA. [*Slamming the heavy suitcase shut and dragging it from the chair.*] To a clean house.

ERNESTO. [*Pathetically.*] To a clean house?

LENA. [*Dragging the suitcase to the door.*] Aie! Where I do not have to listen to your foolish shouting!

[*She exits.*]

ERNESTO. [*Screaming after her.*] Go, then! It is you should have the bad dreams!

[LENA *is heard thumping down the steps.*]

I will sleep smack in the middle of the bed. [*Calling, leaning through the apartment door.*] Mama! I won't dream! I'll sleep all night! [*Wildly.*] Mamaaa!

[*A quick blackout. No music.*]


## SCENE 5

*That night in the shop. No music. A small, soft spotlight finds* ERNESTO *standing dejectedly before the bench, with an old army blanket dragging from under one arm. He drops his blanket on the bench, and sits. Then he takes a can of beans, a fork, and a can opener out of his pocket, and opens the beans slowly. He wearily starts to eat, then speaks.*

ERNESTO. That's all right. It does not matter—at all. When she finds how thin I am growing [*He wipes his eyes on his sleeve.*] yes, someday she will be sorry. Someday they will come and find the body of Ernesto Lippi all pale and thin on his cot. [*He puts aside the beans and stretches himself out, and drags the blanket over him.*]

On this miserable bench, he will be stretched out, too weak

to rise—or to speak, even—unable to speak from starvation and neglect.

[*He sits up suddenly, reaches into his pocket and brings forth a handkerchief and blows.*]

She will be sorry, then. Her heart will be broken.

JOSEPH. [*Appears at the shop door, kicking it open.*] Open up, open up and give me happy greeting!

[*He enters, his arms full of groceries.*]

ERNESTO. What are you doing here, Joseph?

JOSEPH. So! You have been kicked out, eh? Why do you sit in the dark this way?

[*He turns on the lights.*]

ERNESTO. I have not been kicked out, Joseph. My Lena has left *me*.

JOSEPH. Ah ha! I thought maybe it could end this way, and so [*Holding up a bottle.*] I have returned with one excellent bottle of wine—and here in this small package, the pickled feet of a pig—and here cheese—and some fine bread. [ERNESTO *sits drearily.*] So? Must you look so dreary? You make me feel sick to look at you.

ERNESTO. [*Mournfully.*] I want my Lena to come home.

JOSEPH. By all that is holy! I would be happy to be free of such a woman. Even now, when you could at last sleep at night in peace, you play the fool and would sleep on a hard bench instead of in a fine wide bed. You have all the bed to yourself at last! [ERNESTO *moans.*] O my sacred grandmother! [*He calls on the angels.*] You see? You see this fellow, Ernesto? You see him with his weak soul hanging out? This weakling who calls himself a man! This worshiper of woman!

[LENA *comes on stage left, in spotlight.*]

ERNESTO. Hush. Hush, Joseph. Who is this coming?

[*He peers through the window, then rushes to the door. Arms wide, he calls.*]

Mama! You have come back to me!

LENA. [*Regarding him coldly.*] I am only coming back for my toothbrush. That only is why I am coming back.

[*She puts her nose in her arm, and walks away.*]

ERNESTO. [*Following.*] But Mama, you cannot go away from me all the night. We have never stayed away from each other so long.

[*They disappear into darkness, at stage right.* JOSEPH *leaves the shop, which then blacks out, and comes out to sit on the street curb.* ANTONIO *rushes on stage. The spotlight follows* JOSEPH *and* ANTONIO.]

ANTONIO. Joseph! Look at me! I am in love!

[*He passes* JOSEPH *in a bound, and disappears into the blackness, stage right. Lights go up on the apartment, revealing* ERNESTO *tagging* LENA, *and* ANTONIO *bursting in.*]

She loves me! I am the luckiest man in the world!

[*He collapses into a chair.*] My Rosie loves me!

[*He throws his arms over his head with joy.*]

ERNESTO. Go away, Tonio. I got to talk to Mama.

LENA. Tonio, have you been drinking again, too much? I am going to make you some black coffee.

[*She exits to the kitchen.*]

ANTONIO. Women—ah, women. [*He kisses his fingertips into the air.*] The sweetest thing in life is a woman. They are perfection, altogether. [*Growing poetic.*]

> Was ever there
> A rose so fair
> As my sweet Rosie standing there? Ahh!
> Rosie, sweet Rosie, come home with me now!
> The snow is not purer than thy tender brow.

ERNESTO. Tonio, please, I want to talk to Mama.

ANTONIO. Papa, have you ever noticed how a woman touches her hair? How she sits down with just a little—wiggle? How when they sit they cross their legs—so? Ahh, their legs! Is there anything lovelier on God's earth than a woman's legs? [*Hanging over the back of his chair, calling.*] Mama! She loves me!

LENA. [*Entering with coffee.*] I hope so. You are a fine boy. [*She puts down the tray.*]

ERNESTO. Tonio, I got to talk to Mama, *please.*

ANTONIO. Umm, she is such sweetness—such peaches and cream. She is perfection, a-ll-together. Isn't she wonderful, Mama?

LENA. [*Pouring the coffee.*] I don't know is she so wonderful or not. Why does she find some things wrong about my boy if she is so wonderful? Why does she do that, eh?

ANTONIO. Oh, Mama, that is nothing. She is a woman! It means nothing. She is perfect. *Perfect!* Every strand of her hair, every little black eyelash is perfect. Her smile and her frown are all the same. Wonderful! [*Bounding to the door.*] And now goodnight, goodnight, goodnight!

LENA. Tonio! Come back!

ANTONIO. She is waiting, Mama. I have to hurry.

LENA. But your coffee! You didn't drink your black coffee to make the head stop swimming.

ANTONIO. Tonight, Mama, my head may swim all it likes. [*Throws her a kiss.*] Goodnight, beautiful Mama! [*He passes* JOSEPH *in a rush.*] Joseph, come to my wedding! [*He exits.* JOSEPH *remains unmoved.* LENA *has followed* ANTONIO *to the door. She remains there a while, and it is quiet.*]

LENA. [*Very quietly, from the door, her back to* ERNESTO.] Do you not see one fault in me, Papa?

ERNESTO. [*Seated at the table.*] No, Mama, I do not think so.

LENA. [*Still turned away.*] Never? Had I no faults ever?

ERNESTO. [*Gently.*] No, Mama, none that I can remember.

LENA. [*Now turning.*] And for all these years, the same is so?

ERNESTO. Of course, Mama. [*She begins to cry, softly.*] Don't cry, Mama.

[*He half rises, sits.* LENA *walks toward the door, wiping her eyes, stands looking through it, pensively, then turns to him again.*]

LENA. Then why did you have to find this woman, when you stopped the shouting?

ERNESTO. [*In despair.*] No! Not this shouting; we can not be back to this shouting.

LENA. [*Blowing her nose.*] Yes, this shouting. [*She sits at the table.*] And then after so long a time of no shouting—and this woman—then you start the shouting again, and I *know*, then!

ERNESTO. [*Raising his hands in supplication.*] Mama, Mama, you are driving me crazy. Why is it you keep saying, "This woman, this woman"?

LENA. I *hate* this woman, who has stopped you from so much shouting.

ERNESTO. [*Coldly.*] I have not got another woman, Mama.

LENA. [*Wiping her eyes.*] You have not?

ERNESTO. No.

LENA. Then why the shouting and then not the shouting?

ERNESTO. I do not know, Mama. I am all mixed up.

LENA. [*Thoughtfully.*] But if there is not a woman, then the shouting did not mean anything one way or the other?

ERNESTO. Anyway, it was never true. I never did shout very much, anyway. [*Abruptly.*] Look, Mama, would it help maybe if I just *try* a little shouting each morning? Perhaps . . .

LENA. [*Gasping.*] No! Oh, no. [*Very agitated.*] Because every time you were to shout I would think, Papa is showing me there was never this woman, and then I would maybe not believe it any more and I would *hate* this shouting.

[ERNESTO *sits and stares at his hands. He reaches blindly for his cup of coffee, then the salt shaker, and begins shaking salt absently into his coffee.* LENA *screams at him.*] Papa! You are putting salt into the coffee! [*She stares at him. They stare at each other.*] Papa? [*Very tenderly.*] Papa, why is it you *always* salt everything so? [*She rises, as though exalted.*] I cook with plenty of salt and yet you must salt, salt, salt, and now look [*Still very gently.*] you are even salting the coffee. [*Wistfully.*] Maria's husband sleeps all the time. . . . Mrs. Teacy's husband never pays any attention. . . . Mrs. Lark's swears. . . . Mrs. Rollo's . . . [*She hesitates, and regards him fondly.*] but my Ernesto [*She sighs deeply.*] he must *salt everything.* [ERNESTO *sits very quietly.*] Why must you men always have something? [*She sighs softly, and touches his hair lightly, and then takes his coffee cup away.*] Now. You just wait for a minute and I will fix each of us a fresh, hot cup. Look! [*As though to a beloved child.*] I will take the salt from the table. There.

[*She takes the coffee pot and salt, and exits to the kitchen.*

ERNESTO *rises quietly, and pads to the apartment door and peers down at* JOSEPH.]

ERNESTO. [*Softly.*] Joseph? Joseph?

JOSEPH. [*Irritably, not turning.*] Why do you stand up there and say, "Joseph, Joseph"?

ERNESTO. [*Softly.*] Joseph, why is it a woman cannot love a man and let it alone?

JOSEPH. [*Not turning.*] Why do you ask me? I have never pretended to care or know about women.

ERNESTO. [*Stepping out of the apartment a bit.*] I have a small favor to ask you, Joseph.

LENA'S VOICE. [*Singing out sweetly from the kitchen.*] The coffee is coming, Papa; only a minute.

ERNESTO. Only a very small favor, Joseph.

JOSEPH. Ask it, then!

ERNESTO. [*Very earnestly.*] Always remind me, Joseph, whenever you see me, never to forget to salt everything I eat. [JOSEPH *turns now and stares up at him.*] I have no particular liking for salt, but it is better than some things. [JOSEPH *still stares.* ERNESTO *speaks with great dignity.*] You needn't look at me so, Joseph. [*The lights slowly dim. There is a gay run on the mandolin.*]

THE END

# TELLING OF THE NORTH STAR

By

## VINCENT FERRINI

*(Published here for the first time)*

# TELLING OF THE NORTH STAR

## CAST

MA
ALTHEA
CAPTAIN DAN ELIZA
JOE
WILLIS
CAPTAIN MATTHEW ELIZA
THOMAS
TWO OTHER CREW MEN
NEIGHBORS

TIME: The present.
PLACE: A sea city.

# VINCENT FERRINI

FOR the second time, Vincent Ferrini, of Gloucester, Massachusetts, brings us in modern verse form some of the legendary glow that haunts early American seaports in general, and some of them in particular. Last year's work, *Innermost I Land,* was a dramatic reading; *Telling of the North Star* is a verse drama.

Mr. Ferrini edits a poetry magazine, "Four Winds," a quarterly which sometimes comes from London and sometimes from the island of Mallorca; and his own verses get around the world in the Little Magazines of Japan, England, Australia, and Canada, as well as the United States. He has published several collections of verse: "Sea Sprung," "The Infinite People," "Blood of the Tenement," "No Smoke"; and during the last year, "In the Arriving" (Liverpool), and "The House of Time" (London).

Vincent Ferrini, who was born in Saugus, Massachusetts, and educated there, has a wife and three children, and makes his living in Gloucester as a picture-frame maker.

# TELLING OF THE NORTH STAR

*One of the few remaining early houses, with its widow's walk overlooking the harbor. The present inhabitants have it in the manner of the original settlers. The kitchen is blue, modern;* ALTHEA'S *bedroom is a dead red; the living room a deep green. At certain times the night swallows the house, and the rooms breathe like the unseen depths of the ocean. It is such an occasion.* MA *lays the newspaper she is reading on her lap and says almost to herself:*

MA.           something like my father
                  is in the air.
                  so long it is that I
                  felt him, it seems
                  this is another world,
                  his is the real one,
                  and I in between.
                  Dan will be home
                  soon and unlike other times
                  . . . no.

[ALTHEA *comes in expectant.*]

ALTHEA.               yes.
                      this turning
                in myself and those lost.
                strange it is
                and most to my liking
                the hour before dark
                in the attic
                with that old worm eaten
                trunk that smells

of salt and dead men's flesh.
I re-read the love-letters
Captain Matt had written
to his sweetheart
and the unfolding log
books.
                   it is
his presence that is
in this house.
                        my great
grandfather,
                   of me.

MA.          my father's father's father's
grandfather. little is
known of him. he
disappeared; neither he
nor his ship and crew
were ever seen
or heard of.
it is the atmosphere of
their time.

ALTHEA.                    I know, and it
could happen to Joe
and Pa.

MA.                   hardly, these
days, but dont
speak of it.

ALTHEA.              not that
I'm afraid. it seems
like it's already in the
newspapers.

MA.          Althea!
                   what did you
say?

ALTHEA.          I forget.
                 I'm not the self you know.

MA.              the air is thick here.
                 I'd best open a window.

                        *

[*As she rises to do so, a door is heard opening and two fisher-
men loudly enter the kitchen and slap a striped bass and a
basket of lobsters in the sink.*]

CAPT. DAN.       Ma! we're in!
                 and a damn good haul, too!
                 eh, Joe?

JOE.                    yeah.
                 after the next trip
                 Thea and I will be one.

[MA *embraces* DAN *rabidly.* ALTHEA, *distantly, watches.* JOE *goes
to* ALTHEA *to wrap her in his arms, but feels a chill in her attitude.*]

MA.              Dan!
CAPT. DAN.          what's the matter?
                 anything happen?

MA.              no. just extra happy.

CAPT. DAN.       you act as though
                 we escaped death's claw.

JOE.             yeah.
                        maybe that animal's
                 stink is on me.

[*He hoops* ALTHEA *violently, and is abashed at the impenetrable
mood.*]

                 Thea! we just got in.
                 arent you wanting to see me?

ALTHEA.          the present is so sudden.

JOE.             Ma, what's coming into her?

MA.        she's in a world of lost
love letters and
log books.

CAPT. DAN.       on
the ships of the past,
by the looks of her.

ALTHEA.     leave me alone
all of you.

[*She runs to her bedroom,* JOE *following.*]

*

CAPT. DAN.    come on, Ma, let's boil
those lobsters; it's a
gift to us from an
unknown friend.

MA.              again!
someday the law
will knock our door down.
why must you do this,
Dan? when you know
how much it distresses me.

CAPT. DAN.   they all do, Ma.

MA.        does that mean
you have to be a petty thief
like all of them
and keep me on the rack of
worry?

CAPT. DAN.     okay, Ma, promise
never to do it again.

MA.        a man can become haunted
by stealing
and obsess others. . . .
old Capt Matt would never
touch another man's
goods.

CAPT. DAN.    how do you know
he's no different than
any of us. come on.
the last time.

MA.                                it's
your word!
[*She goes to the sink to start the late supper; suddenly she stops
and turns to him.*]
                              Dan,
you said "he's no
different than any of us."

CAPT. DAN.    what's news about that?

MA.            you put Matt in the living
tense.

CAPT. DAN.    Ma! what's undermining here?
if you dont keep
her out of the attic
I swear I'll burn
that trunk, letters,
log books, clothes, trinkets
and all! people
getting bewitched by
junk!
              and now you
making me a part of it.
not in my house!
                        Joe'd
better give her
something else to occupy
that mind of hers.

MA.            dont you stir sin
up unnecessarily.
why, you're almost
afraid to let us
speak as we feel.

CAPT. DAN.    not if you talk
sense, but no crazy
jigsaws.

MA.                            but Dan,
doesnt it make
you wonder
                           about Matt,
and all the other ships
that have vanished?
and the last one, only
two years ago, the
GUDRUN?

CAPT. DAN.    sure it does.
but not when you make off
as though the boat
and crew still live.

MA.            who can say they dont?

CAPT. DAN.    I do.
                         this is what happens
to women when they are
left alone with too damn
much time on their
minds.
                         where's the jug?
there's a man's meat!

[*After looking about, he finds it in the pantry, fills one glass
full, dumps it, and fills another, and trudges into the living
room, picks up the newspaper.*]

*

[JOE *and* ALTHEA *are seen talking in her bedroom.*]

JOE.            the bell at the harbor
light was never
as heartwarming as
tonight. the sound of
it still churns in me.

need no longer dream
or count the days—
I have you now.
                     Althea,
we are nearly one.

ALTHEA.      just before the curtain
of night came down
I saw the full sails of
the HARRIET come
over the horizon of the
hooked moon.

JOE.      "mother ann!"
not the HARRIET!
it was dusk
and the sun's shaft was
bloody in the sea.

ALTHEA.      [*Not having heard.*]
I could see
the torn sails
as it came past the
Dogbar . . . and a white
haired man at the wheel,
. . . his eyes alive
flashing hard as
light in diamonds
and a tale to tell
beyond what is written
about that ship
or anyone on it.

JOE.      how could you see
his eyes a good two miles
away? and the sky
blackening!

ALTHEA.      surrounded it was

in a halo
of light, yellow, and as
close to me as the
spearmint in the window box
outside.

I heard them
talking . . .

[*She moves toward the window.*]

JOE.                             Althea,
if you must day-dream
do it about us.

[*He reaches for her, but she steps away in the direction of her thoughts.*]

in a week or two
you'll be leaving this house
and making ours!
and we havent even found
a place to start in.

ALTHEA.      they'd been on high seas
for most two hundred years
without ever sighting love
and now docking
at Cain's Wife.
a crew no wharf
or people have ever seen
nor such a ship!
they've finally come
back home.

home?

who
will recognize them
or accept them?

JOE.      no!
only stars and masts and
hulls come to rest

and other lit windows
welcoming the weary.
[*Lays his hands on her shoulder, touching her hair.*]

ALTHEA.          a driftwood ship.
whole, worm eaten, and
stranger than any dream.
and alive, the men
bone white, leathery and
questioning, their movements
like evening winds,
smooth as kelp
and tough as the tales
their tongues are
tied with.
          each
gesture a song
of places no books
have known.
          (and that
is where I am,
in them
as they come to take
the burden of the lost
from the back of my mind)
they will know
because it is for me
they have come
down all the rages of those
years.

JOE.          I cannot follow
you. Althea, Althea,
listen to me.

ALTHEA.          I have to
journey with them
to learn the peace they

will teach me

          and divine

the quest

      in the offing.

JOE.      leave me?

         now that I

have found you?

[*Frantic, he seizes her passionately, madly intent as a desperate lover who sees his approaching loss and knows the only way to stay her.*]

ALTHEA.    [*beating him back.*]

      no. no. no.

[*In the wrangling, he flings her onto the bed, rips off her bodice, she sobbing with heartbreak, as in the tidal passion he brings her to earth, the sobs dying uneasily in the night.*]

CAPT. DAN.    [*knocking on door.*]

    Joe! Althea!

    the lobsters and wine are

    waiting.

JOE.            we're coming—

Thea mine,

        and

married.

[*He rises, fixes himself, strokes her gently, she still shaking.*]

      put on that

yellow dress I love

you in. I'll be

waiting

    with them.

\*

CAPT. DAN.    [*tasting wine and lobsters.*]

better than the Town

Landing's!

JOE.                it's what we come home
                        for, besides our wives.

CAPT. DAN.      yeah. what did you say?

JOE.                because of Ma
                        and my wife to be.

MA.                 soon and
                        before another fog.

JOE.                [*eating voraciously.*]
                        never tasted anything
                        so sweet.
                        hope we have enough.

MA.                 there's the striped bass.

JOE.                this the last crawler?

MA.                 have it yourself, Pa's
                        had all he can hold and
                        Thea doesnt care for it.

CAPT. DAN.      if I had seen you gorge
                        like that before, I'd say
                        you were on a bully haul.
                        Thea'd better hurry
                        or she'll have the table to
                        herself.

[ALTHEA *appears in black.* MA *motions her to sit and eat, but she shakes her head and broods into the living room.*]
                        what's she
                        in sad clothes for?
                        in another mood, or
                        the same one, blacker?

MA.                 leave her be.

JOE.                fog'll clear,
                        always does.

CAPT. DAN.  something peculiar
about her.

MA.  you're asking what
the weathervane cant
tell.

CAPT. DAN.  feels like the ice
is broken
and the air from that
water
colder than the ice.
none of em want it
that way
and years after
that's how they hunger
for it.

MA.  Dan!
how can you!
and be so wrong!

CAPT. DAN.  she'll change
and get used to it
and then like it,
eh, Joe?

JOE.  [*sheepishly.*]
dont know what you're
steaming about.

CAPT. DAN.  dont—much.

MA.  Dan,
let them alone.
[*A rap on the door, a member of Dan's crew,* WILLIS, *enters.*]

WILLIS.  the HARRIET's tied in!
what mad
squealing of gulls!

a ghost ship
if ever these eyes beheld one.
a black masted schooner!
white winded and blowing
alive as you
and me
and yet not alive.
the men are aghast.
they say that haunted
crew is intent in this
direction! it's the look
of your house in the
silence that sheathes
them!
            the town is dazed
and bereft of air
moving away from that sight
as from a plague.

CAPT. DAN.    are you touched, Willis?
              and ranting mad?

JOE.          it cant be!

WILLIS.       the crew from the HARRIET
              that's not been heard of
              since 1791 . . . rigger
              and men!
                        a reality
              no one living will ever
              tell and stand
              believed! and
                              heading
              here!

CAPT. DAN.    [*Strides over and grabs* WILLIS
              *and smells his mouth.*]
              you're drunk, man.
              and from the broth of a fairy

tale some barfly
is spinning for excitement.
always thought you had
a soft spot in your bean!

MA.    it can be, Dan,
that what he says can
bear listening to.
                    my
father, when we were children,
related many a happening
that none in his straight
mind would give his belief
to, and we accepted
because his crewmen swore
their lives upon it
when we asked them.
it could be that Captain Matthew
your ancestor generations
in the beginning of Gloucester
is back and with the
HARRIET!

CAPT. DAN.    now you, too!
start a rumor
and who knows where it
will gutter? well this
one will be stamped out quick!
the dead are dead
and no one in his sane
mind doubts it.
and all you here
will mind the business of
living!
            as long as
I am at the wheel
of this house and its
destiny!

[ALTHEA *enters, radiant.*]

ALTHEA.     it's he!
Captain Matthew and
crew
      luminous as the riding
moon!
the townspeople edging
after
with purple faces
incredulous, and drawn by
a force outside them,
like the very leaves flying
from the tree of them
and bitten by curiosity
wanting to get back
to know and start
again in a new
knowledge. . . .
        but fear
is snake in them
        eating
. . . thrown stones
of the kids
going through them!
they have come to prove me!

WILLIS.     this is one time
a mutiny will triumph
and with a Captain's
consent!

CAPT. DAN.     over me, dead!

JOE.     and me, too, Capt!
I'm staunch with you
against this madness
that has crept
here in a dreadful contagion

that will sweep us all
if we dont crush it down!

[*A scuffling of feet outside the door and a strange muffled knocking. Everyone is in suspense except* ALTHEA, *who is beautiful with anticipation.*]

CAPT. DAN.    a settlement soon and
one for the log book.
enter!

[*The door is opened gently as though by no hand, and there, white as bones that have been saturated by wind, time and salt sea, the spiritual outlines (in a physical aspect) of* CAPTAIN MATTHEW, THOMAS, *his first mate, and two* CREWMEN.]

Who are you?

CAPT. MATT.    is there no reflection?

CAPT. DAN.    none but intruders.

CAPT. MATT.    one who enters another
tone of his own land home
is no trespasser!

CAPT. DAN.    who are you?

CAPT. MATT.    Captain Matthew of Gloucester
of the ship HARRIET
ELIZA,
with my first mate, Thomas,
and two men of my crew
who return to our ancestral
grounds to verify
one existence and another
after a hundred sixty three years
absence!

CAPT. DAN.    you are all dead!

CAPT. MATT.    you hear us!
and very much alive
as anything is!
four times removed

your grandfather!
and no recognition in your eyes
except for those who want
us.

CAPT. DAN.  you are dead.
a hallucination brought
by the trouble of feverish
females and a drunken
fisherman!
                    to get the
attention of us
who keep the business
of living going!

CAPT. MATT.  only because we havent
been wanted in the longest
of continuing years.
only two here
drawing us homeward.
finding the townspeople
screeching at us,
our own families hysterical
and insulting us with
"go back where you came
from." throwing rocks
and names, giving us
hate and fear
instead of love.
the life we know on the
kingdom of water
is clean
and takes one as he is
for what he can give.
our bones are in the salt,
the foam, fog is our breath
and the fishes our
living eyes looking through

death
            and being the life
we can never die.
                        thirst
nor desert, the furnace of
the sun, the boiling seas
nor the white terrible
waste of the moon
can age us but the
weather recreates us
in another dimension
that waits to be found,
as we are here
and can share . . .
but the willing is hate
corrosive and crippling
and an end comes. . . .
                        of what
manner of men
                        those
that leave and go on
voyages other vessels
cannot fathom or fear to?
ELIZA is in me
and harks back to a past
that is the future
and the present of our
meaning.
                . . . there is a sickness
here
        of ships and people
dying a slow living!
who eulogize the past
refusing us
are frozen in terror of the
present.
                we

are the future
and have come to take
back the momentoes of our
other living
            to continue

THOMAS.                                    with Althea.

JOE.        over my dead self!
            you ghoulies of hell!
            no reflection of mine
            are you
            and you'll never get over the
            threshold!

THOMAS.     you are as wind only.
            you storm as a beast
            and kill the very flower
            you need and do not
            know the nourishing of,
            and no woman can be yours
            by the trampling,
                            especially
            Althea.
[ALTHEA *is drawn toward* THOMAS.]
                a life here
            you are not ready for
            if you ever will be.

JOE.        no ghost
            will judge, stop,
            or ruin my life
            if I can help it.

[*He lunges at the first mate. For a shocked moment there is a
physical tussle between two men, more like two irreconcilable
enemies, when* JOE *is felled with a knife in his midriff. All is
consternation and incredulity.*]

CAPT. DAN.   murderer!

[*He rushes to* JOE, *and sees he is done.*]
dead
and by a ghost's hand!
that I would ever say it!

THOMAS.        more his own hand
than mine!
Althea, come, let us
be off!
Captain Matthew!

CAPT. MATT.    yes.
before more of what we do
not want comes
wholly out of their
misunderstanding.

[*Voices outside crowd into the house as* CAPT. MATT *and* THOMAS,
ALTHEA *in his arms and their men after them, leave.*]

MA.        Althea! Althea!
come back!
[*To herself.*]
much
as I believe
this will never be the end
of her
or us.

CAPT. DAN.    Willis!

WILLIS.        aye?

CAPT. DAN.    get the men and warn
the townspeople.
hurry!

WILLIS.        aye!

[*They fly out.* MA *at* JOE'S *side, with the help of a* NEIGHBOR,
*picks him up and takes him to* ALTHEA'S *bedroom and covers
him.*]

*

MA.   [*Weeping.*]
     a double sorrow!

NEIGHBOR.  one no one
     will ever believe.
     oh, what is the truth
     of it, or what does
     it mean?
       who will ever
     believe the tale of it?

MA.    that it has finally
     happened
     and to us.
     o, we go back
     into them
     so far we reckon not
     with the wheeling of the lives
     that make us
     so deep in us.
     we know not
     what we see!
     double sorrow and more
     sorrow,
       there is no end
     of it.
      this mystery moving
     in our living.

NEIGHBOR.  rest your poor head,
     dear, it is more
     than should descend on
     the devil himself.

[*It is near midnight.* MA *and the* NEIGHBOR *are in each other's
arms, when voices are heard excitedly.* CAPT. DAN *and* WILLIS
*come in.*]

CAPT. DAN.  who will believe it?

WILLIS.  you have to.

CAPT. DAN.    I don't know.
                          it is more than
              my soul ever had to wrestle
              with.

WILLIS.       they shot at that crew
              as they boarded
              and took off,
              some leaping at it
              touching it
              through it
              into the black water
              like logs and lead!
              that taking off!
                               full
              sails
              ghostly
                      ghostly
                              and in a strange
              glory.

CAPT. DAN.    Thea looking back
              her hand raised almost
              like a shadow
              much as I never
              noticed
                      her . . .
                              O
              to unload this
              burden
                      and refind her
              and myself.
                      crippled
              is my conscience. . . .
              how can I die
              now?

# JOHN TURNER DAVIS

By

## HORTON FOOTE

*A television script*

*(Published here for the first time)*

# JOHN TURNER DAVIS

## CAST

*John Turner Davis* was originally produced by the Philco Television Playhouse, November 15, 1953, over the National Broadcasting Company's network, with the following principals in the cast:

JOHN TURNER DAVIS ............. Cliff Tatum
PAUL ....................... John Marriott
HAZEL .................... Katherine Squire
THURMAN .................... Larry Gates
SHERIFF ..................... Frank Overton
INEZ
MISS FANNY
OLD MAN
MISS SARAH
MAN

OTHERS: Nan McFarland, Ruth Hope, Georgia Simmons, Paton Price, Sudie Bond, Harold Grau, William Hickey.

Produced by Fred Coe, with Gordon Duff as Associate Producer.

Directed by Arthur Penn.

TIME: Midsummer of 1933.
PLACE: Harrison, Texas.

# HORTON FOOTE

THERE have been many good original short plays produced on television during the year, and probably each viewer has his and her own favorite among them. Sometimes the acting of a skilled player in a principal role, a Margaret Wycherly, a Maria Riva, a Walter Hampden or an Otto Kruger will assure a play's reception as an outstanding production. There are also those dramas and documentaries that do not feature well-known performers, but in which the story is so well contrived or factual that the television viewer is kept interested throughout the play.

Occasionally, there is a short script which stands on its own endowment, which has something to say and its own persuasive way of saying it. It could not have been written by any other than the author. Such a play is Horton Foote's *John Turner Davis*. In fact, throughout the year, Mr. Foote has contributed substantially to the originality, honesty and clarity of television drama.

Other recent television plays by Horton Foote, all on NBC-TV, have been: *The Old Beginning* (the Psychiatric Institute in Washington asked for permission to use this script for use by undergraduates in psychiatry, as the best example of a father-son theme expressed through drama); *The Trip to Bountiful,* starring Lillian Gish; *The Rocking Chair,* in "The Doctor" series; *Young Lady of Property, The Oil Well,* starring Dorothy Gish; *Expectant Relations, Death of the Old Man, Tears of My Sister,* and *The Midnight Caller.*

The following full-length plays have been published and produced on Broadway: *Only the Heart* (1944), *The Chase* (1952) and *The Trip to Bountiful* (1953).

# JOHN TURNER DAVIS

## ACT ONE

*The year is 1933; the scene a dusty country road in the middle
of summer on the outskirts of Harrison, Texas. A young boy of
twelve is sitting by the road, looking around as he takes a stone
out of his shoe.*
*A man in the distance can be heard stopping a team of horses.
He calls back to the boy. The man is* PAUL, *a negro. He is
delivering ice.*

PAUL. Hoa . . . ! Hoa . . . ! Hey, Boy!

JOHN TURNER. Yep?

PAUL. Where are you goin'?

JOHN TURNER. Into Harrison.

PAUL. You want a ride?

JOHN TURNER. I sure would.

PAUL. Hurry up an' get on the wagon.

[*The* BOY *runs down the road and climbs onto the waiting
wagon.*]

You look hot. Why don't you git yourself a piece of ice before
we git started? Bring me a piece.

JOHN TURNER. I thank you.

[*He runs around to the back of the wagon and takes a piece of
loose ice. He runs back to the front and climbs up on the seat
with the man.*]

PAUL. Thanks. All set?

JOHN TURNER. Uh-huh!

PAUL. All right. [*The* BOY *chews his ice.*]

There are two houses out on this river road. I may have to
stop and deliver ice to one of 'em, but I'll git you to Harrison
quicker'n you kin walk it. You didn't look like you was in too
much of a hurry, anyways.

JOHN TURNER. I'm in a hurry. I just didn' know the way, so I couldn' go too fast.

PAUL. Where you comin' from?

JOHN TURNER. The river.

PAUL. Been fishin'?

JOHN TURNER. Nope.

PAUL. I hope you ain't been swimmin'. That river's not safe to swim in. There's whirlpools in that river an' suck holes an' alligators . . .

JOHN TURNER. I know all about that. I ain' been swimmin'.

PAUL. What were you doin' down there?

JOHN TURNER. I been livin' down there.

PAUL. Oh. [*He jerks the horses' reins once more.*] Gee up!

[*They go on, as the scene dissolves to the living room of a cottage. The living room, as well as the rest of the house, has had excellent care. There are Reynolds' copies on the walls; and cats' tails and castor bean pods, dried and painted gold and silver, in vases about the room.*
*A woman in her early forties,* HAZEL, *is there dusting the furniture. She has a towel tied around her head. She is a plain woman, but with a great deal of kindness in her face. After a moment, she goes to the window and looks out. She takes the towel off her head, wipes her face of any perspiration, puts the towel down and goes outside on the porch.*
*The porch is covered with vines, and seems very cool. She stands on the steps looking out into the front yard.* INEZ *calls to her from the distance.*]

INEZ. [*Calling.*] Hazel! What are you doin' standin' out in that sun? [INEZ *comes up the front gallery steps. She has a parasol over her head.*] You're gonna have a sun stroke, honey.

HAZEL. I just came outside. I'm lookin' to see if the ice man is in sight.

INEZ. Well, I wouldn't put a foot off that porch without somethin' over my head. I let Horace take the car to work this mornin', so I had to walk to town for my mail, and I swear to you I had to stop and rest four times makin' it back home—

parasol and all. Oh, I think this sun is gonna burn us all up.

HAZEL. I know.

INEZ. It's just ruinin' the cotton.

HAZEL. I know. Can you sit down for a minute?

INEZ. Just for a minute. I've got to go home and get my dinner on the table.

HAZEL. I'm sorry I can't offer you anything cool to drink, but I'm all out of ice.

INEZ. That's all right. [*A pause.*] I don't see why you live out on this old river road, Hazel. If I could find me a house in Harrison big enough for my family, I'd move so fast!

HAZEL. Well, some people like town and some people don't.

INEZ. But how do you stand it? I'd think you'd get so lonesome . . .

HAZEL. No ma'am. I was born here, you remember. The river road is home to me. When our house burned and my daddy had to move us into town, I just didn't feel right. I told Thurman when we were courtin' that I wanted one thing understood if I married him: that the first money we got ahead— that I didn't want diamonds and I didn't want cars—I wanted him to build me a house on the River Road.

[*She looks around the porch.*]

It's cooler out here, too, you know. At least it is on my front gallery. I'm so grateful for my front gallery. I know I said to Thurman when we were plannin' the house, I didn't care what else I had as long as I had me a cool front gallery, and I must say I have it.

INEZ. It is cool. But lonely. I never sit on my front gallery because there is nothin' to see. What's the use of a gallery if nobody passes by to speak to?

HAZEL. Well, I like it. [*A pause.*] It's gonna change our luck livin' out here. I told Thurman that. I said I haven't had any luck and my papa didn't have, nor no one in my entire family, since our house burned and we moved away from the River Road. Move me back there and watch my luck change . . . !

INEZ. Has it changed your luck?

HAZEL. No, ma'am, but it will. It will change our luck. I

prophesy that Thurman's business is gonna improve and I prophesy that . . . Well, you just wait and see. All kind of things are gonna happen to us out here.

INEZ. Do you think there's oil out here?

HAZEL. I don't know about that. But all kinds of things are gonna happen to us out here. You just wait and see. . . . Inez, I got some new cut glass yesterday. Do you want to see it?

INEZ. All right, but I hate to go into your house.

HAZEL. Why?

INEZ. Because it's always so spotless. My kids have just made a shambles out of my house. But what can you do? I've just given up tryin' to have anything nice any more.

HAZEL. Oh, yonder comes Paul. [*She calls.*] Paul! Paul! Ice! Fifty pounds! [*Then to* INEZ.] Come on with me to the back porch. I want to see if there's room in my ice box for the ice.

INEZ. Everything always looks so pretty and fresh in your house. It makes me so ashamed.

[*They have reached the back porch.* HAZEL *goes to the ice box. She opens it.* PAUL *comes in, carrying the ice. He is followed by* JOHN TURNER.]

PAUL. I was about ready to pass you by, M's Whyte. I said to myself, I said, surely M's Whyte don't need no ice today.

HAZEL. Oh, yes, I do! It goes so in this heat.

PAUL. Heat's burnin' up the cotton. It better rain 'fore the week is out, or there's gonna be no cotton in this county again this year.

INEZ. Oh, don't say that, Paul!

PAUL. I don't have to say it. Just look around you! Cotton is burnin' up, everywhere you look.

INEZ. Whose little boy is that, Paul?

PAUL. I don't know 'm. I met 'm walkin' into town along the river road. He says he belongs to some of them people camped out along the river bank.

INEZ. What's your name, little boy?

JOHN TURNER. John Turner Davis.

HAZEL. What's your mama and daddy thinkin' about, lettin' you walk aroun' in this heat, with no hat on your head?

JOHN TURNER. I don' have no mama an' daddy.

HAZEL. You don't?

JOHN TURNER. No, ma'am. I belong to my Uncle Delbert an' my Aunt Velma. They went off in the truck to try an' find some cotton to chop, day before yesterday. They left me with the Culpeppers. They said they'd be back las' night. They didn' show up, an' when I woke up this mornin' the Culpeppers was all gone. I didn' know what to do, an' a man down there told me to git into Harrison an' tell the Sheriff an' let him git word to my Aunt an' Uncle.

INEZ. Paul, you leave him with me. . . . I'll take him to my house. He'll have a sun stroke ridin' aroun' in this sun.

JOHN TURNER. Oh, no, ma'am, I wouldn' have no stroke. I picked cotton in worse sun than this, an' no hat on my haid.

INEZ. I know. But you come on to my house and I'll give you some dinner and I'll call the Sheriff . . .

JOHN TURNER. Thank you, ma'am. But I'll go on an' find the Sheriff, myself.

INEZ. Well, all right.

PAUL. Well, come on, boy, if you're comin' with me. My ice is meltin' out in that wagon. You want ice tomorrow, M's Whyte?

HAZEL. Tomorrow? This afternoon! I'd like more ice, I know, this afternoon.

PAUL. Yes'm. Come on, boy!

[*He goes out.* JOHN TURNER *follows after him.*]

INEZ. Poor little thing! I bet he hasn't had a good meal in a month. They live on fish and meal and fat back down at that river camp.

HAZEL. I know; I've seen the way they live down there. Did you ever see the way they have to live?

INEZ. Yes, it's pitiful, isn't it?

HAZEL. Yes, it is. I guess they just follow the cotton crop from place to place.

INEZ. I guess.

HAZEL. Makes you grateful, doesn't it?

INEZ. Yes, it does. . . . Well, let me see your cut glass.

HAZEL. Oh, yes. I'd forgotten all about that.

[*They go out toward the living room, as the scene dissolves to the store of* THURMAN WHYTE. *It is a general dry goods store. Inside the door, sitting under a ceiling fan, is* MISS FANNY DEE; *she clerks in the store. Standing in the doorway is* THURMAN WHYTE. *He is a heavy man in his late thirties.*]

MISS FANNY. Business is terrible all over town, Thurman. You can just shoot a cannon ball down the streets. All the merchants are standin' at the doors of their stores, with their faces down to here! [*She points down to her knees.*] I've never known it so quiet.

THURMAN. Well, they can say what they want to me about the oil and the rice and whatever else they think they've got in this country—when the cotton crop fails, the merchants starve to death.

MISS FANNY. I know.

THURMAN. Well, it can't get any worse; that's for sure.

MISS FANNY. That's for sure!

THURMAN. I laugh and kid Hazel. You know, she always said when we moved back out to the river road our luck was gonna change. Well, we've been there three years now and I've had a crop failure facin' me every year. But she still says our luck is gonna change. And she believes it.

MISS FANNY. I know. [*She wipes her brow in desperation.*] Isn't it hot?

THURMAN. Yes, ma'am. But I'll tell you, Miss Fanny, like I tell my wife: talkin' about it never helped.

MISS FANNY. I wasn't talkin' about it. I was just remarkin'. How is Hazel standin' the heat?

THURMAN. Pretty well. It gets quite cool at nights over at our place. [PAUL *comes into the store.*] What can I do for you, Paul?

PAUL. I've come to collect for the ice.

THURMAN. All right, Paul.

[PAUL *hands him a bill, and he reaches into his pocket and takes out some money.*]

PAUL. Thank you. . . . Did M's Hazel tell you about that little boy that was with me when I took the ice to your house this mornin'?

THURMAN. The one that came from the river?

PAUL. That's right.

THURMAN. Yep. She was tellin' me about it at dinner.

PAUL. I was just talkin' to the Sheriff. He tells me he thinks his peoples has just run off and left 'm. He said he'd been down to the River askin' the people down there about it, and they all said they thought his folks had run off and left 'm.

THURMAN. Is that so? Too bad!

PAUL. It sure is. He was a nice little boy.

THURMAN. Hazel said so.

PAUL. Well, bye, y'all.

[PAUL *goes out.* THURMAN *stands there for a minute, thinking.*]

THURMAN. Isn't that awful? What gets into people to run off and leave a little boy like that? I don't understand it. Seems like people that don't want or care anything about children have a plenty. And you take a couple like me and Hazel, just eatin' our hearts out for a child—and we have none.

MISS FANNY. I know. There's not much justice in that.

THURMAN. Miss Fanny, I think I'm gonna take a walk to the drug store.

MISS FANNY. Nobody else is doin' any business, I can tell you that. You can just save yourself a trip.

THURMAN. I'm not goin' to see if anybody else is doin' business, Miss Fanny. I'm goin' to get myself a Coca-Cola. I'll be back in fifteen minutes, in case I'm needed.

MISS FANNY. Which drug store are you gonna be in?

THURMAN. Thornton's. And Miss Fanny, will you call Hazel and remind her tonight is my poker night! I won't be home for supper.

MISS FANNY. Yes, sir.

[*He goes.* MISS FANNY *starts to rise, then sinks into a chair, as the scene dissolves to the front gallery of the Whyte house.* HAZEL *is sitting there, rocking, and fanning herself. It is nearly sundown.* JOHN TURNER DAVIS *comes up into the yard.*]

JOHN TURNER. Howdy do, ma'am!

[HAZEL *looks up and sees the boy standing there.*]

HAZEL. Yes?

JOHN TURNER. I'm tryin' to find my way back to the River. I got lost. How far is it back to the River?

HAZEL. About a mile. And you're headin' in the wrong direction to find the River. You have to go back *that* way!

JOHN TURNER. Yes, ma'am.

HAZEL. Aren't you the boy that was here this mornin' with the ice man?

JOHN TURNER. Yes, ma'am. . . . I guess I'd better git started before dark comes on. I'm liable never to find that old river in the dark.

[*He starts out of the yard.*]

HAZEL. Excuse me, boy. What's your name again?

JOHN TURNER. John Turner Davis. [*A pause. He looks around at the porch.*] It's cool on your porch.

HAZEL. Yes, it is. The vines keep it cool. There's a breeze from the Gulf startin', that helps . . . [*It begins to rain.*] That's rain.

JOHN TURNER. Yes, ma'am. [*The rain is falling very hard now.*] That's a good thing. Might give the folks some cotton to pick. I sure hope it's not too late for the cotton crop. We could all stand a good cotton crop. Rich and poor alike . . .

HAZEL. Did the Sheriff get hold of your Aunt and Uncle for you?

JOHN TURNER. No ma'am, not yet.

HAZEL. That's too bad.

JOHN TURNER. Yes, ma'am. But I'm not discouraged.

HAZEL. Won't you sit down until the rain is over?

JOHN TURNER. Yes, ma'am. I guess I better wait here until the rain stops, if you don' mind.

HAZEL. Why, no, I'd be so glad to have you. [*He sits down.*] I love the sound of rain. When I was a little girl, John Turner, I used to always dress up and play lady on the days that it rained. I'd get dresses down that belonged to my mama and my grandma and my great-aunts. I lived in a big old house out here on the River Road, with lots of rooms in it—and my mama was a saver. She would save dresses and shoes and petticoats and —I don't know what all.

JOHN TURNER. I never lived in a house longer than a month at a time. I like to live in a house someday. [*A pause.*] The sheriff says he don' hold out any hopes of findin' my aunt an' uncle. He tried to discourage me about it. He wanted to send me to a home. So I thought to myself: this jail is no place for me. An' I left. Sheriff says he'd bet his last dollar they've run off an' left me. Well, he's wrong.

HAZEL. Why, I'm sure he's wrong.

JOHN TURNER. Anyway, I ain' no orphan, you know. I got a mama an' papa somewhere. I don' know where, but somewhere. I asked Uncle Delbert an' Aunt Velma where, but they never would tell me. I asked them if they were ever gonna tell me. An' they said they would, someday. But that day never came. I don' reckon I'd know my mama an' my papa if I passed them right on the street. 'Course, I don' know if they want me now, if I did find them.

HAZEL. Why, of course your mama and papa would want you.

JOHN TURNER. Then, why did they give me away in the first place? Aunt Velma says it was because they felt sorry for her. An' that may be. But I still don' think they must have cared much about me. I've seen the poorest kind of people, with enough kids to make you dizzy thinkin' about it, but try to take one of them kids an' they'd fight you until they killed you or you killed them. Aunt Velma fought to keep me once. Uncle Delbert had to go off an' leave us because he had no money to buy gas for the truck, an' he had to hitch himself a ride to get himself a job to make a little money, an' a Sheriff come along and says they couldn' raise me right an' he was gonna take me and put me in a home; an' then my Aunt took a gun an' said if they touched me she'd kill him or he'd have to kill her; an' he knew she meant it, too. He backed right away. [*A pause.*] That's why I know they haven' left me now. I don' care what that Sheriff or fifty Sheriffs says—or what the fool people down at that river say. Aunt Velma an' Uncle Delbert are comin' back here to get me.

HAZEL. I'm sure they will, son.

JOHN TURNER. You got a husband?

HAZEL. Yes.

JOHN TURNER. Where's your husband?

HAZEL. He isn't here. He's off playin' poker.

JOHN TURNER. Oh. [*A pause.*] Where are your children?

HAZEL. We don't have any.

JOHN TURNER. Yes, ma'am.

[*A pause.*]

HAZEL. The rain's over.

JOHN TURNER. Yes, ma'am. But that wasn't no rain; that was a shower. That's worse than havin' the dry spell. That'll just rot what's left of the cotton.

HAZEL. I guess . . . [*He whistles a tune softly to himself.*] That's a pretty little song. What's the name of that song, son?

JOHN TURNER. I don' know, ma'am. It's just a song Uncle Delbert always was whistlin'. They call a song like that a reel song, you know. [*He laughs to himself.*] There's an old lady livin' down at the river bottom an' she thinks it's a mortal sin to sing or to whistle one of them songs. She thinks the only thing fit to sing is a hymn. If anyone starts to sing one of them reel songs around her, she'll pick up a rock and chuck it at you. She hit Uncle Delbert once—right in the back of the head. He cussed until Aunt Velma told him *she* was gonna hit him in the head with another rock, if he didn't stop.

[*A hoot owl is heard in the distance.*]

Listen to that old hoot owl! Don' ever kill a hoot owl!— That's the wuss kind of luck there is. That's wuss than crossin' ten black cats.

HAZEL. John Turner . . .

JOHN TURNER. Yes, ma'am.

HAZEL. When was the last time you ate today?

JOHN TURNER. Noon time. Sheriff fed me.

HAZEL. Aren't you hungry?

JOHN TURNER. Well, I'm pretty hungry . . .

HAZEL. Why don't you let me fix you a sandwich, and get you a glass of buttermilk?

JOHN TURNER. Well, that would be mighty nice—but I wouldn'
care to put you to any trouble.

HAZEL. Wouldn't be puttin' me to a bit of trouble.

JOHN TURNER. Yes, ma'am.

HAZEL. You wait here. I'll bring it out to you.

JOHN TURNER. Yes, ma'am.

[*She goes.* JOHN TURNER *sits on the steps, whistling his song to himself.*]


## ACT TWO

*It is the gallery of the Whyte House.* JOHN TURNER *is sitting there.* PAUL *calls,* "Ice! Ice!" *from the distance.* HAZEL *calls outside,* "John Turner, tell Paul I want fifty pounds this morning."

JOHN TURNER. Yes, ma'am. M's Hazel says she wants fifty pounds, please.

[PAUL *comes up to him.*]

PAUL. Ain't you the little boy that I brung into town yestidy?

JOHN TURNER. That's right.

PAUL. What's happened to you?

JOHN TURNER. Nothin'. I just had me a bath an' got my hair slicked down with some of Mr. Thurman's hair oil. I'm livin' here with M's Hazel an' Mr. Thurman until my aunt an' uncle come an' git me.

PAUL. How're they gonna find you, sittin' here on M's Whyte's front gallery—when they left you at the River?

JOHN TURNER. Well, I worried about that some. But M's Hazel figured that out. She called the Sheriff an' got him to go down to the River and tell everybody down there where I could be found, when my aunt an' uncle come for me. I been sittin' here lookin' for them up an' down the road. I got it all figured out. They're comin' today. Today is the fourth day. Once before they went off an' stayed four days. Their ole truck broke down, an' it took Uncle Delbert that long to earn the money to git it fixed up. You can hear that ole truck a mile away —chokin' and sputterin'. . . . I'm gonna hear it, an' then I'm gonna jump off this porch an' run down the road to meet them.

. . PAUL. Well, I hope you're right. [HAZEL *comes out on the gallery*.] 'Mornin' M's Hazel.

HAZEL. 'Mornin', Paul.

PAUL. I'll get your ice right away.

HAZEL. Thank you. And just go in the back porch. I've made plenty of room for it in the ice box.

PAUL. Yes, ma'am.

[*He goes out of the yard.*]

HAZEL. Well, John Turner, what have you been doin'? Countin' your money?

JOHN TURNER. [*Laughs.*] No, ma'am. I've been sittin' here waitin' for my folks to come up the road. Won't they be surprised when I tell them what's happened to me! You do think the Sheriff went down to the River an' told them people?

HAZEL. Yes, I do.

JOHN TURNER. Yes, ma'am. I just would hate for anything to happen wrong. I woke up last night an' I thought: what if they come in during the night an' saw I wasn' there an' went off again. It gave me the cold creeps thinkin' about that. I almost got up out of bed an' went on down there. Then I was afraid you an' Mr. Thurman would worry about me. I just don't know what to do. [*He jumps up.*] Is that a truck?

HAZEL. I didn't hear anything.

JOHN TURNER. I guess it wasn' nothin'. I been hearin' trucks all mornin'.

HAZEL. Now, you're gonna wear yourself out, waitin' this way. You've been sittin' here three hours. They may come today and they may not, but sittin' here and waitin' like this won't help a bit.

JOHN TURNER. Yes, ma'am. But I know they're comin' today. Today is the fourth day, an' you see before . . .

HAZEL. And if they come, they're gonna find you. The Sheriff has taken care of that. Now, why don't we walk downtown and get some new clothes for you, and get your hair cut . . .

JOHN TURNER. Thank you, ma'am. But I just as soon stay here, if it's all the same with you.

HAZEL. It's fine with me, if that's what you want to do.

JOHN TURNER. Yes, ma'am. That is what I want to do.

[PAUL *comes out.*]

PAUL. Want to ride up the road on the wagon with me for a piece?

JOHN TURNER. No, thank you. I'm gonna sit right here an' wait.

PAUL. Well, good luck.

[*He goes.* JOHN TURNER *is sitting on the steps, looking up and down the road as the scene dissolves to the* SHERIFF's *office. The* SHERIFF *is sitting at his desk, reading his paper.* THURMAN *comes in.*]

THURMAN. Sheriff . . .

SHERIFF. Hello, Thurman.

THURMAN. Sheriff, have you heard any word about that little boy's folks?

SHERIFF. No. Now I told you, Thurman, I'd call you.

THURMAN. I know, but—Hazel is wartin' me to death about it.

SHERIFF. I'm sorry, Thurman. There's nothin' more I can do. I've gotten in touch with all the officers from here to Lou'siana and down to the valley. Now, I think they've run off from the boy . . .

THURMAN. Yes, sir. But you understand he doesn't think that. Hazel says . . .

SHERIFF. And I can't help about what he thinks. I told him right here yestidy—but he wouldn't listen to me, and left.

THURMAN. Yes, sir. But if you're right, what's to become of him?

SHERIFF. Well, there are homes for boys, we can get him into. I know a good one out in West Texas. They turn out fine boys out there.

THURMAN. Yes, sir.

SHERIFF. Would you like me to talk to him again?

THURMAN. No, sir, I'll talk to him. Or Hazel will. You understand, he's a nice boy.

SHERIFF. I understand that. But this happens all the time, you know, especially when times git hard and people have trouble makin' ends meet. They just go off and leave their kids . . .

THURMAN. I see. Then you don't hold out any hopes at all?

SHERIFF. I'd say one in a thousand.

THURMAN. Then there still is hope?

SHERIFF. I said one in a thousand. Now if you can call that hope, you're welcome to it.

THURMAN. Yes, sir. Hazel says he's been sittin' on the Gallery all day just lookin' up and down the road—waitin' . . .

SHERIFF. Well, I'd be glad to talk to him again.

THURMAN. No. We'll talk to him.


[*Scene dissolves to the front gallery.* JOHN TURNER *is still sitting on the steps.* HAZEL *comes out the front door. She sits beside him. It is twilight.*]

HAZEL. It's quiet out here, isn't it?

JOHN TURNER. Yes, ma'am.

HAZEL. My neighbor down the road can't stand it out here because of the quiet. But I like it that way.

JOHN TURNER. Yes, ma'am.

[*A pause.*]

HAZEL. Soon be time for Mr. Thurman to be home.

JOHN TURNER. What time is it?

HAZEL. About six. He's always home by six fifteen, unless he stays in town for something.

JOHN TURNER. Yes, ma'am. . . . Ole sun is about to set. When I used to be ridin' the highways with my aunt an' uncle, we'd race the sunset sometimes. We always would camp out at night, an' Uncle Delbert liked to settle down before dark. He said he could tell more about the ground we was gonna sleep on, if he looked it over before the sun was down. . . . Aunt Velma says she looks forward someday, to stay in one place, sun rise an' sun set, winter an' summer for the rest of time. . . . Uncle Delbert said he didn' know when that day was gonna be. Because she was like him, an' if you tried to tie the two of them to one place for more than two weeks they both was champin' at the bit. . . . Aunt Velma said, well, she was gettin' less an' less like that as time went by. . . . Well, I hate to admit it, but it looks like they're not comin' today. I guess they gonna set a new record. I guess they gonna stay away this time for five days. I know they're worryin' about me. I'm glad they don' know the Culpeppers have gone off an' left me all alone. They'd plum die. . . . I'm gonna get up at six o'clock tomorrow mornin'. I'm gonna dress, an' I'm gonna be sittin' here. . . . I know what they been doin': sittin' by the side of some old road. You see, that old truck broke down, an' it took money to haul it into town and git it fixed, an' Uncle Delbert he had to go some place, maybe walk ten or twelve miles to git the work to earn the money to git the truck fixed or . . . [*Pause.*] Oh, I'm just whistlin' in the dark. It's got me worried. I don' know what could have happened to 'em.

[THURMAN *comes up to the porch, with a package.*]

THURMAN. Hey!

HAZEL. Hello, honey.

[*They kiss.*]

THURMAN. How are you, John Turner?

JOHN TURNER. Pretty fair.

THURMAN. I brought you some clothes.

JOHN TURNER. Yes, sir. Thank you. But you shouldn' have bothered.

THURMAN. It was no bother. Why don't you go in and try them on and see how they fit?

JOHN TURNER. Yes, sir. Thank you.

[*He takes them and goes into the house.*]

THURMAN. I think I got him the right size. I got him a set of clothes for Sunday and a set for every day.

HAZEL. That was nice. I tried to get him downtown. I wanted to get his hair cut, but he wouldn't budge off this porch. He's been sittin' right here lookin' up and down that road since seven this mornin'. Did you talk to the Sheriff?

THURMAN. Yes. He says there's one chance in a thousand they'd turn up.

HAZEL. But did you tell him that the boy's convinced they're coming back?

THURMAN. I told him.

HAZEL. What did he say about that?

THURMAN. He said he'd bet anything he had, that they didn't turn up. He says he'd be glad to come over here and talk to the boy again. He says the boy has to understand they won't come back.

HAZEL. Is he gonna come talk to him?

THURMAN. No, I said you or me could tell him.

HAZEL. But he just said . . .

[JOHN TURNER *comes out dressed in new overalls. He seems a little awkward and shy.*]

THURMAN. Come on out here, boy, and let us have a look at you. [*He comes up to them.*] Well, that's a pretty good fit, if I do say so myself. Do they feel comfortable?

JOHN TURNER. Yes, sir.

THURMAN. Turn all the way around. [*The boy does so.*] How does it look to you, Hazel?

HAZEL. It looks just fine. Are they good and sturdy?

THURMAN. Yes, the best thing I had in the store. Do you like them, boy?

JOHN TURNER. Yes, I do.

[HAZEL *starts for the house.*]

HAZEL. I think I better get supper started.

[*She starts through the door.* JOHN TURNER *calls to her.*]

JOHN TURNER. M's Hazel, I'm gettin' worried. I'm gettin' awful worried. I don' know what could have happened to my folks. If you all don' mind, I think I'd feel better if I slipped down to the river, an' just spoke to somebody down there, myself. You see, I know the Sheriff talked to people down there, but I'd feel better if I spoke to them, myself. People can be funny an' they may not remember . . .

HAZEL. John Turner, I'm sure . . .

JOHN TURNER. I just gotta go down there. I didn' sleep all last night for fear they would drive up at night an' look around an' not see me an' turn around an' leave again.

HAZEL. Why would they do that?

JOHN TURNER. I don' know, but I gotta go down there. I gotta talk to people, myself.

HAZEL. Well, all right.

JOHN TURNER. An' I gotta wait on, down there. I gotta be there when they come. It was nice of you to have me here, but I can't enjoy myself now for worryin' about them missin' me someway. [*A pause.*] I'm sorry I put you to all the trouble about the clothes, but I'll take 'em off now . . .

HAZEL. You can have the clothes, boy. We meant for you to have them.

JOHN TURNER. Yes, ma'am. But I'd feel better if I didn't take 'em. My aunt an' uncle might not like it. I'll just git in my own clothes, if you don' mind . . .

THURMAN. John Turner!

JOHN TURNER. Yes, sir?

THURMAN. Sit here beside me!

JOHN TURNER. Yes, sir.

THURMAN. Well, I don't know how to tell you this, boy—but I've had another long talk with the Sheriff—and he tells me . . .

JOHN TURNER. Yes, sir.

THURMAN. He tells me—that in his honest opinion . . .

JOHN TURNER. Yes, sir.

THURMAN. That he doesn't look for your aunt and uncle back.

JOHN TURNER. Yes, sir.

THURMAN. Now, I know how you must feel; you're not gonna be satisfied with his opinion or anyone else's . . .

JOHN TURNER. No, sir.

THURMAN. So why don't you let me take you to the River, and we can talk to the folks down there, and you can satisfy yourself about whether they've come or not, and whether they'll be told the proper things when they do come, and then I can bring you on back here to wait.

JOHN TURNER. No, sir.

THURMAN. But, boy . . .

JOHN TURNER. No, sir. Because I know what'll happen—if it ain' already happened. It come to me just in there, while I was puttin' my clothes on, an' it's scarin' me nearly out of my mind. They're gonna come back, an' hear about me, an' drive by in the night, an' see what a nice place you have, an' figure you all will take good care of me, maybe, an' then ride off again without me.

HAZEL. Why would they do a thing like that, John Turner?

JOHN TURNER. I don' know why. I don' know why. . . . Because they're afraid they can' git enough to feed me. They're afraid . . . [*A pause.*] I'm sorry now I ever come into town. I wouldn' have come at all, but I got hungry. An' I made it all up about the Culpeppers. There's no Culpeppers down there. I told you a lie, an' the Sheriff a lie. My aunt and uncle slipped off from me; that's why they didn' take me. They slipped off from me, like they done three times before when times was hard an' they didn' have no money to buy food. But always before, their consciences got to hurtin' them, so they'd turn aroun' an' come back for me. I kep' thinkin' they would this time. I kep' thinkin' . . .

HAZEL. Did they tell you that's what they were gonna do?

JOHN TURNER. Yes, ma'am. They always get to talkin' that way when times are hard an' they don' have much to eat. They say they're gonna put me in a home, where I can git good food an' clothes; an' then I git scared an' slip away in the brush until they git over feelin' that way; an' most times they git over it by mornin', an' this is one of the times they didn'. I heard the truck leavin' from out in the brush, an' I run after them, hollerin' for them not to leave me, but they wouldn' stop. I heard Aunt Velma cryin', but they wouldn' stop, an' I couldn' catch them.

[*He is crying now.* HAZEL *holds him close to her.*]

HAZEL. John Turner. John Turner. They'll come tomorrow. You said, yourself, they always come back. They'll come tomorrow. Maybe even tonight. Maybe tonight while we're havin' our supper, there'll be a knock on the door and we'll go to the door and they'll be standin' there . . .

JOHN TURNER. No, ma'am. I just can't take the chance. I'm scared. I've gotta go on back down there. I should've thought of this last night.

HAZEL. John Turner . . .

JOHN TURNER. I thank you both for all your kindness, but I

gotta go.

HAZEL. John Turner . . .

THURMAN. Hazel, the boy knows what he has to do.

JOHN TURNER. I'll go in an' take off the clothes now.

THURMAN. You don't have to do that, boy. We want you to have them. It would make us feel bad if you didn't take them.

JOHN TURNER. Yes, sir.

THURMAN. Please, take them!

JOHN TURNER. All right. Thank you. [*A pause. They look uncomfortably at each other.*] I guess I better git started, if I'm goin'.

HAZEL. Can't you just have supper first?

JOHN TURNER. No, ma'am. I'll just go on now.

THURMAN. Let me drive you in my car.

JOHN TURNER. I'd rather walk, if you don' mind.

THURMAN. All right.

[JOHN TURNER *goes to* HAZEL; *he holds out his hand.*]

JOHN TURNER. I sure do thank you for your kindness.

HAZEL. That's all right.

[*He turns to* THURMAN.]

JOHN TURNER. And thank you for your kindness.

THURMAN. That's all right, boy.

[JOHN TURNER *turns and goes down the steps.* THURMAN *and* HAZEL *stand watching him go. After a moment,* HAZEL *stands, waving in the distance. She calls.*]

HAZEL. Good-bye, John Turner. Good-bye!

[*He does not hear her, so there is no answer. She and* THURMAN *sit down on the steps together.*] Was it hot in town?

THURMAN. Yes, it was.

HAZEL. Cool out here!

THURMAN. Yes, it is. [THURMAN *stands up and looks off into the distance.*] He's out of sight now. He's clean out of sight now.

HAZEL. Are you ready for your supper?

THURMAN. No, I'll wait a little while.

[*He sits down again. They look out into the yard.*]

HAZEL. Really, we have a lot to be thankful for, Thurman, when you come to think of it. We own our own home, and we have our car, and your business isn't makin' us rich, but we get along . . .

THURMAN. I know.

HAZEL. And we have a happy marriage, and we should be thankful for that . . .

THURMAN. I'm thankful for it. I wouldn't trade places with any man in this world.

HAZEL. I wouldn't, either. [*He takes her hand.*] I pray, for his sake, they're there. I pray—I pray—I pray.

THURMAN. I know.

[*They sit in silence.*]


## ACT THREE

*The scene is again the front gallery, later that night,* HAZEL *comes out in her dressing gown. She sits on the steps. After a moment,* THURMAN *comes out.*


THURMAN. What are you doin' up, Hazel?

HAZEL. I just couldn't sleep.

THURMAN. I couldn't, either.

HAZEL. I thought you were asleep.

THURMAN. No. I've been tryin' to fall asleep, but I couldn't. I heard you get out of bed, and I almost called to you—and then I heard you come out here. [*He looks up at the sky.*] If I know anything about clouds, it's gonna rain hard before this night is through.

HAZEL. It wouldn't surprise me at all. I've known all along we were gonna make a cotton crop.

[*The hoot owl is heard.*]

THURMAN. Listen to that old owl! Looks like we've got a permanent visitor.

HAZEL. I know. He appears about sundown and stays the night.

THURMAN. You mean, he wakes *up* then. He's probably here all day, too, sleepin' up in that old pecan tree.

HAZEL. I hadn't thought of that. [*A pause.*] I heard it was bad luck to kill one of those. Did you ever hear that?

THURMAN. Yes, I have.

HAZEL. John Turner told me that last night.

THURMAN. I guess he's been at the River long ago.

HAZEL. Oh, long ago! I hope he feels more easy in his mind, now.

THURMAN. I hope. . . . It looks like rain and it smells like rain.

HAZEL. Yes, it does.

[*They sit in silence for a moment, then* THURMAN *gets up.*]

THURMAN. Hazel, I can't sleep until I find out what's happened to that boy. I'm goin' on down there and see how he's made out.

HAZEL. I wish you would. I'd certainly feel better.

THURMAN. I'll get my clothes on. Do you want to come?

HAZEL. No, I'll stay here.

THURMAN. All right.

[*He goes into the house.* HAZEL *is sitting, as the scene dissolves to a camp by the River. Four or five ragged and hungry people are sitting around a bonfire, staring at the flames. An* OLD WOMAN *is there, quietly singing a hymn to herself. An* OLD MAN *is near her, chewing a twig.*]

OLD MAN. How many hymns do you know, Miss Sarah?

MISS SARAH. More'n I could count, or you could count, or any known man could count.

OLD MAN. I reckon.

[*She goes back to singing.* THURMAN *comes up to the group. He goes over to the* OLD MAN.]

THURMAN. Excuse me.

OLD MAN. Shh! Miss Sarah is singin' us a hymn.

THURMAN. I'm sorry. [*He looks around the group for someone else to talk to. He goes over to a* MAN *at the edge of the group.*] Excuse me.

MAN. Uh huh!

THURMAN. I'm tryin' to locate a little boy. John Turner Davis is his name. He was livin' here with his aunt and uncle, and they went off and left him . . .

MAN. They come back, though.

THURMAN. When?

MAN. Last night about sundown. They asked about him, and we told them what the Sheriff said, and they got in their truck and went off, and they come back in about an hour and put up a tent. When I got up at daybreak, they had gone off again. Then, about two hours ago, the boy come here lookin' for them. I told him they'd come and gone. He didn't say nothin'. He just turned around and went off. My wife says she thought he was cryin', but it was gettin' dark by then and I couldn't see.

THURMAN. You don't know which way he went?

MAN. No, sir. [*He turns to* WOMAN *by him.*] Do you know which way that little boy went?

WOMAN. He went back up the road. A man stopped him and asked him why he was cryin', an' he said, "For no reason"— and just kept a goin'. Then I went after him and hollered and said: wouldn' he like to share our supper with us? But he said he wasn't hongry—and kept on.

THURMAN. He went down that road?

WOMAN. Yes, sir.

THURMAN. Thank you.

[*He goes. The* OLD WOMAN *is still singing. The* MAN *and the* WOMAN *are listening to her as the scene dissolves to the front gallery of the Whyte house.* HAZEL *is seated there. She is looking anxiously up the road. We hear a car pull up and stop. She gets up and looks out into the night.* THURMAN *comes in.*]

THURMAN. I got there too late.

HAZEL. Too late?

THURMAN. Yes, he'd gone. He was right. His folks came yesterday about sundown, and they were told where he was, and they must have come by here and thought we were gonna keep him, and they went off again without him; and when he got to the River he was told that, and they say when he heard that he just went off back down the road. I went up and down every road leadin' to the River, drivin' my car slow as I could, callin' his name. . . . But he wouldn't answer, if he heard me. [*A pause.*] Did you ever ask him to stay on here?

HAZEL. No, I didn't think we had the right to.

THURMAN. I guess we didn't. . . . Oh, honey, we don't have no luck. We don't have no luck at all.

HAZEL. Don't say that!

THURMAN. We don't.

HAZEL. You said yourself we had a lot to be grateful for . . .

THURMAN. I know, but I wanted to keep that little boy, Hazel—the worst kind of way.

HAZEL. I know, but we couldn't have kept him, Thurman. It wouldn't have been right, as long as there was a chance his folks were comin' for him.

THURMAN. I know. . . . I'm gonna call the Sheriff. Maybe he can find him. He just can't go wanderin' around the country by himself—a twelve year old boy!

HAZEL. I know.

THURMAN. I'd look the rest of the night, if I thought I could find him. But I don't know where to find him.

HAZEL. I know.

[*He goes inside.* HAZEL *covers her face with her hands.* JOHN TURNER *comes up on the steps. She hears him and looks up.*]

John Turner? Is that you?

JOHN TURNER. Yes, ma'am. I was comin' by here, an' I seen you on the steps.

HAZEL. I'm so glad you came. Let me call Thurman. [*She calls into the house.*] Thurman! Thurman! We've got company! We were worried about you, John Turner.

JOHN TURNER. Were you?

HAZEL. Yes, we were. You see, Thurman went down to the River to find out how you were gettin' along, and couldn't find no sign of you anywhere—and then he went up and down all the roads in his car callin' to you . . .

JOHN TURNER. Yes, ma'am.

[THURMAN *comes out.*]

HAZEL. Look who's here, Thurman!

THURMAN. Where did you come from, boy?

JOHN TURNER. I was just walkin' down the road, an' I said to myself: "Is that M's Hazel sittin' on them steps?" an' I come up to see, an' it was. [*It begins to rain.*] There's rain. That ought to be good for the cotton.

THURMAN. I prophesied rain. Didn't I prophesy rain, Hazel?

HAZEL. Yes, you did. Are you hungry, John Turner?

JOHN TURNER. Yes, ma'am.

HAZEL. Let me get you something.

[*She goes into the house.*]

JOHN TURNER. That's a hard rain. That's a growin' rain. That rain will make enough cotton to keep everybody busy. I'm glad about that.

THURMAN. So am I.

JOHN TURNER. Seems like every time I come here we get a rain of some kind. Last time it was a shower.

THURMAN. I know.

JOHN TURNER. Well, my aunt an' uncle have gone off for good, I guess. Now I got no mama an' papa an' no aunt or uncle. I got 'em, I guess, but I don' know where they are. So, might as well not have 'em, for all the good they doin' me. . . . I thank you for comin' after me. I heard you callin' me, but I was cryin' so hard at the time, I was ashamed to answer. I'm over my cryin' now. I'll set here a while, if you all don' mind, until the rain is through. Then I'll go on into town an' see the Sheriff—see if he can figure out what's gonna become of me. I thought, there for a while, I'd run around on my own, but that's a lonesome kind of life, I decided after about four hours in that dark woods. Everybody tells me there's a home that boys can go to, where they can give you an education and teach you a trade. . . . The Sheriff said yestidy I'd be better off there. I couldn' see it, of course, at the time.

THURMAN. John Turner, we don't want you to go to any place. John Turner, we don't have a boy; and we're lonesome, John Turner; and if you'd like to stay here, we'd sure like for you to stay here.

JOHN TURNER. Yes, sir. I wouldn' care to put you out any . . .

THURMAN. You wouldn't be puttin' us out. You'd be doin' us

the biggest kind of favor.

[HAZEL *comes out with the sandwich.*]

JOHN TURNER. Yes, sir.

HAZEL. Here you are!

JOHN TURNER. Thank you. [*He eats the sandwich.*] All my life I wanted to live in a house. I reckon I could get used to livin' in a house, same as anyone.

THURMAN. 'Course you could. [*He turns to* HAZEL.] I asked John Turner to stay on here with us, Hazel.

HAZEL. Oh, I'm so glad. Will you stay, John Turner?

JOHN TURNER. Yes, ma'am. If you want me. [*The rain has stopped.*] Doggone if that isn't just another old shower! That's hard on the cotton.

THURMAN. Yes, it is. Well, I was wrong; I thought sure this would be a real rain.

HAZEL. It's gonna rain.

JOHN TURNER. How do you know?

HAZEL. Because—I know. I know.

THURMAN. And she might be right, John Turner. She might be right. You see, livin' on this road has always been lucky for her, and she says the luck is to be passed on to me, and now I guess to you.

JOHN TURNER. I certainly hope so. I could use some luck.

[*The rain has started again, harder than before.*]

THURMAN. You see?

JOHN TURNER. Yes, sir.

THURMAN. Are you tired, boy?

JOHN TURNER. Yes, sir. I'm tired, but I'm not sleepy.

THURMAN. Neither am I. I'm happy, but I'm not sleepy.

HAZEL. Well, why don't we just sit here then, and listen to the rain?

[*The three of them sit quietly, listening to the sound of the rain.*]

CURTAIN

# A REMITTANCE FROM SPAIN

## By

## THEODORE APSTEIN

*(Published here for the first time)*

# A REMITTANCE FROM SPAIN

## CAST

*A Remittance from Spain* was originally done by the One-Act Play Workshop at Brander Matthews Theatre in New York City, on June 24 and 25, 1953, directed by the author and with the following cast:

DOROTHY ................ Patricia Carnegie
CARL PETERS .............. Tom DeGaetani
LUBOV STEWART ............. Anne Hegira
KREYDON ............... Joseph Pisacane
MRS. RANDALL ............. Joan Lightdale
MR. RANDALL ................. Jim Egan

TIME: The present.
PLACE: Acapulco, Mexico.

# THEODORE APSTEIN

THEODORE APSTEIN brings to these annuals his sixth play, *A Remittance from Spain*, interpreting the Mexican scene. His previously published plays have been: *Making the Bear, Before the Bullfight, Fortunata Writes a Letter, Paradise Inn,* and *The Beams of Our House*. His play, *Fortunata Writes a Letter,* has been produced in Danish, Norwegian, and Afrikaans, as well as in English.

In addition to the short plays which have appeared in these volumes, Dr. Apstein is the author of eight long plays and several translations, and other short plays. He has written scripts for CBS's series, "Lamp Unto My Feet," for "Theatre Guild on the Air," for the "Schlitz Playhouse of Stars"; and his long play, *Illusion,* produced by the Morganthau Workshop in New York, will be produced professionally in Mexico City this spring under the title, *Breve Kermesse*.

Dr. Apstein was born in Kiev, Russia, received most of his early education in Mexico, and has also lived in Argentina, Columbia, and Peru. He made a two year investigation of Latin American theatres on a Rockefeller Foundation grant, contributed to magazines in Buenos Aires and Mexico City, wrote a paper on "Higher Education in Mexico" for the Pan American Union, and is at present teaching at Columbia University and at the American Theatre Wing.

# A REMITTANCE FROM SPAIN

*The cocktail lounge of a swanky new hotel in Acapulco, Mexico, extends into the terrace which overlooks Caleta beach. To one side, we see the swinging, cushioned doors leading to the cocktail lounge and bar proper. The other side leads to the dining room. In the rear, there is a railing and a staircase which eventually ends on the beach. The bay and the ocean are in the distance, and a very blue, star-clad sky. It's a very warm winter evening.*

CARL PETERS *is seated at one of the tables on the terrace, having a long, cool drink.* DOROTHY TURPIN *is at the railing, looking down at the beach. Both are attractive young people in their late twenties.* DOROTHY *is wearing a beach robe over her bathing suit.* CARL *is in his swimming trunks, with a towel wrapped around his neck. Juke-box music is heard from the bar.*

DOROTHY. With the lights on, the ocean looks green. I like it better when it's blue—in the daytime. [*She comes back to the table and sits down.*] There's supposed to be folk music on the beach tonight.

CARL. What kind of folk? If it's that typical Mexican stuff, I've had enough of it.

DOROTHY. I keep forgetting you're practically a resident. But remember I'm just a tourist. I've been here only a few days and I find Mexican songs very exciting—and certainly better than that juke-box in the bar.

CARL. I get homesick for juke-box music.

DOROTHY. And you a musician! Oh, Carl, you're funny—and it's good to see you again. Only—only what am I going to report back to your mother?

CARL. That's easy. Dear Mrs. Peters, I saw Carl, and all your predictions were right. He should've gone to work at that factory like you wanted him to. No, of course he's not a musician; he's a bum.

DOROTHY. Your mother thought I might be able to . . . I guess it was silly of her, and of me, too. I've never had much luck with you. Is it because we grew up on the same block? [CARL *smiles, says nothing.*] Carl, your family's willing to pay for the trip back.

CARL. What have I lost in Cleveland?

DOROTHY. Your mother, your brothers . . . [CARL *sneers.*] You could go to school there—get some training in music. How long can you stay in Acapulco?

CARL. I've been going strong for three months. I'm a beachcomber and I like it. You can tell my mother I'm happy for the first time in my life.

DOROTHY. That's a lie.

CARL. As you well know, it's very pleasant to eat.

DOROTHY. Not off Mrs. Stewart, it isn't.

CARL. You ought to try it sometime. You always insist on paying your own check.

DOROTHY. She gives me the creeps. Especially when I think of her with you.

CARL. What about her with me? We're just great friends— even though she tries hard to make you think otherwise; you and everybody else, for that matter. If she wants to cherish that myth, why not let her? It doesn't hurt me. I have no reputation to worry about. And I get to eat and drink.

DOROTHY. Has she been paying your hotel bill, too?

CARL. That I don't know. But it's submitted to her, yes.

DOROTHY. Oh, Carl, how long do you think you can stall that awful woman?

CARL. Until she asks me point blank, and I'll either say, "Yes," and go on eating, or I'll say, "No," and come back to Cleveland. [*He laughs.*] To the old block. Will I still have a chance with you?

DOROTHY. I told you I'm going to marry my boss after this vacation.

CARL. Funny you had to take a vacation first.

DOROTHY. I wanted to see you again before I got married.

CARL. Well, now you've seen the bum . . .

DOROTHY. You enjoy that thought, don't you?

CARL. Maybe. I just take my pleasure wherever I can find it. Oh, there she comes!

DOROTHY. Your pleasure?

CARL. For the time being, she has the means to provide me with it.

[LUBOV STEWART *appears from the dining room. It's hard to determine her age. She could be anywhere from forty-five to sixty. She wears an inordinate amount of make-up and tries to be coy, which she thinks makes her seem considerably younger, but it doesn't. All her clothes—dress, shawl, shoes, bag and gloves— have seen better days. They are all very expensive items, but out of style and a little ragged at the edges. In that, they match their owner.*]

LUBOV. Carl, dear, am I terribly late? Dorothy, how are you? [*She kisses* CARL *on the cheek, then proceeds to kiss* DOROTHY, *who almost turns away, but still gets a peck.*]

Dorothy is so shy with me, isn't she, Carl? Please don't be! I like to kiss everybody, don't I, Carl? We always did in Europe . . .

CARL. What'll you have?

LUBOV. Oh, darling, you know I always let you decide.

CARL. Daiquiri be all right?

LUBOV. No, I want a tequila cocktail. [*She sits down and smiles coyly at* DOROTHY.] Isn't the heat unbearable? Anybody who comes to Acapulco should have his head examined. To think it's snowing in New York now!

DOROTHY. Are you from New York, Mrs. Stewart?

LUBOV. Upstate. And, darling, please, don't call me Mrs. Stewart. I never did like the name on checks, and the man who bears it is the most repulsive creature on the face of the earth. I have to sign that name, but I use it as little as possible. Carl, where's my drink?

CARL. I'm trying to attract a waiter.

LUBOV. Can't you get it yourself?

CARL. Yes, yes, I can.

[*He goes into the bar.*]

LUBOV. Now, darling, will you promise to call me Lubov?

DOROTHY. Is that your first name?

LUBOV. Yes, dear, *Lu-bov.*

DOROTHY. I've never heard of it.

LUBOV. [*Laughs.*] It means love. It's a Russian name. I was born with an ugly name; I daren't mention it to you. But I met a Russian dancer in Barcelona once. I was still married then. He was with the Ballet Russe. I guess all Russian dancers were in those days. He said—enough of that stupid name your father gave you, "You are Lubov"—and he put a wreath of garlands in my hair. My husband thought it was priceless, and I've been Lubov ever since. A Polish count once told me I should use Luba, short for Lubov, but I like Lubov better, don't you?

[DOROTHY *wants to react, but doesn't know what to say.*]

I'm so glad. You know, Dorothy, the moment I saw you, I knew we'd understand each other—because we do have something in common. Of course you're from the Middle West and I simply abhor the Middle West, but we have something in common.

DOROTHY. Do we?

LUBOV. We're both terribly fond of Carl. [*Short pause.*] Aren't you?

DOROTHY. Of course I'm fond of him. We grew up together. But I hadn't seen Carl in eight years. He went to New York, he was in the army, then he came down to Mexico.

LUBOV. He's so terribly talented. Don't you think he's talented, darling?

DOROTHY. I have no idea, Mrs. St . . .

LUBOV. Uh-uh.

DOROTHY. I have no idea. I know he's wanted to be a composer for a long time, but I've heard he needs training badly.

LUBOV. Oh, that's what I keep telling him—training, that's what makes a musician. In my house in Madrid we used to entertain all the great musicians—De Falla, Strauss, Ravel—

they all said the same thing—training.

DOROTHY. I don't imagine Carl has much of a chance for training in Acapulco.

LUBOV. Of course not. But I'm taking him to the States with me.

DOROTHY. I didn't know you were going back.

LUBOV. Didn't Carl tell you?

DOROTHY. No.

LUBOV. Oh, absolutely. I've got to go—and soon. You see, my father—bless his heart, I haven't seen him in almost twenty years—he's frightfully ill, and I'd never forgive myself if I didn't see him before he died.

DOROTHY. And then you'll stay in the U.S.?

LUBOV. Hah? Oh, I don't know. I imagine . . . I came to Mexico before the war and then one winter I moved to Acapulco to be warm, and I've stayed here. Ever since my divorce, I've preferred not to keep track of time. [CARL *returns with her drink.*] Thank you, darling. I love the color of the tequila cocktails, don't you?

DOROTHY. Yes, it's a nice orange-pink. [*She turns to* CARL.] Mrs. Stewart was telling me she's going to the States soon.

LUBOV. [*With a straw in her mouth.*] I should think you would've told Dorothy.

CARL. Well, I didn't know when.

LUBOV. You do, too, know when. As soon as humanly possible. I'm only waiting for a remittance from Spain. It's been frightfully difficult to get large sums out of Spain, and of course, I need a large one to make this trip and take Carl, too.

CARL. You don't have to.

LUBOV. Oh, now darling, you know perfectly well I wouldn't leave you behind. [*She takes his hand into hers.*] And you need training, Dorothy and I are agreed on that.

CARL. I've told you—I'm a beachcomber, not a musician.

LUBOV. Nonsense! I don't like to hear you talk like that. He loves to tease me. Sometimes I get furious at him and won't speak to him for hours.

DOROTHY. Have you had your swim this evening?

LUBOV. I wish I could—but I've gained simply too much weight in this horrible town. People eat like pigs here, and its contagious. When I get back to New York, I'll have to lose at least fifteen pounds. Then I can wear a bathing suit again. I wouldn't be seen dead in it now. But if you and Carl want to go for another swim, don't let me keep you—please don't!

DOROTHY. I think I will.

[*She gets up.*]

CARL. I'll join you after a while.

DOROTHY. All right. Excuse me.

[*She goes down the steps to the beach.*]

LUBOV. Dorothy doesn't like me. [CARL *says nothing.*] You could try to deny it—at least that would be the polite thing to do. Oh, I don't know why I have to put up with people like you!

CARL. As I said before, you don't have to!

LUBOV. All right, maybe I won't! You'll be sorry when I leave for New York and you'll be stuck in this tropical paradise.

CARL. That's a threat I've heard once too often. Is that remittance from Spain ever coming?

LUBOV. How dare you question me? How dare you? [CARL *gets up and starts to leave.*] Darling, forgive me, I'm very nervous tonight. The heat and the dampness . . .

CARL. It's hot and damp every night.

LUBOV. All right, and I'm nervous every night. I'm not used to associating with people from the other side of the tracks— like your friend, Dorothy.

CARL. She's not from the other . . . Maybe she doesn't come from a fine upstate New York family, but neither do I.

LUBOV. Darling, you're an artist. That's different. Artists have always had patrons from the upper classes. [*He sighs.*] In Madrid, I used to help little ballerinas who came from nowhere, literally nowhere. God, that was my mistake. My husband decided to patronize one of them himself—oh, how he patronized her—she's now the second Mrs. Stewart—a filthy little gypsy named Encarnacion.

CARL. Lubov . . .

LUBOV. Yes, darling?

CARL. Don't say any more to Dorothy about going to the States.

LUBOV. I'll say anything I want to say. Why not?

CARL. Because she's going to tell my family, and I don't want them to expect me.

LUBOV. Darling, you don't mean you'd rather stay here?

CARL. No, I'd like to go with you, but I don't want Dorothy to tell my mother that . . .

LUBOV. What? That we're friends?

[*She takes his hand and presses it against her bosom.*]

Well, we are, and there isn't a thing Dorothy—or your mother—can do about it.

CARL. Just don't give her the impression that you've completely overpowered me.

LUBOV. You don't really like me, either, do you?

[*This is said in the manner of a petulant child demanding affection.*]

CARL. Yes, I like you, Lubov, or I wouldn't spend so much time with you.

LUBOV. In preference to younger women like Dorothy— girls who can show their bodies on the beach. Darling, if you want me to . . .

CARL. No.

LUBOV. I'm not terribly unattractive in a bathing suit. Let me tell you a secret. [*In a loud whisper.*] I've been asked to model the new spring fashions at the style show they're having next week. Of course I refused. Imagine what my father would say if he heard I'd become a model!

CARL. Yes, imagine!

[JAN KREYDON, *a middle-aged man, nicely dressed in a summer suit, appears from the dining room.*]

LUBOV. *Monsieur* Kreydon, what a pleasure to see you again! You're so busy with your new clientele, you pay no attention to me . . .

KREYDON. [*Kisses her hand, since she has extended it.*] Madame Stewart, no customer will force me to neglect you. Good evening, Mr. Peters.

[CARL *nods to him.*]

LUBOV. Carl, bring me another tequila cocktail.

KREYDON. But you can call a waiter.

LUBOV. Oh, my dear *Monsieur,* the service on the terrace is simply intolerable. It's all right in the restaurant, but out here —of course, I don't care—I've got Carl, but the rest of your clientele might object. Carl, will you please?

[CARL *picks up her glass and his, and goes into the bar.*]

Oh, that boy—he's an American, of course, and I've gotten so out of touch with my countrymen, having lived in Spain and France most of my life. That's why I like to talk to you, *Monsieur;* I've always adored the French.

KREYDON. I'm a Dutch Jew, *Madame.*

LUBOV. Well . . . [*She gives him one of her coyest smiles.*] You're still European, and Europeans—all of them—have a great deal of charm. Whatever made you come to this hell-hole to open up a hotel?

KREYDON. I do not consider it a hell-hole, especially after what I escaped from. And since Americans have discovered Acapulco as a resort, it is a very productive business.

LUBOV. Acapulco's been ruined by American tourists.

KREYDON. That is the opinion of some of my Mexican friends. I am not in a position to share it. I make my living from Americans.

LUBOV. I dare say they swarmed to this hotel when I moved in, didn't they?

[KREYDON *tries to ignore this remark by looking away.*]

That old hotel across the bay made me sick, literally sick. I couldn't stand those damp walls and leaking roofs. It's a dreadful place, really. They tell me no one stays there any more.

KREYDON. Oh, during the season, every hotel in Acapulco is full.

LUBOV. Yes, but full of what? That's what I mean.

KREYDON. A hotel keeper can't afford to be a snob.

LUBOV. [*Laughs.*] You mean I can? Oh, I know I am. I like to be a snob. I like to associate only with my kind of people.

KREYDON. Of course. Then, perhaps this hotel, where I allow anyone to stay, is no longer adequate for you.

LUBOV. [*Looks at him with terrified eyes, then says arrogantly.*] I'll be the judge of that, *Monsieur* Kreydon.

KREYDON. Except, *Madame,* you have such a deep scorn for my hotel that you have refused to pay your bills—yours and Mr. Peters'—for five weeks.

LUBOV. Five weeks? [*An almost hysterical, forced laugh.*] Do you know I had credit for five *years* at the best hotels in Biarritz?

KREYDON. And I, *Madame,* had a baronial mansion in Rotterdam. Those were other days. Now I am a hotel keeper, and you are a paying guest who has not paid.

LUBOV. Very well, *Monsieur.* I'll pay as soon as possible.

KREYDON. That is what you have said to the clerk several times, *Madame.* May I ask when?

LUBOV. I'm expecting a remittance from Spain. My ex-husband is supposed to send me a handsome check every month, but something has gone wrong with the Spanish exchange—or the banks—I don't understand those things.

KREYDON. It is unpleasant for me to remind you that you were also expecting money from Spain when we insisted on the last bill, and you paid us with a watch.

LUBOV. Didn't it cover the amount?

KREYDON. Practically. A small balance of a hundred and some pesos is still due on that bill.

LUBOV. Well, that should be easy; you can add it to the new one.

KREYDON. *Madame,* against my will I have checked with the last hotel where you stayed . . .

LUBOV. Have you?

KREYDON. I have been informed that you paid the first bill with a ring, but moved out owing them three thousand pesos.

LUBOV. This is offensive, *Monsieur.* You asked for references —of me—and from that cheap, fat Mexican?

KREYDON. He has been very kind in not prosecuting you. I, for instance, could not afford to lose three thousand pesos. Nor would I care to have an incident in my hotel . . .

LUBOV. An incident?

KREYDON. If *Madame* will remember under what circumstances she left that last hotel—and the one before that.

LUBOV. It was an accident, *Monsieur,* not an incident.

KREYDON. These accidents always seem to happen when you decide to change hotels.

[MR. *and* MRS. RANDALL *have appeared on the terrace.*]

MRS. RANDALL. Jim, isn't that the woman we met last year at the . . .

RANDALL. I believe it is, by golly.

[LUBOV *has noticed them, tries to hide her face in her shawl, and speaks to* KREYDON *intensely and rapidly.*]

LUBOV. You needn't worry, *Monsieur,* everything will be taken care of. My husband has tremendous holdings in Spain.

MRS. RANDALL. [*Approaching the table.*] Pardon me.

LUBOV. One of your customers, Mr. Kreydon.

[*And she turns away.*]

MRS. RANDALL. I'm sure we met last summer—a year and a half ago. Aren't you Mrs. Stewart?

LUBOV. Huh?

RANDALL. We were staying at the hotel across the bay. You had the suite overlooking the ocean.

MRS. RANDALL. And we got very high on tequila cocktails one night . . .

LUBOV. [*As if trying to recollect.*] Oh . . .

KREYDON. You will excuse me, please.

LUBOV. But *Monsieur* Kreydon . . . [*He bows and leaves.*] Yes, I'm Mrs. Stewart. You must forgive me if I don't remember you, but of course one meets so many people in Acapulco. They come and they go, all year round.

RANDALL. You've been here a long time.

MRS. RANDALL. I'm so glad we ran into you.

LUBOV. Yes . . .

[*She seems embarrassed, doesn't quite know what to say.*]

MRS. RANDALL. You mind if we join you for a moment?

LUBOV. No, no—not at all. Please sit down.

RANDALL. [*As he sits down.*] Whatever happened to that nice young man?

LUBOV. Young man?

MRS. RANDALL. Oh, yes, the medical student . . .

[LUBOV *looks bewildered.*]

RANDALL. He escorted you to all the nightspots. Let me see, what was his name?

MRS. RANDALL. Hector.

LUBOV. Oh, Hector—oh, my dear, he wasn't a nice young man at all. He wanted me to help him through medical school, and of course I was perfectly willing, but after all . . .

RANDALL. After all—what?

LUBOV. [*Smiles.*] Well, you know—one night on the beach he said he was a man and I was a woman—and, my God, he was a Mexican, you know.

MRS. RANDALL. Oh.

RANDALL. I see.

[CARL *appears with two drinks.*]

LUBOV. Oh, thank you, darling. This is Mr. Peters and . . .

RANDALL. [*Shakes hands with* CARL.] Randall. Pleased to meet you.

LUBOV. And Mrs. Randall.

CARL. How do you do! Will you have a drink?

MRS. RANDALL. [*Looking at her husband for help.*] Why . . .

RANDALL. No, thanks, our party's waiting for us at the Copa.

LUBOV. Oh, you're doing the nightclubs again?

MRS. RANDALL. Well, we did cover them all a year and a half ago, but it seems . . .

[*Again she looks for help to her husband.*]

RANDALL. Say, you know, Mrs. Stewart, we've been expecting you . . .

MRS. RANDALL. Oh, she doesn't remember, Jim. We gave you our address—and you promised to look us up.

CARL. [*Casually.*] Where do you live?

RANDALL. Irvington. Just outside of New York. Westchester.

MRS. RANDALL. I suppose when you did go up, you were too concerned about your father to . . .

LUBOV. No. [*There is a pause. She hopes someone will speak, but she realizes it's still her turn.*] I didn't go up. I haven't been to the States.

RANDALL. But you told us as soon as that remittance from Spain . . .

CARL. Hm.

LUBOV. [*Very nervous.*] I couldn't make it, that's all.

MRS. RANDALL. I'm sorry to hear that. I guess it was too late. Your father?

LUBOV. My father's all right.

CARL. Is he, Lubov?

LUBOV. He's frightfully ill, of course, but it's one of those things that go on and on.

CARL. As a matter of fact, Mrs. Stewart is still planning to go up to see him. Maybe she'll call on you then. Have you still got their address, Lubov?

LUBOV. I'm sure I do.

RANDALL. [*Takes out his wallet.*] Well, just in case, here's my card again.

LUBOV. Thank you, thank you so much.

MRS. RANDALL. Would you care to join us at the Copa?

LUBOV. Thank you, but I've stopped going to the usual places.

RANDALL. Well, dear . . .

[*He takes her by the arm.*]

MRS. RANDALL. Yes. Maybe we'll see you on the beach in the morning.

LUBOV. I hope so. Good night.

RANDALL. Good night, Peters.

CARL. So long.

[*The* RANDALLS *go out.*]

LUBOV. [*Grabs her drink and finishes it.*] Those dreadful, dull tourists! I have no idea who they are or when I met them. You speak one word to them and they feel you're an old friend.

CARL. You met them a year and a half ago.

LUBOV. Stop looking at me like that. It's not my fault.

[*Her fingers are dancing nervously on the table.*]

CARL. You've been kidding me.

LUBOV. No, no, darling . . .

[*She goes to him and puts her arms around him, then tries to rest her head on his shoulders, but he steps away from her.*]

You know I need money— I need money desperately. [*She walks away from him.*] I've got to go to New York; I really must. I must see him before he dies. [*She touches her hair.*]

I've got to spend some time in Mexico City first—go to a beauty parlor—order some new clothes. My father hasn't seen me in twenty years. He expects me to be young and slim and . . .

CARL. You can't let him see the wreck you've become, huh?

LUBOV. Yes—huh. Since you're such a gentleman, I can tell you the truth. My father is a gentleman, a gentleman of the old school. He doesn't approve of drinking or smoking—or keeping a young man. God, I don't remember anything I've done in twenty years he does approve of. But I've got to see him once more before he dies! He's an old man, frightfully old —eighty, I think. Oh, but he has a good mind, darling; he can see through me.

CARL. How do you know, if you haven't seen him in twenty years?

LUBOV. I remember him—oh, so clearly.

CARL. People change.

LUBOV. Not my father.

CARL. You've been *running* for twenty years, haven't you?— trying to find affection?

LUBOV. [*Indignant and again arrogant.*] Trying to find affection! Really, the nerve of the young man! I was the most sought-after heiress in New York State. I had dozens of suitors before I picked my husband. And when I lived in Madrid, six Spanish noblemen—six that I know of, there may've been more—but six Spanish noblemen lost their lives in duels over me. A member of the royal family wanted to elope with me, and the crown prince of Albania! Trying to find affection, indeed! Just because I was faithful to that dreadful man who finally betrayed me with a gypsy named Encarnacion. I had more affection than any woman in Spain. And even here, in this God-forsaken tourist resort . . .

CARL. [*Interrupting her.*] There've been young men like me, trying to take advantage of you. Maybe laughing at you behind your back.

LUBOV. Carl! [*And then pitifully.*] Don't you like me at all? [*She follows him.*]

CARL. Tonight I do, Lubov, I like you very much.

LUBOV. [*Trying hard to be playful.*] Not the way I want to be liked. You feel sorry for me.

CARL. Yes, a little.

LUBOV. [*Touching him, hoping for an embrace.*] No real affection?

CARL. I think it's real—as real as I'm capable of.

[*But he can't go through with the embrace, and rejects her.*]

LUBOV. [*Slaps him hard across the mouth.*] Indeed!

CARL. Lubov, how long have you been going back?

LUBOV. [*Stunned by the question.*] What?

CARL. How long has your father been on his deathbed?

[*She moves away from him, escaping as he starts attacking her with his questions.*]

Are you sure he isn't dead already? You were waiting for that remittance a year and a half ago. For all I know, you were waiting for it ten years ago, too!

LUBOV. No. [*She's at the railing now, staring down at the water.*] Before the war it was simple to get money from Europe.

CARL. Why didn't you go up then?

LUBOV. Oh, for God's sake, leave me alone! Get me another drink! Please, darling, I need another drink. I can't stand to have all these questions asked, to have my word in doubt. I'm not used to your tactlessness!

CARL. You better set a date for our departure.

LUBOV. I see. All right. I suppose the time has come to . . . [*She has managed to work up some artificial excitement.*]

Carl, darling, we're going to New York. We really are! I'm not fooling you. I've just thought of a way. I can scrape the money together. Once I get home, my father will help me out. I'll tell him everything—what I've done, how I've lived—and I'll hope for his mercy. Darling, please go call the airlines. Find out what connections we can make in Mexico City; we'll leave Acapulco early in the morning.

CARL. We don't have to leave tomorrow.

LUBOV. Oh, yes, tomorrow! Even tonight, if possible. It's not often I have a fit of courage, darling.

CARL. All right, I'll get the information.

[*He kisses her on the cheek, and leaves.*]

LUBOV. [*Sits for a second making faces, still enjoying the one kiss* CARL *gave her of his own free will. Then she rummages through her purse, produces the mirror again, looks at herself, deliberately musses her hair. She puts the mirror back in the bag and pulls her dress over one shoulder, as though it had been torn.*]

*Monsieur* Kreydon!

[*There is desperation in her cry for the manager. She gets up and runs to the bar.*]

*Monsieur* Kreydon!

[*She opens the swinging door, looks inside. The juke-box music becomes very loud for a second. Then she rushes to the terrace again and to the dining room door.*]

*Monsieur* Kreydon!

KREYDON. [*From the dining room.*] Yes, *Madame* Stewart? [*He appears on the terrace.*]

LUBOV. [*In a frenzied voice, clinging to his coat.*] Oh, *Monsieur*, I'm in dreadful trouble, and you must help me. Only you could possibly help me . . .

KREYDON. *Madame*, you're trembling.

LUBOV. And for a good reason. That frightful young man!

KREYDON. Who?

LUBOV. Who? Who do you think? Carl Peters! He's been annoying me dreadfully.

KREYDON. But *Madame* . . .

LUBOV. [*Walks away from him, wringing her hands.*] It's a result of your admitting all sorts of riff-raff into your hotel.

KREYDON. *Madame*, you brought Mr. Peters here. It was you who asked me to give him the room adjoining yours.

LUBOV. [*At the top of her voice, and bringing her fists down on the table.*] Will you shut up? Don't you see the state I'm in?

KREYDON. Yes, I do, *Madame,* and I think you should retire to your room and . . .

LUBOV. I can't. I'm frightened. Oh, *Monsieur* . . .

[*She holds on to his coat again.*]

You and I should understand each other. Because I'm really more European than American—and here I am in the midst of natives and wolves. I don't know how these people think, how they act. Please help me. Carl Peters is trying to take advantage of me. I thought he was a talented musician, and I might be able to help him through the people I know. I know some of the . . .

[*She realizes she is making no impression on* KREYDON.]

Anyway, there was no romantic interest, and suddenly this young man—oh, really, you know what I mean, *Monsieur*—I simply can't tolerate that kind of behavior! Please keep him away from me!

KREYDON. I will try my best, *Madame.*

LUBOV. To be completely safe, *Monsieur,* I'm going to move to another hotel at once—tonight!

KREYDON. That, of course, is as you wish. But before you do . . .

LUBOV. I'll sign something—anything.

KREYDON. At the last hotel you signed . . .

LUBOV. That cheap fat Mexican!

KREYDON. As I said, I can't afford . . .

LUBOV. I must move tonight!

KREYDON. I'm afraid I can't allow that, *Madame.*

LUBOV. [*Like a frightened animal.*] You can't keep me here by force!

KREYDON. Not here, *Madame.* But perhaps the authorities . . . [LUBOV *emits a cry, a frail, thin cry of realization.*]

I am terribly sorry.

LUBOV. No, it's all right. You're a very smart business man. How much do I owe you?

KREYDON. Including Mr. Peters' bill?

LUBOV. I said I'd pay for him, didn't I?

KREYDON. Yes, *Madame.* At the special rate I arranged for you, it comes to—in pesos or in dollars?

LUBOV. Suit yourself. I haven't the cash, anyway.

KREYDON. Close to twenty-eight hundred pesos, some three hundred dollars.

LUBOV. [*Slips off her bracelet.*] Will you accept this as security?

KREYDON. This? [*He examines it.*] Certainly.

LUBOV. You know a good thing when you see one.

KREYDON. I imagine this is worth more than what you owe. I shall accept it only as security, not as a payment.

LUBOV. Well, that depends . . .

KREYDON. I will be glad to send you a check for the difference.

LUBOV. That's very nice of you.

KREYDON. It is a lovely piece. You should try to recover it when you receive your remittance from Spain.

LUBOV. There are so many I haven't recovered . . .

KREYDON. But this is the last piece of jewelry.

LUBOV. Have you been rummaging through my trunk?

KREYDON. No, *Madame*. But I have been informed. A costly necklace to a fancy dressmaker in Mexico City, an antique brooch to a hotel in Cuernavaca, a ring to the last hotel, a watch . . .

LUBOV. Don't tell me the story of my life, *Monsieur*. Keep the bracelet and remember me well. That cheap fat Mexican could've gotten it, you know. But I didn't like him. [*She goes to the railing.*] Carl Peters is making a phone call. Please tell him not to look for me. I never want to see him again.

KREYDON. Very well. [*She goes to the steps leading to the beach.*] Madame . . . ?

LUBOV. Yes?

KREYDON. I have changed my mind. I will not take the bracelet. It is already making my hand burn.

LUBOV. Don't tell me you, too, are sorry for me!

KREYDON. I don't want any accidents . . .

LUBOV. You won't in your hotel, *Monsieur*.

KREYDON. [*Goes to her with the bracelet.*] Please . . .

LUBOV. No. I've always scorned pity, *Monsieur*. *Au revoir.*
[*She goes down the steps.*]

KREYDON. *Au revoir.*

[*He looks after her, then starts towards the dining room and runs into* CARL *at the door. He stops.*]

CARL. Yes? Have you seen Mrs. Stewart?

KREYDON. She gave me a message for you.

CARL. Oh?

KREYDON. I hope this will not come as a shock. She is moving out of this hotel tonight.

CARL. No, it's tomorrow we're leaving.

KREYDON. She is leaving the hotel tonight. Without you, Mr. Peters. She asked you not to annoy her any more.

CARL. Aren't you overstepping . . . ?

KREYDON. This is a very unpleasant task. But I think I understand Mrs. Stewart's dilemma. She does not want you to see her broken—and she is broken now. She had promised to go away with you?

CARL. Why—yes.

KREYDON. She will never go away, you see.

DOROTHY. [*Appears on the steps.*] Carl, I ran into Mrs. Stewart on the beach and she didn't see me. I mean, I spoke to her and she ignored me; she was glassy-eyed. There's something very strange . . .

CARL. [*Runs to the railing.*] Look, she's going into the ocean —with her clothes on! Lubov!

KREYDON. [*Puts his hand over* CARL's *mouth.*] Don't!

CARL. [*Pushing* KREYDON *away.*] She can't swim!

KREYDON. Let her get in. We will drag her out before she drowns. [*He calls.*] Lorenzo! Alvaro! *Al agua!* [*To* CARL.] She is in the habit of attempting suicide. It gives her much attention.

CARL. The least I could do . . .

[*He starts down the steps, but now* DOROTHY *stops him.*]

KREYDON. But she does not wish to see you again. There— Lorenzo and Alvaro will get her out of the water. But first she must get in far enough.

DOROTHY. How awful!

KREYDON. Do not worry. She will be all right.

CARL. How often has this happened?

KREYDON. Every time she has moved out of a hotel. Every time she has to break with a young man. Every time she gives up a piece of jewelry.

CARL. This is horrible. We've got to stop this! I'm not going to stand for it!

[*He goes towards the dining room.*]

DOROTHY. What can you do?

CARL. I'm going to wire her father right away. She ought to be taken home . . .

KREYDON. Her father? But do you not know?

CARL. What?

KREYDON. Her father died six years ago.

[CARL *collapses into a chair.* KREYDON *looks towards the beach.*]

Lorenzo and Alvaro are going into the water. She has been rescued every time.

DOROTHY. Do you think that's merciful?

KREYDON. Who knows, who knows!

**CURTAIN**

# SALT FOR SAVOR

## By

## PERCIVAL WILDE

*(Originally published in the Christmas, 1953, issue of* Esquire, *and now reprinted by courtesy of* Esquire *and its Editor, Frederic A. Birmingham.)*

# SALT FOR SAVOR

## CAST

PATRICK
PATRICK, JUNIOR
MR. JENKINS
MR. NOSWORTHY
MR. McDOUGAL
J. B.
A LEPRECHAUN

TIME: The present.
PLACE:  A business office.

# PERCIVAL WILDE

PERCIVAL WILDE was born in 1887, was graduated from Columbia University in 1906, and during the intervening years until his death in 1953, he wrote more one-act plays than any other American. More than one hundred of his plays have been produced, some many times, and one was acted by two hundred and sixty-one different organizations in a single calendar month.

Many students are acquainted with his book, *The Craftsmanship of the One-Act Play* (revised as *Primer of Playwriting*), and other readers know his *Rogues in Clover* (short stories), *The Devil's Booth* and *There is a Tide* (novels), *Inquest* (a mystery), and his anthology of *Contemporary One-Act Plays from Nine Countries*.

The collected volumes of his own one-act plays are: *Dawn, and Other One-Act Plays of Life Today; Confessional and Other American Plays; The Unseen Host and Other War Plays; Eight Comedies for Little Theatres; The Inn of Discontent, and Other Fantastic Plays; Three Minute Plays; Ten Plays for Little Theatres; Comrades in Arms and Other Plays for Little Theatres.*

His one-act plays which do not appear in collections include: *The Line of No Resistance, The Reckoning, The Toy-Shop, Reverie, The Enchanted Christmas Tree, Kings in Nomania, Alias Santa Claus, To Kill a Man, Nanny, Blood of the Martyrs, Ordeal by Battle, Mr. F* (retitled as *Night of Miracles*) *Legend,* and *Salt for Savor.*

*Salt for Savor,* included here, is the fourth play by Percival Wilde to appear in a collection by this editor. The first was *A Question of Morality,* in *Representative One-Act Plays by American Authors* (early edition; then *Pawns* in the later edition of the same book.) *Mr. F* was included in *The Best One-Act Plays of 1940.*

# SALT FOR SAVOR

*A business office whose main piece of furniture is a handsome flat-topped desk on which are a large block of push-buttons, a carafe of water, a glass, and a bottle of pills. Part of the floor is covered by a thick, dark rug. There are such chairs as would be expected. At one side are windows or a window; elsewhere are two doors, one leading to the outside and the other to the inside of the building. The glass of one door may be lettered in reverse,* PRESIDENT. *Prominent on a wall is a chart some three feet high by five feet long, and it is largely headed* SALES. *A heavy black line zigzags across it, rising impressively for the most part, but ending with an abrupt nose-dive one-third from the right. Elsewhere on the walls may be placards:* THINK; DO IT NOW; BOOST— DON'T KNOCK; SELL AND REPENT.

*At the rise of the curtain,* PATRICK, *a coatless, middle-aged cleaning-man, is at work. He is armed with a mop, and a large drying cloth is thrust into his belt. Near the outside door is a pail of water, obviously part of his equipment.* PATRICK *is mopping the floor not far from the desk, when the outside door opens, and* PATRICK, JUNIOR, *a lad of twelve, enters with a lunch box which he brings to the desk.*

JUNIOR. Hey, Pop!

PATRICK. Well?

JUNIOR. I brought your lunch.

PATRICK. Ye did, did ye?

JUNIOR. Mom was busy with the baby, so I fixed it myself. There's sandwiches with peanut-butter.

PATRICK. Ugh! How I hate that stuff!

JUNIOR. A bottle of beer.

PATRICK. It will be warm, I'm thinkin', by the time I'm ready to drink it.

JUNIOR. Keep it in the box, Pop. . . . And there's a hard-boiled egg.

PATRICK. Now there's somethin' that sounds good! If there's one thing I like, 'tis eggs, an' if there's one way I like 'em better than another, 'tis hard-boiled!

JUNIOR. Mom boiled the egg for you last night, and I put it right here on top. See?

PATRICK. [*Inspecting.*] An egg, that it is—an' if ye say 'tis hard-boiled, well then, 'tis hard-boiled. But where's the salt?

JUNIOR. The salt?

PATRICK. Ye wouldn't be expectin' me to eat the egg wit'out no salt, would ye? 'Tis the salt that gives the savor to the egg! 'Tis the salt that makes t'other things worth the eatin'.

JUNIOR. Pop, I got something funny to tell you about the salt.

PATRICK. Ye mean ye forgot it?

JUNIOR. No, Pop, I didn't forget it. I put it in the box before I left the house. I'm positive of that; and it was in the box when I opened it on the bus, just to make sure everything was there.

PATRICK. An' the salt was gone!

JUNIOR. Pop, it was right on top—in a saltcellar—and then I saw a funny little fellow, all in green, grinning at me from the other side of the bus and waving a butterfly net: Pop, a butterfly net in a bus! And when I got here the salt was gone.

PATRICK. An' ye think the funny little feller took it?

JUNIOR. Pop, he must have taken it—though he didn't come within six feet of me.

PATRICK. Give me the box. . . . Junior, I don't mind yer bein' forgetful; boys are like that, an' I used to be a boy meself; but when ye try to lie to yer old man . . .

JUNIOR. Pop, I'm not lying!

PATRICK. Ye're expectin' me to believe that story about the little feller, all in green, with the butterfly net?

JUNIOR. That's right, Pop.

PATRICK. Junior, ye ought to be ashamed o' yerself! Tell the truth, an' take the consequences! Don't be makin' up stories that no man in his right senses would be believin'! Mebbe ye're me own son, but ye're not the man for me! I say it with sorrow

in me heart, but I say it an' I mean it: ye're not the man for me!
An' now get out o' here before I lift ye out on the toe o' me boot!

JUNIOR. Pop!

PATRICK. Out! Out!

[*At* PATRICK's *threatening move,* JUNIOR *departs hastily, by the
outside door.* PATRICK *shakes his head in anger, dips his mop in
the pail, and swinging it too widely, sloshes water over the
freshly polished boots of the immaculate assistant superintendent who enters by the identical door at that unlucky moment.*]

MR. JENKINS. Damnation!

PATRICK. Oh, I'm sorry, sir!

MR. JENKINS. All over my boots!

PATRICK. Here, let me, sir.

[*He tries to wipe off the boots with his cleaning cloth.*]

MR. JENKINS. You know how particular the big boss is about
our appearance. They say you can tell the people in our organization because they're forever getting their boots polished.
That's what I've just been doing—downstairs—and now look!
Stop it, will you? I think you're making them worse.

[*He marches about the room, inspecting. He runs his finger over
the desk and evidently finds dust. He shows his finger.*]

What's this?

PATRICK. I haven't dusted it yet.

MR. JENKINS. At this time of day? [*He indicates the box.*] What
is this disgusting object?

PATRICK. My lunch box.

MR. JENKINS. Are you proposing to eat your lunch at the president's desk—with the president, perhaps?

[*In his progress around the desk, he collides with the pail.*]

Damnation! No, don't say a word! Patrick, this isn't the first
time I've found you slack in your work, but it's going to be the
last! Patrick, in the words which our president uses when necessary, and which you have doubtless heard him address to former
employees, you're not the man for me.

PATRICK. Mr. Jenkins!

MR. JENKINS. Patrick, in plain English, you're fired. [*As* PAT-
RICK *drops his mop.*] Here, take that with you!

PATRICK. Not if I'm fired. Ye c'n do what ye please wit' it yerself.

[*He goes out, via the outer door.* MR. JENKINS, *with obvious distaste, picks up the pail and the mop and starts to carry them to the side of the room, when there enters, via the inner door, the superintendent,* MR. NOSWORTHY.]

MR. NOSWORTHY. Jenkins!

MR. JENKINS. Yes, sir?

MR. NOSWORTHY. *Mr.* Jenkins, what on earth are you doing? *You* with a mop and a pail?

MR. JENKINS. I can explain, Mr. Nosworthy.

MR. NOSWORTHY. I doubt it; I doubt it greatly. Do you think we're paying you a salary to mop floors? Certainly not! You're supposed to hire cleaning-men to do that.

MR. JENKINS. Mr. Nosworthy!

MR. NOSWORTHY. I presume you will tell me that the laboring-man makes more than the man in the white-collar job these days. Perhaps he does; perhaps he does—sometimes—but it doesn't excuse your actions. You're the man in the white-collar job. You're supposed to remember your place.

MR. JENKINS. Mr. Nosworthy, I came in here and found Patrick wasn't through cleaning the president's office . . .

MR. NOSWORTHY. And you offered to help him, I dare say: to slosh around with the mop while he carried the pail; or perhaps you carried the pail while he sloshed around with the mop! And look at your boots, Mr. Jenkins! Just look at them, I say.

MR. JENKINS. Patrick spilled some water on them.

MR. NOSWORTHY. Of course he did! An occupational hazard, Jenkins! If you must be a cleaning man while paid to supervise what a dozen cleaning-men are doing, you must expect revolting little accidents like this. Faugh! Jenkins, you're not the man for me.

MR. JENKINS. Mr. Nosworthy!

MR. NOSWORTHY. Jenkins, I say it with sadness, because I know that you have a wife and children, but you are not the man for me.

MR. JENKINS. Mr. Nosworthy!

MR. NOSWORTHY. On your way out, you may stop at the cashier's window and collect your salary until the end of the month [*With sudden anger.*] and get going, Mr. Jenkins, without giving me any more back-talk, or I will discharge you for cause, which would mean that your salary stops this instant! Well?

[MR. JENKINS *goes hastily, outer door. With quite as much distaste as* MR. JENKINS *exhibited before him,* MR. NOSWORTHY *takes up the mop and the pail and starts to carry them out through the inner door. He almost collides with the general manager,* MR. MCDOUGAL, *a fussy little man with a gold pince-nez, who enters.*]

MR. MCDOUGAL. Mr. Nosworthy! Bless my soul, I *am* astonished!

MR. NOSWORTHY. Amusing, isn't it?

MR. MCDOUGAL. Curious choice of a word, Mr. Nosworthy, curious indeed. I can only remark, in the language attributed to Queen Victoria, "We are not amused."

MR. NOSWORTHY. This pail doesn't belong in the center of the room.

MR. MCDOUGAL. No; naturally not.

MR. NOSWORTHY. This mop isn't an ornamental article in the office of our respected president.

MR. MCDOUGAL. Mr. Nosworthy, I couldn't have put it better myself.

MR. NOSWORTHY. This lunch box . . .

MR. MCDOUGAL. [*With distaste.*] Is that what it is? [*He examines the contents with the aid of his glass.*] Sandwiches . . .

MR. NOSWORTHY. I believe that is what they are.

MR. MCDOUGAL. A bottle of beer. So you drink during business hours, Mr. Nosworthy?

MR. NOSWORTHY. No; certainly not.

MR. MCDOUGAL. The evidence is against you. An egg. I suppose you break the egg into the beer.

MR. NOSWORTHY. [*Trying to pass it off with a laugh.*] I don't think that would improve it, Mr. McDougal.

MR. MCDOUGAL. Probably you know more about it than I do.

[*He shakes the egg next to his ear; he tries its shell with his knuckles.*] Apparently a hard-boiled egg; no, you wouldn't break it into the beer.

MR. NOSWORTHY. Mr. McDougal, that is not my lunch.

MR. MCDOUGAL. No? Then what is it doing in your possession?

MR. NOSWORTHY. [*Becoming desperate.*] It isn't in my possession.

MR. MCDOUGAL. Worse and worse, Mr. Nosworthy; it is on the president's desk. I have heard that the younger generation goes in for pranks. Is this one of them? Do you consider it a prank to indulge in such activities in the office of the president of a company whose products are used in every quarter of the globe, whose sales mount up into the millions every year [*With a sad look at the chart.*] I mean, whose sales used to mount up into the millions every year?

MR. NOSWORTHY. [*Desperately.*] Mr. McDougal, you haven't let me say a word!

MR. MCDOUGAL. [*Not unkindly.*] It is because I don't want to make your offense worse than it is already. Actions speak louder than words, and believe me, Mr. Nosworthy, they have spoken. They are speaking now. They are saying, in the language of our respected president, "Mr. Nosworthy, you are not the man for me." I look at you, and I hear those words spoken in a voice of thunder, "You are not the man for me!" You are an eccentric. You are a jester. You are a clown—in an organization which can get along nicely without comedy relief. If our sales have fallen off, it is doubtless because our salesmen have imitated your vagaries, thus accounting for [*With a wave of his hand toward the graph.*] that nose-dive, that precipice, that catastrophe! Not another word, Mr. Nosworthy! When I come back here tomorrow, I don't want to see you on the premises. You are not the man for me! And now, sir, let me be rid of you!

[*As* MR. NOSWORTHY *starts for the inner door.*] Here: take those loathsome objects away with you!

MR. NOSWORTHY. As you said, they have nothing to do with my work. Take them away yourself.

[*He goes, slamming the inner door.*]

MR. MCDOUGAL. [*Much upset, sits at the desk and pours himself a little water, completely emptying the carafe.*] My word! My word! My word!

[*He sips the water.*]

J. B. [*Enters at the outer door. He is the president of the company, and is a corpulent, elderly man in golfing togs. He takes a single look at the office.*] Brrh! Brrh!

[*He crosses to the desk chair which* MR. MCDOUGAL *hastily vacates.*]

MR. MCDOUGAL. Good morning, J. B.

J. B. Brrh! Brrh! Grrow!

MR. MCDOUGAL. I hope you're feeling better.

J. B. [*Indicating the graph.*] With that on the wall?

[*He opens the bottle of pills and gets one out. He tries to pour water from the carafe, but it contained only the little which* MR. MCDOUGAL *drank, and the glass, too, is quite empty.*]

MR. MCDOUGAL. I'll get you a glass of water, J. B.

J. B. It's not your place to get me a glass of water. You are the general manager of this company. Stay where you are! Sit down. [*He has opened the lunch box.*] I have always been known for my resourcefulness. Observe me carefully, Mr. McDougal.

[*He takes out the bottle of beer, opens it with an opener which he produces from a vest-pocket, and pours the beer into the glass. He downs the pill, washing it down with the beer.*] Brrh!

[*The combination evidently does not taste good.*]

The brand is one which I particularly dislike.

[*He investigates the lunch box again, finding the sandwiches and beginning to eat them.*]

A little too thick, but tasty, very tasty.

[*He discovers the egg, takes it out, examines it, but returns it to the box.*]

MR. MCDOUGAL. Better now, J. B.?

J. B. Grrow! [*With a wave at the graph.*] I will never feel better while that exists! Just look at it! Our sales passed a million two years ago. They passed a million and a half last year. They started off magnificently this year—and then? Crash! Smash! Blam! Blooie! Kerflop! [*Munching a sand-*

*wich.*] I've lost my appetite! I don't sleep well at night. My game of golf has gone to pieces. I slice my drives. When I get into bunkers I don't get out. A child can putt better than I do. When I hear the ball fall into the cup, I think of that [*Another wave at the graph.*] and I wonder if our sales are going to make the same sound, "Plunk! Plunk!" when they hit bottom.

MR. MCDOUGAL. It's just too bad, J. B.

J. B. Is that all you can say? I was thinking, on the way here in my car. I've got to get rid of the dead-wood. I've got to turn the screws. I've got to tighten up the organization. This is the president's office. Well, look at it, with a mop and a pail in the corner, and a tin lunch box on the president's desk!

MR. MCDOUGAL. I didn't put it there, J. B.

J. B. Don't try to dodge the credit, Mr. McDougal. You meant well, I'm sure, and I can take a hint: with sales gone to pot and no dividends for our stockholders, the president of the company shouldn't take three hours off for lunch, and he shouldn't eat in expensive restaurants. He should bring a lunch box with him, just as he did when he was a penniless youngster thirty years ago with nothing—nothing . . .

MR. MCDOUGAL. Except ideas.

J. B. Brrh!

MR. MCDOUGAL. Imagination.

J. B. [*Tackling the second sandwich.*] Grrow!

MR. MCDOUGAL. An ambition to get to the top!

J. B. [*Again investigates the lunch box. He removes the egg and replaces it, but there is a paper napkin, and this is evidently what he wants, for he takes it out and uses it.*] A general tightening up, that's what I was saying to myself in the car. Out with the dead-wood; prune it away, root and branch! Away with the fuddy-duddies! Let us have fresh blood, young blood! Does this look like the office of the president of a successful corporation—or does it resemble the headquarters of some little enterprise in one of the rural districts? Mr. McDougal, I'm afraid the fault lies at your door.

MR. MCDOUGAL. [*Surprised.*] At mine, J. B.?

J. B. It came to me when I saw that mop and that pail. Mr.

McDougal, you're not modern. You are younger than I, but you are old-fashioned. You smack of patriarchal times. You are a living antique. What did I say? "Living?" Mr. McDougal, you don't know you're alive! I like you personally—I always did—but I must think of the example you set our entire organization. You are not the man for me. No, Mr. McDougal, you are not the man for me! I won't discharge you, after your long service—you've been with me nearly twenty years, haven't you?—but I will suggest that you retire on your pension—it isn't much, but it's better than nothing—at the end of the quarter.

MR. MCDOUGAL. J. B., this is a dreadful shock to me.

J. B. To me, also. Brrh! It was the mop and the pail—and the lunch box—well meant, I do not doubt, but oh, such a wrong philosophy!—that pointed up the situation. Mr. McDougal, you are not the man for me—and now leave me. I want to think. [*He waves his hand dramatically at the large signs,* THINK, DO IT NOW, SELL AND REPENT, *as* MR. MCDOUGAL *is about to say something.*] Grrow!

[MR. MCDOUGAL, *quite crushed, to'ters out via the inner door.* J. B. *finishes his sandwich and takes a second pill, washing it down with the last of the beer. Then he walks to the graph, standing before it, studying it. He raises both fists heavenward in protest. He remarks audibly.*] Brrh! Grrow!

[*From the neighborhood of the desk, there appears a little man, only the size of a boy, garbed in green from head to foot. He wears a conical green hat and his green cloth shoes come to a point. His face is framed by greenish-white whiskers: no mustache and no real beard. Various objects, subsequently referred to in the dialogue, are thrust into his broad leather belt or are attached to it. He brandishes a huge pair of shiny scissors, nearly as large as himself, and with them he falls to his knees immediately behind* J. B. *and begins snipping along the rug just back of the president's heels.* J. B., *suddenly conscious of the newcomer's presence, wheels abruptly.*]

THE LEPRECHAUN. Shh!

J. B. What?

THE LEPRECHAUN. Stand still! Don't jiggle me!

J. B. What are you doing?

THE LEPRECHAUN. There! I snipped it off.

J. B. You snipped what off?

THE LEPRECHAUN. [*Raising from the rug a large, recognizable black cut-out, and displaying it.*] Yer shadow. I cut off yer shadow.

J. B. [*Incredulously, accenting each word.*] You—cut—off—my—shadow?

THE LEPRECHAUN. That's right.

J. B. What are you going to do with it?

THE LEPRECHAUN. [*Placing the scissors on the desk; folding the shadow tenderly and stowing it in a wallet attached to his belt.*] I'm goin' to cut it up for bait. . . . If I had a hook—and a line—an' some good bait, I could catch me a fish—if there was a fish. . . . Do ye know the lake about a mile from here?

J. B. Of course.

THE LEPRECHAUN. There's halibut in that lake.

J. B. Yes; yes.

THE LEPRECHAUN. [*Slapping his wallet.*] Ye could catch halibut with a bait like this.

J. B. [*Emphatically.*] There isn't any lake a mile from here!

THE LEPRECHAUN. Don't I know it?

J. B. Halibut isn't a fresh-water fish. You would never find halibut in a lake.

THE LEPRECHAUN. Don't I know that, too?

J. B. You won't catch any halibut with that!

THE LEPRECHAUN. Who said I wanted to catch halibut? I don't like halibut. I prefer smurgeon.

J. B. What is smurgeon?

THE LEPRECHAUN. A smurgeon is a cross between a sturgeon and a smelt.

J. B. That's utterly ridiculous!

THE LEPRECHAUN. [*Nodding.*] Isn't it? The smurgeon thinks so, too. That's why he climbs the nearest tree and dies laughing at himself.

J. B. [*Pointing.*] What's that you've got at your belt?

THE LEPRECHAUN. This? A pendulum.

J. B. What do you want with a pendulum?

THE LEPRECHAUN. [*Mildly.*] Who knows but some day I might find a clock.

J. B. And that?

THE LEPRECHAUN. The net? Do ye ever have butterflies in yer stomach?

J. B. Sometimes.

THE LEPRECHAUN. I catch 'em with this. Moreover, 'tis handy when I want somethin'; 'twas handy this mornin' in the bus.

J. B. And that?

THE LEPRECHAUN. The saltcellar?

[*It dangles from his belt on a cord.*]

J. B. Yes, the saltcellar.

THE LEPRECHAUN. [*Shaking his head wearily.*] What would a saltcellar be for if 'twere not for salt? An' what would salt be for if 'twere not for somethin' to eat with it?

J. B. You're a leprechaun, aren't you?

THE LEPRECHAUN. A leprechaun, that's right.

J. B. What's a leprechaun doing out of Ireland?

THE LEPRECHAUN. Ye might as well be askin', "What's a leprechaun doin' *in* Ireland?" We're doin' the same things everywhere: we're doin' good to the children of men.

J. B. Cutting off my shadow? You call that doing good?

THE LEPRECHAUN. Why not? Ye won't be needin' it any more.

J. B. [*Aghast.*] You mean—you mean . . . ?

THE LEPRECHAUN. [*With a lovely smile.*] That's right! Yer heart ain't been actin' like it should: ye said that yerself, didn't ye? Ye lose yer temper. Ye take pills. Ye say cruel things, like "You are not the man for me." Mebbe so; an' then, one fine day, ye learn ye're not the man for somebody else. Mebbe ye learn ye're not the man for anybody else.

J. B. But my shadow! My shadow!

THE LEPRECHAUN. Leprechaun law don't let me take more than one thing at a time: that's why I've got the salt an' nothin' to put it on; but after yer heart has stopped beatin', ye won't need a shadow.

J. B. [*With his fingers to his wrist.*] I—I don't believe I feel my pulse.

THE LEPRECHAUN. No; naturally not.

J. B. I feel queer without my shadow, like a big kite without a tail.

THE LEPRECHAUN. Some of 'em feel worse than that at the start.

J. B. [*Getting down on the rug and hunting.*] I don't see that shadow anywhere!

THE LEPRECHAUN. How could ye, when I've got it safe in me wallet?

J. B. [*Still on the rug.*] Look here. I'm a business man. I'll buy my shadow back from you!

THE LEPRECHAUN. Yes? What have ye got to offer?

J. B. Leprechauns want crocks of gold, don't they?

THE LEPRECHAUN. Naturally; to ransom themselves when humans catch them.

J. B. [*Rising.*] Well, I'll give you a crock of gold.

THE LEPRECHAUN. I've got one.

J. B. I'll give you another, a bigger one.

THE LEPRECHAUN. One's enough; a second would be a headache.

J. B. I'll make you rich!

THE LEPRECHAUN. Who ever heard of a rich leprechaun?

J. B. I'll give you a car! A yacht! A suit of clothes! A dozen suits of clothes!

THE LEPRECHAUN. [*Indicating the graph.*] With *that* on the wall? Why, ye poor man, what have ye got yerself?

J. B. [*For the first time, feebly.*] I want my shadow. I've lived with it a good many years. I'm used to it. I've grown attached to it. What use is my shadow to somebody else? I feel lost without it.

THE LEPRECHAUN. [*Scathingly.*] Ye mean ye'd rather go on gaspin' for breath, an' takin' pills, an' visitin' the doctors?

J. B. Yes; a thousand times rather.

THE LEPRECHAUN. Ye might be dancin' over the hills an' down the dales; ye might be listenin' to the beasts an' the insects an' the fowls of the air; ye might be hearin' what the beech tree says to the mountain laurel that grows near its roots;

an' ye might be learnin' the secrets that the great god Pan whispers to all Nature's creatures. Ye might be skippin' about between the snow flakes, or ridin' on a bolt of thunder, or sinkin' into the warm heart o' the earth with the summer's rains. . . . Ye don't want to come along with me?

J. B. I'm afraid.

THE LEPRECHAUN. Afraid o' what?

J. B. Afraid of giving up the things I know for the things I don't. My life is here.

THE LEPRECHAUN. [*Shaking his head and opening his wallet.*] Then ye're not the man for me! No, ye're not the man for me! Well, what have ye got that's worth so little that it'll make an even trade?

J. B. [*Looking about wildly.*] This . . .

THE LEPRECHAUN. [*Examining it.*] A beer bottle. I'd swap, but it's empty.

[*He hurls it into the wastebasket.*]

J. B. These.

THE LEPRECHAUN. [*Smelling.*] Papers where there used to be sandwiches—peanut butter sandwiches—my favorite kind—only ye et 'em. No.

J. B. This.

THE LEPRECHAUN. [*With growing excitement and satisfaction.*] An egg! A hard-boiled egg! It needs just a bit of salt—an' I've got the salt! . . . An' all ye want for it is yer shadow?

J. B. That's all. That's all.

THE LEPRECHAUN. Take it quick before ye change yer mind! Here ye are!

J. B. [*Unfolding the shadow tenderly; holding it up.*] I'm a business man.

THE LEPRECHAUN. Naturally ye are that.

J. B. What's to prevent you from snipping it off again?

THE LEPRECHAUN. I'll make ye a free gift o' the scissors. See? [*We see, as* J. B. *carefully smooths out the shadow, holds it up again, and fits it on the rug where it was formerly; but suddenly we no longer see* THE LEPRECHAUN, *who, taking advantage of a moment when the shadow has hidden him, has vanished.* ]

J. B. I see.

[*He pats the shadow into place and gives a preliminary caper.*]
Yes, I see.

[*He looks about; wipes off his spectacles.*]
I mean, I don't see.

[*He looks about again. The big pair of scissors is on his desk. He takes it up stealthily, and watching out to make sure that he is unobserved, tiptoes across the room to the chart on the wall.*]
I see; I mean, I see perfectly.

[*With one bold snip, he cuts off the nose-diving part of the graph. It acts as if it were black adhesive tape, for when he fits it back, at a pleasantly ascending angle, it adheres at once, climbing to a new high, a new prosperity, a new everything-as-it-should-be.*] There!

[*He opens a desk drawer and conceals the scissors. Then he takes up the large block of push-buttons, selects one, and presses.*]

MR. MCDOUGAL. [*Entering timidly through the inner door.*]
You rang, J. B.?

J. B. [*Indicating the chart.*] Mr. McDougal, look!

MR. MCDOUGAL. [*Delighted.*] No?

J. B. Yes!

MR. MCDOUGAL. No?

J. B. Yes!

MR. MCDOUGAL. Not really?

J. B. Can you doubt the evidence of your eyes? Mr. McDougal, a few minutes ago I addressed you hastily. Your conservative ideas have always been valuable, extremely valuable. What I meant to say—what I really meant to say—was that you *are* the man for me.

MR. MCDOUGAL. [*Touched.*] J. B.!

J. B. Let that be understood once and for all; and now, with our sales clicking like that, I believe I might play a few holes of golf.

MR. MCDOUGAL. Best thing in the world for you, J. B.

J. B. Carry on while I'm gone, Mr. McDougal. Carry on.

[*He goes through the outer door, looking back and ceremoniously opening the door for his shadow.*]

MR. MCDOUGAL. [*Examines the block of push-buttons, and in his turn, presses one.* MR. NOSWORTHY *enters by the inner door, is fascinated by the chart, and marches up to it.* MR. MCDOUGAL *chuckles.*] Hard to believe, isn't it?

MR. NOSWORTHY. Incredible! Quite incredible!

MR. MCDOUGAL. Mr. Nosworthy, we are a great team!

MR. NOSWORTHY. Mr. McDougal, under your leadership . . .

MR. MCDOUGAL. In the event that I have not said so before, Mr. Nosworthy, you are the man for me. Continue as you have begun. Carry on.

[*He goes via the outer door.*]

MR. NOSWORTHY. Aye, aye, sir.

[*He presses a button.*]

MR. JENKINS. [*Entering through the outer door at once.*] You rang for me, sir?

MR. NOSWORTHY. [*Indicating the chart.*] In view of the excitement which this has created, I can quite understand . . .

MR. JENKINS. [*Very happily.*] Yes, sir.

MR. NOSWORTHY. Which is to say, Jenkins . . .

MR. JENKINS. It's perfectly clear, sir.

MR. NOSWORTHY. That you are the man for me: but definitely; definitely. Carry on.

[*He goes, via the inner door.*]

MR. JENKINS. Oh, how can I thank you, sir?

[*He examines the push-buttons, but there is evidently none for one so humble as* PATRICK, *and he shouts.*] Patrick! Patrick!

PATRICK. [*Offstage.*] Coming! [*He enters through the outer door.*] Yes, sir?

MR. JENKINS. The president's office is quite spotless—as it always is after you've cleaned it. You might begin work on the vice-president's.

PATRICK. Yes, sir. Yes, sir.

MR. JENKINS. Patrick, you are efficiency itself! You are certainly the man for me!

[*He goes, through the inner door.*]

PATRICK. [*Taking up the mop and the pail.*] Yes, sir. That's what I always say meself. I always knew it.

[*He is on his way out when* JUNIOR *enters.*]

JUNIOR. Hey, Pop! Salt!

PATRICK. What salt?

JUNIOR. I ran home and got some more salt for the egg.

PATRICK. What egg?

JUNIOR. Why, have you forgotten, Pop? [*He runs to the desk and opens the lunch box.*] Pop, it's empty!

PATRICK. So 'twould be. Yes, so 'twould be. Junior, it's come back to me this second, for we've had a busy mornin' here: yep! I et me lunch, an' then I forgot all about it!

JUNIOR. Why, Pop!

PATRICK. Junior, ye are me own son, an' there's been times when ye've been a sore trial to me; but I'll say this, Junior: "Ye're the man for me!" . . . Bring along the lunch box, Junior, will ye?

[*He goes through the outer door.*]

JUNIOR. [*Takes up the lunch box. A sound makes him turn his head. Facing him near the other end of the desk is* THE LEPRE-CHAUN, *salting and nibbling at the last of a hard-boiled egg, for all the world like an overgrown squirrel.*] Hello.

THE LEPRECHAUN. Hello.

JUNIOR. I saw you in the bus this morning.

THE LEPRECHAUN. I saw *you* in the bus this mornin'!

JUNIOR. What have you been doing here?

THE LEPRECHAUN. Who? Me?

JUNIOR. [*Shaking his finger at him.*] Yes, you!

THE LEPRECHAUN. What have I been doin' here? I've been havin' fun; just havin' fun.

[*He giggles;* JUNIOR *giggles.* THE LEPRECHAUN *squats, hands on knees, and laughs heartily;* JUNIOR, *facing him, does the same. Their laughter echoes through the room.*]

**CURTAIN**

NOTE: The Author has been astonished to learn that in this day and age there are persons who do not know how shadows should be "snipped off." It is unnecessary to follow the outline of the shadow on the rug, an old-fashioned method which takes time and whose results are uncertain; it is sufficient to snip a straight line behind the feet of the person casting the shadow, after which the latter is free of its moorings and may easily be raised from the rug—particularly if a black cut-out of the correct size and shape has been placed on the rug before the curtain rises.

# THE FORGOTTEN LAND

By

## JOHN SHEFFIELD

*(Published here for the first time)*

"Naked and alone we came into exile. In her dark womb we did not know our mother's face; from the prison of her flesh have we come into the unspeakable and incommunicable prison of this earth."

Thomas Wolfe

# THE FORGOTTEN LAND

## CAST

SUZY JONES
SAMMY LOU BERRY
MR. BERRY

TIME: The present.
PLACE: The action takes place on a stretch of barren countryside outside a town of Southern Kansas.

# JOHN SHEFFIELD

*The Forgotten Land* is the second play by John Sheffield to appear in these annuals. Last year his play, *The Imploring Flame,* was included.

Mr. Sheffield was born in New York City in 1927, was educated in its public schools, at New York University and the University of Texas. In Texas, he wrote short stories and contributed a column of verse to the "Daily Texan," played football and was a member of the Southwestern swimming team. A back injury forced him to give up hopes for an athletic career, and thereafter, while working at odd jobs in the South and West, he continued writing short stories and poetry. Several of his short stories have appeared in small Western publications, and a horror story, "Derelicts of the Moon," appeared in Horror Stories Yearly of 1950. Interest in dramatic writing finally prevailed, and Mr. Sheffield is now working on a number of short plays, and one long play, *Far Away, the Dawn.* He is employed as a physical instructor in a Manhattan gymnasium.

# THE FORGOTTEN LAND

## SCENE 1

*This is a stretch of barren countryside just outside a town of Southern Kansas. The Missouri-Kansas-Texas Railroad tracks are in the near distance, offstage left. Broken ground lies in the rear, with several dying, forlorn reminders of trees. An old billboard, advertising* DR. PEPPER IS THE DRINK FOR ME *lies where a Norther has deposited it—in a clump of rocks, ashes and garbage. Along stage left, a large sign happily announces,* WELCOME TO CARSONVILLE—POP. ONE THOUSAND—HOME OF CARSON'S JUTE PRODUCTS. *At stage right, rear, we see the outside of and wooden steps leading into an old deserted railroad shack, unpainted, rotting, the windows fallen out. Desolation pervades the atmosphere, as if interminable time has passed, leaving behind ruin, decay and sterility.*

*As the curtain rises, the shrill whistle of a passing train cuts into the austere silence. The train passes quickly, the whistle recedes, a death-like calm covers the stage. A pallid, late afternoon sun is slowly declining in a portentous, cloudy sky. There is a pause. The door of the shack opens and a young girl appears at the threshold.* SUZY JONES *is sixteen years old, pretty, with a very white complexion and long dark hair. She is dressed in an old calico housedress; she stands at the door for a few moments, then comes down and seats herself on the second step of the porch. She raises her eyes and stares capriciously at the sky. She murmurs to herself, "Damn his hide!" Another pause. From offstage, left, comes the sound of a resonant male voice raised heartily in song.* SUZY *quickly jumps up, a look of expectancy flashing across her face.* SAMMY *enters from the left, a tall, husky young Kansan, broad-shouldered, sinewy, nineteen years of age. His face is bronzed, and his skin is a metallic brown. He wears dungarees and a dirty white sweatshirt. When he speaks, the*

133

*words come slowly, carefully, with a strong Kansan drawl. He is singing loudly.*

SUZY. [*Reproachfully.*] I been waitin' fer yuh near pas' an' hour.

SAMMY. [*With a broad smile.*] Yuh have?

SUZY. Watcha been doin'? Drinkin'? [*No answer. He continues singing.*] Sammy Lou Berry, yuh stop that an' answer me right this minute!

SAMMY. I been havin' a real good time down at th' Las' Chance.

[*He sings.*]

SUZY. [*Quickly.*] Yuh stop this crazy carryin' on right this minute! Yuh been drinkin' agin! An' at *that* place!

SAMMY. [*Happily.*] Jus' two little nips. Shore! Why not?

SUZY. I been settin' here waitin' like a durn fool while yuh been drinkin' wit' alla them dames at th' Las' Chance!

SAMMY. [*Firmly.*] Now, Suzy, yuh be quiet! [*Proudly.*] A *man* ain' a *man* till he c'n hol' his likker.

SUZY. Who says so?

SAMMY. I says so!

SUZY. If m' folks knowed I been comin' down here tuh meet cha, I'd a have m' Paw down m' neck awready.

SAMMY. [*Casually, feigning unconcern.*] I ain' assed yuh tuh come.

[*She glares at him angrily. He approaches her and attempts to embrace her. She repels him.*]

SUZY. Yuh breath smells worse 'n slop!

SAMMY. That's th' likker—an' chewin' terbacca.

SUZY. Yuh oughta be ashamed a yuhseff!

SAMMY. [*Throwing his shoulders back, proudly.*] Like hell I am! I'm findin' out thin's ev'ry day. I c'n out-drink any guy at th' Las' Chance. Out-drink, out-run, out-fight 'em. An' they knows it, too. They's all a scared a me. They all wanna be m' pal an' buy me drinks.

SUZY. Yuh jus' big an' dumb! [*Pointing to her head.*] Nothin' up here! Yuh ain' got nothin' up here.

SAMMY. Says who?

SUZY. Says ev'rybody.

SAMMY. [*Flexing his biceps.*] I got muscles, see? They does m' thinkin' fer me. [*Rubbing his muscles.*] These here, Baby. See 'em? [*She turns away, annoyed.*] I done a couple a stunts fer ev-rybody at th' Las' Chance t'day. They seen quick enuff I ain' jus' no plain guy. I betcha cain't guess wha' I done?

[*He looks at her, hoping for a response. She has turned her back on him and looks away.*]

Huh? Yuh wanna hear? [*No answer.*] Then I guess I'll tell yuh. I rassled wit' Joe Simpson an' I knocked 'im down three times. Jus' in fun, but I throwed 'im three times till he give up. Joe Simpson weighs more 'n two hun'red an' fifty poun's. Picked 'im up wit' one han' an' held 'im in th' air. [*Proudly.*] How's that fer somepin? [*No response from* SUZY.] Then I wen' an' let Mamie Stewart sit on m' shoulders. I bend down an' let 'er get on. She sets down—Mamie ain' no feather, neither—an' I run aroun' th' bar wit' her on m' shoulders. Twen'y times. How's that fer somepin? I didn' even get out a win'.

SUZY. [*Sarcastically.*] Very nice!

SAMMY. [*Smiling.*] Ain' it? Ev'rybody was fightin' tuh buy me drinks.

[SUZY *turns and faces him, hands akimbo.*]

SUZY. I thought yuh said yuh had on'y two drinks?

SAMMY. Mebbe three.

SUZY. Or four. Or five.

SAMMY. I c'n hol' m' likker.

SUZY. [*Angrily.*] Keepin' me waitin' while yuh drinkin' an' carryin' on wit' Mamie Stewart—that ol' slut!

SAMMY. [*With a wink.*] She's shore takin' a likin' tuh me.

SUZY. [*Jealously.*] I bet she called yuh up tuh her room, too.

SAMMY. [*Flatly.*] Shore did!

SUZY. [*Aghast.*] An' yuh wen'?

SAMMY. [*Feigning proudness.*] Nope. Tol' 'er I had a date fer t'night awready. I promised mebbe some other time.

[SUZY *is infuriated. She stands there, speechless.*]

She says she ain' gonna charge me nothin', neither.

[SUZY *is enraged. She bends down, picks up a large rock and heaves it at him. He laughs wildly and ducks, the rock missing him. He jumps forward and seizes her around the waist, lifting her high into the air and swinging her around. She strikes his head and shoulders with her fists, but the blows have no apparent affect on him. He laughs wildly. Finally he puts her down, giving her a resounding smack on the bottom. She utters a wild shriek, one hand going behind her back to soothe the soreness. He stands there, laughing riotously.*]

SUZY [*Furiously.*] Sammy Lou, yuh—jus' a brute! [*He laughs loudly.*] I hate yuh! I hate yuh!

SAMMY. Cain't yuh take a joke?

SUZY. [*Rubbing her soreness.*] That ain' no joke.

SAMMY. Yuh shore look funny!

SUZY. Mebbe Mamie Stewart likes when yuh do that tuh her, but I don'. I have a good mine tuh go right home.

SAMMY. [*Casually.*] Why don' cha?

SUZY. 'Cause—'cause I'm here awready.

[*He crosses to her and takes her in his arms. She makes no effort to stop him, rather letting herself be taken. He strokes her hair lightly.*]

SAMMY [*Softly.*] Like silk. Jus' like silk.

SUZY. [*With a hurt, humbled tone.*] Mamie Stewart ain' got no nice hair. [*No answer.*] Has she?

SAMMY. [*Stroking her hair.*] I dunno.

SUZY. B'sides, she's ugly an' ol'.

SAMMY. [*Teasing.*] She ain' too bad.

SUZY. I been tol' she's near thirty.

SAMMY. [*Uninterested.*] Is she?

SUZY. She got pimples on her face.

SAMMY. She ain' nice as you.

SUZY. I bet yuh tol' 'er that she's beautiful.

SAMMY. Hell! I never tol' 'er nothin'.

[*He lifts her head, and kisses her squarely on the mouth. She raises herself slightly, her hands going around his neck. The kiss is a long one; they break slowly.*]

SUZY. [*Hoarsely.*] Sammy . . . ?

SAMMY. Yeah?

SUZY. [*Slowly.*] Yuh didn' go up tuh Mamie's room, didja?

SAMMY. Naw. I tol' yuh I didn'. I on'y got one girl—an' that's m' baby here.

SUZY. Do yuh mean it?

SAMMY. Shore I mean it.

SUZY. Are yuh sorry fer keepin' me waitin' so lon'?

SAMMY. Shore.

SUZY. Yuh know wha' m' paw said?

SAMMY. Wha'?

SUZY. Preacher Sims tol' him yuh no good, jus' like yuh paw.

SAMMY. Yeah?

SUZY. Preacher Sims says yuh been carryin' on somepin terrible all over town. Says yuh never come tuh church, an' th' devil's got yuh soul. Jus' like yuh ol' man!

SAMMY. Preacher Sims been sayin' that?

SUZY. That's wha' Paw says he tol' 'im. . . . He said somepin else, too.

SAMMY [*Ominously.*] Wha' he say?

SUZY. [*Slowly, hesitantly.*] He said—yuh ain' never had no maw. He said yuh maw—was a tramp—an' she carried on wit' yuh paw. After yuh come, she run off—leavin' yuh paw all alone.

SAMMY. [*Furiously.*] Lyin' son of a . . .

SUZY. Sammy. [*She places a finger over his mouth.*] Yuh oughtn' tuh speak that way 'bout Preacher Sims.

SAMMY. That's wha' he is! Fer sayin' somepin so mean, that's wha' he is.

SUZY. [*After a pause.*] It don' make no diff'rence tuh me, Sammy. I don' care wha' folks say 'bout yuh maw or yuh paw.

SAMMY. [*Slowly.*] Paw's okay.

SUZY. [*Softly.*] Preacher Sims says yuh ain' never had no home or folks tuh love yuh, 'r care fer yuh.

SAMMY. [*Bitterly.*] I got Paw!

[*She crosses and sits on the steps of the porch.*]

SUZY. Come an' set by me, Sammy.

[*He crosses to her and seats himself next to her. She raises her eyes and stares at the sky.*] A cold sky. Cold an' dark. I don't like cold skies.

SAMMY. [*As if he weren't listening.*] Huh?

SUZY. Yuh ain' been listenin'?

SAMMY. Naw.

SUZY. Thinkin'?

SAMMY. Yeah.

SUZY. M' paw says a girl like me oughta look fer a rich man.

SAMMY. Yeah?

SUZY. Fine a rich city man, mebbe f'om Dallas. Man wit' a car, an' a house, an' lotsa money. Paw says any rich man 'd be lucky tuh get me. I got th' looks, he says. . . . Paw don' know 'bout us. I ain' gonna tell 'im, neither.

SAMMY. Yuh paw don' like me, does he?

SUZY. He ain' never said nothin' bad agin yuh.

SAMMY. Yuh maw don' like me any. I knows that fer certain. I seen 'er on th' Drag th' other day. I says, "Good mornin', M's. Jones." She jus' passes me by, like she ain' seen me.

SUZY. Paw tol' 'er wha' Preacher Sims said 'bout cha.

SAMMY. [*Perplexed.*] Wha' does folks have agin me an' m' paw? Not th' folks who hang aroun' th' Las' Chance—they never say nothin'. They like me. It's other folks, like yuh paw an' maw. Like Preacher Sims. Other folks f'om town. When I sees 'em on th' street, I a'ways greet 'em all. They turns away an' makes out like I ain' even there. Wha's folks got agin Paw an' me? We never done nothin' tuh nobody. We ain' white trash. We're jus' as good as alla 'em.

SUZY. Folks is funny.

SAMMY. They sure is.

SUZY. Folks is afraid a yuh paw an' you.

SAMMY. Why? Why is folks afraid a us?

SUZY. [*Hesitantly.*] 'Cause—they say—yuh paw done bad thin's.

SAMMY. It ain' true. Paw done nothin' wrong.

SUZY. Now—folks is sayin' bad 'bout cha, too, Sammy.

[SAMMY *rises irritably and bangs his fist against the stanchion.*]

SAMMY. Damn 'em all! Damn 'em all!

SUZY. [*Rising.*] Sammy! Don' talk that way.

SAMMY. We done nothin' tuh no one. We never took no charity f'om none a them. Why cain't they leave Paw an' me be? Why don' they mine their own affairs?

SUZY. [*Comfortingly.*] People jus' likes tuh mine other folks business.

SAMMY. Let 'em keep out a mine . . . Mebbe Paw drinks more 'n he should. Mebbe we ain' got no fine clothes like other folks. Paw never took nothin' f'om nobody; an' he ain' gonna hafta, s' lon' 's I live. I'm gonna take care a him. He's a man who ain' never had th' breaks. . . . B'sides—Paw's sick. He cain't wuk no more. [*Softly.*] Paw's dyin'.

SUZY. Dyin'?

SAMMY. Yeah. Th' likker. Th' likker's burned up his insides. [*A train whistles in the distance,* SUZY *looks off left.*]

SUZY. Here she comes—*Th' Silver Comet*—St. Louis right through tuh San Antone. Waco, Dallas, Austin, San Antone— alla them big places. Big cities wit' lots a folks, lots a cars, big de-part-ment stores fulla dresses an' nice thin's.

[*The train whistle grows louder and nearer.*]

Right through. Gee, it mus' be great tuh see alla big places. [*The train roars by, drowning out her voice. Then the train disappears into the distance.*]

SAMMY. [*Dreamily.*] One a these days I'm gonna hop a freight an' hit th' road. Gonna see alla them big places. I'm jus' gonna get on a freight an' go tuh alla th' big cities. I been itchin' tuh do it fer a lon' time now. I been wantin' tuh do it, on'y I been a scared tuh say it tuh Paw—that I been waitin' tuh go. Paw might take it th' wron' way; it mebbe 'd hurt 'im bad. I don' wanna hurt 'im. That's why I been stayin' on here.

SUZY. [*Slowly.*] Wha' 'bout—you an' me?

SAMMY. Yuh c'n come wit' me, if yuh wanna.

SUZY. [*Happily.*] C'n I, Sammy?

SAMMY. Shore. Yuh c'n come. It ain' gonna be Heaven in them boxcars. Hoppin' freights ain' kid's play. At fust, till yuh get sorta used tuh it, it's hard.

SUZY. I don' mine, Sammy. I'm not made a soff stuff.

SAMMY. Wha' 'bout yuh folks?

SUZY. I don' care 'bout m' folks.

SAMMY. They won' let yuh go.

SUZY. I won' ass 'em.

SAMMY. [*An arm about her waist.*] We won' say nothin' tuh nobody. Jus' go off alone some day.

SUZY. [*Smiling happily.*] I love yuh *so* much, Sammy. Yuh make me feel good all over.

SAMMY. [*As he bends to kiss her.*] I love yuh, too. More 'n alla worl' put t'gether.

[*They kiss.*]

SUZY. [*Softly.*] I got somepin tuh tell yuh, somepin secret.

SAMMY. Yeah?

SUZY. [*Coyly.*] Betcha cain't guess?

SAMMY. Wha'?

SUZY. Try an' guess.

SAMMY. [*Puzzled.*] Hell! I cain't guess.

SUZY. Come on over here an' set.

[*She leads him to the porch steps. He sits, then she seats herself comfortably upon his lap.*]

SAMMY. What're yuh actin' so mis-terious fer?

SUZY. [*Beaming.*] I been feelin' sick lately.

SAMMY. Sick?

SUZY. I been gettin' dizzy durin' th' day, an' I been throwin' up wha' I been eatin'.

SAMMY. Huh?

SUZY. Yuh know wha' that means, Sammy? It means I'm gettin' a baby.

SAMMY. [*Incredulously.*] A baby?

SUZY. Doc Benson tol' me so.

SAMMY. Doc Benson?

SUZY. I wen' tuh see 'im t'day.

SAMMY. A baby . . . ?

SUZY. He promised not tuh say nothin' tuh nobody. [*He sits there, stunned. She runs her fingers through his hair.*] Cain' yuh say somepin? Ain' yuh happy?

SAMMY. [*Falteringly.*] Jesus.

SUZY. [*Laughing.*] Yuh big boob!

[*She kisses him on the forehead.*]

SAMMY. [*Ominously.*] What're yuh folks gonna say?

SUZY. [*Independently.*] I don' care no more. I don' care wha' no one says.

SAMMY. But—yuh still goin' tuh school.

SUZY. I ain' goin' back. Never agin. I'm gonna live here, wit' yuh paw an' you.

SAMMY. [*Musing.*] A baby.

SUZY. Doc Benson said so. He said I con-ceived a month ago. He knows we ain' legal married, so he kinda looked at me funny-like. He said I should tell m' folks 'bout it. But I ain' gonna. It's nobody's business. [*Pause.*] Are yuh—sorry it happened?

SAMMY. Folks 'll say bad thin's 'bout cha now.

SUZY. I don' care. I love yuh, Sammy. That's alla counts. Yuh lovin' me, too. That's important.

SAMMY. [*Compassionately.*] I *do* love yuh, Suzy. Yuh don' hafta ass that.

SUZY. [*Softly.*] Yuh ain' gonna flirt wit' Mamie Stewart no more?

SAMMY. She don' mean nothin' tuh me . . . Gee, I near for-got. I got somepin fer yuh.

SUZY. [*Excitedly.*] Yuh bought me somepin?

SAMMY. Uh-huh.

[*He removes a small, thin package from his back pocket. It is a handkerchief, wrapped delicately in pink tissue paper.*]

SUZY. [*Seeing him take it out.*] Wha' is it?

SAMMY. Yuh guess fust.

SUZY. I dunno.

SAMMY. Guess.

[*She grabs for it, and he pulls his hand away. She tries to grab it out of his hand; he catches her wrist and holds it behind her back.*] Yuh gotta gimme a big fat juicy kiss fust.

[*He reaches for her mouth.*]

SUZY. [*Teasing him.*] Nope. Yuh ain' gettin' nothin'.

[*She pushes his face away. He releases her hand, pulls her face down, quickly kisses her.*] Now gimme.

[*He gives her the package. She accepts it as if it were something priceless. She holds it in her hand for a moment, staring at it intently, then she proceeds to unwrap it. She does so slowly, carefully. She parts the paper and removes a multi-colored handkerchief. She utters a deep sigh of amazement; her face lights up; in her happiness, she finds it hard to speak.* SUZY *suddenly throws her arms about* SAMMY *and kisses him fervently.*]

SAMMY. [*Releasing himself.*] Hey! Watcha doin' tuh me?

SUZY. [*In ecstasy.*] Oh, Sammy, it's beautiful! Jus' lovely. Why didja buy it fer me? There ain' no occasion . . .

SAMMY. I saw it in th' store winda on th' Drag, an' I figgered I'd like yuh tuh have it. Ain' it purty?

SUZY. [*Smelling it.*] It is, it is. It smells f'om per-fume, too. It's th' mos' beautiful presen' I ever got—ever. I'm gonna keep it fer wearin' tuh church on Sundays.

SAMMY. Naw. I wancha tuh wear it alla time.

SUZY. It's too purty.

SAMMY. It's fer wearin', ain' it? Not keepin' jus' fer Sundays. [*She wraps it up again and puts it in the pocket of her dress.*] Do yuh really like it?

SUZY. I do. It has alla th' colors a th' rainbow on it—like th' sky jus' affer a storm. It's very beautiful. It mus' be very expensive. Yuh shouldn' go aroun' spendin' yuh money so foolish.

SAMMY. It didn' cos' so much. B'sides, I ain' never bought yuh nothin' b'fore. Now—now that yuh gettin' a baby, it's like yuh was—m' wife. Ain' it?

SUZY. Shore. Like we was married.

SAMMY. When th' baby comes, it'll be half you an' half me. What'll yuh folks say?—yuh stayin' here wit' Paw an' me.

SUZY. I ain' goin' back no more. I got nothin' tuh get.

SAMMY. When yuh don' come home, they'll get th' sheriff lookin' fer yuh.

SUZY. It ain' nobody's business wha' I do. I'm ol' enuff tuh do wha' I please.

[SAMMY *rises, picks up a stone, heaves it with all his might.*]

SAMMY. See that. I c'n throw farther 'n any guy in town. I bet. Jus' b'fore I left high school couple years back, Mr. Cabot—he's th' coach—he come ovah tuh me an' says, "Sammy, how 'bout goin' out fer football this year? We c'n a'ways use good men on th' team." "I ain' got time," I tol' 'im, " 'cause I wuks after-noons. An' another thin', I'm quittin' soon's I'm ol' enuff. Yuh don' make a helluva lot jus' wukin' part time affer school." Paw was night watchman ovah at Carson's Mill then, but he wasn' makin' much. Then Paw los' his job, an' it was up tuh me tuh take ovah. [*Proudly.*] I started on'y wit' ten a week at Carson's. Three years back. Nigger wuk—cleanin' th' place, porterin'. But I wuk up fass. Betcha don' know how much I'm makin' now? [*She shakes her head.*] Twen'y bucks. Twen'y bucks a week. I sure wuked up fass. Now I c'n run any machine in th' place. It ain' sissy's wuk, neither. It's man's wuk. An' yuh know wha'? I been savin' wha' I c'n out a m' money. I been puttin' some away ev'ry week. Paw's been holdin' it fer me. I a'ways give 'im alla th' money an' he saves fer me. He takes wha' he needs fer hisseff, th' res' he hides in th' house. He tol' me we been able tuh save a nice little pile. Says we got more 'n a hun'red bucks. I on'y been gettin' th' twen'y a week fer pas' three months, else we coulda mebbe saved more. . . . Paw wen' in tuh town this mornin' tuh buy grub. Mebbe tuh look fer a new place tuh live. This place is kinda run-down. . . . I tol' Paw tuh get hisself a new Sunday suit. He ain' got but one, an' it's real shabby an' ol'. I made 'im put it on this mornin' 'cause it's near worn out awready.

SUZY. Yuh oughta get *yuhseff* a suit a clothes. Yuh ain' got much.

SAMMY. I ain' got nothin', b'sides another pair a jeans.

SUZY. Them yuh wearin' 're bad worn out, Sammy.

SAMMY. I don' need any suits. I never go nowhere.

SUZY. Why don' cha ever come tuh church on Sundays, Sammy?

SAMMY. I ain' got no reason tuh go tuh church.

SUZY. Why does alla folks go?

SAMMY. I dunno. On'y I ain' never liked it. God ain' never done nothin' fer me. Tell it tuh Jesus, Preacher Sims a'ways says. I tol' Jesus plen'y—on'y he never done nothin' tuh he'p Paw or me.

SUZY. [*Seriously.*] Yuh gotta be-leeve in Jesus.

SAMMY. I ain' said I don' be-leeve. On'y Jesus an' nobody never don' care fer Paw an' me.

SUZY. Preacher Sims says yuh gotta drive yuh sins away an' be ready tuh meet yuh maker any time he's ready tuh call yuh.

SAMMY. [*Turning to her.*] Yuh know, it's funny—funny as hell.

SUZY. What's funny?

SAMMY. [*Kicking up his heels.*] Them same folks as go tuh church—they're th' ones who're a'ways talkin' 'bout savin' yuh soul an' gettin' ready tuh meet yuh maker. Them's th' folks been talkin' mean thin's 'bout Paw an' me. They's th' ones been gossipin' 'bout us, an' sayin' I'm a bastard an' ain' had no real maw. They go tuh church ev'ry Sunday an' pray tuh Jesus tuh fo'give 'em their sinnin'. Then soon's they leave church, they starts in agin, all ovah.

SUZY. Folks is nacheral int'rested in other folks business.

SAMMY. Not down at th' Las' Chance. Down there nobody ever said nothin' 'bout me. They like a guy fer hisseff—an' there's on'y two kinds, good an' bad. Nothin' in b'tween.

SUZY. Preacher Sims is aimin' tuh get th' Las' Chance closed up. He says th' lowest sorts a people hang out there. He calls it a "den a sin an' evil."

SAMMY. I ain' never seen no sinnin' down there. Far as I'm con-cerned, it ain' nobody's business if th' girls wanna have a good time wit' th' fellas. They don' harm no one. Some folks jus' ain' happy till they c'n hurt others.

SUZY. [*Slowly.*] If it's a boy, I'm gonna call 'im Sammy Lou Berry, Junior. Yuh like that, don' cha, Sammy?

SAMMY. [*Casually.*] Sure.

SUZY. It's a real nice name.

[SAMMY *attempts to lift a huge rock to his shoulder.*]

SAMMY. Betcha I c'n get this on m' back.

[*His muscles strain as he gradually lifts the rock; then he lowers it back down to the ground.*]

SUZY. [*Wonderingly.*] Sammy, wha' was yuh maw like?

SAMMY. I don' 'member m' maw.

SUZY. Don' yuh paw ever say nothin' 'bout 'er?

SAMMY. Naw.

SUZY. He never tol' yuh 'bout 'er?

SAMMY. Naw. Paw don' talk much 'bout wha' was.

SUZY. I bet she musta been real purty.

SAMMY. Paw never said.

SUZY. Don' he have no pitchers a her?

SAMMY. Naw.

SUZY. [*Thoughtfully.*] Sammy, let's take some pitchers a us.

SAMMY. Pitchers?

SUZY. Case I die when th' baby comes. . . . I wan' cha tuh have m' pitcher tuh show 'im.

SAMMY. Yuh ain' gonna die.

SUZY. 'S possible. A lot a wimmen die when their babies come. . . . Do folks really go tuh Heaven when they dies?

SAMMY. I dunno. I suppose some a them goes tuh Hell.

SUZY. Th' bad ones. That's wha' Preacher Sims says . . . D' yuh think Preacher Sims 'll go tuh Heaven—bein' as he's God's Messenger?

SAMMY. More rightly tuh Hell—fer sayin' th' thin's he does.

SUZY. [*Looking at the sky.*] Wonder where Heaven is! Th' sky's so durn big an' empty. Ev'rythin' looks so lonely up there.

SAMMY. [*Looking up.*] Kinda dark t'day. Like it was th' end a th' worl'.

SUZY. Gonna rain t'night.

SAMMY. Rain's good fer th' earth. Sorta makes ev'rythin' breathe.

[*He crosses over and seats himself on the ground at her feet. He draws his legs up to his chin and broods moodily.*]

SUZY. [*Carefully.*] Sammy, it ain' true—'bout cha maw—is it?

SAMMY. Wha'?

SUZY. Wha' folks been sayin'.

SAMMY. Sometimes, when I'm in bed at nights, I get tuh thinkin' 'bout thin's. Folks in town never liked me much. Th' kids at school a'ways use tuh keep away f'om me—like they was tol' tuh hate me. I never done no harm tuh them. . . . One day I was playin' in th' school yard, an' some kid get in th'

way. Th' ball hit 'im, so I wen' ovah tuh say I didn' mean it—
hittin' 'im. He was mad as anythin', an' he started tuh say bad
'bout Paw. He said: "Yuh paw's a no good drunk bum, an' yuh
maw was a tramp. Yuh jus' a bastard wit' no maw." I got red
in th' face an' tried hard not tuh do nothin'. Th' other kids
were laffin' loud. I sorta—sorta fergot ev'rythin'. I jus' wanted
tuh kill 'em, alla 'em. I grabbed one a them an' started tuh hit
'im. I hit 'im in th' nose a couple a times. Th' other fellas
jumped all ovah me. 'Bout ten a them. They gimme th' wust
beatin' I ever got. . . . I never wen' there agin. I use tuh love
tuh play ball in th' school yard durin' lunch hour. But I never
wen' back there agin. [Softly.] I was ashamed. Not that they
beat me up. 'Cause wha' they said 'bout Paw—an' m' maw. I
hated them, alla them! They got no right tuh say wha' they did!

SUZY. Why does yuh paw drink so much? Folks say he spen's
alla th' money yuh give 'im fer likker. They say he ain' never
sober.

SAMMY. I dunno why Paw drinks so much. I ain' never assed
'im. When he ain' home by late, I go lookin' fer 'im. I sorta
know where tuh fine 'im. Then I bring 'im home an' put 'im
tuh bed. He's like a baby. [Then, desperately.] Paw's good!
He ain' mean an' hateful. He don' hate no one. An' plen'y
folks in this town sure stepped all ovah him. They look at Paw
like he's worse 'n dirt. He ain'! He's good as gol'. Kinda'n alla
them put t'gether.

SUZY. [Gently.] Don' hol' no grudges, Sammy.

SAMMY. [Bitterly.] I don' hol' no grudges agin no one. . . .
They all afraid a me now [Touching his biceps.] 'cause I got
this tuh perteck me. I c'n beat 'em all—take 'em on all at th'
same time. I'm stronger 'n alla them. They respeck me. A guy
gotta be strong tuh get respeck—they gotta fear yuh. They
gotta know yuh tuff, an' yuh c'n take all they got tuh dish out,
an' yuh c'n give 'em some yuhseff. I ain' afraid a no man.

SUZY. [With compassion.] Yuh cain't be fightin' a'ways. Yuh
cain't live that ways.

SAMMY. [Shaking his head.] I c'n live that way. I shore c'n.

SUZY. [*Looking at him intently.*] Ferget wha's been said. Ferget it.

SAMMY. [*Hesitantly.*] I try—awful hard. But it don' wuk. Sometimes I keep rememberin' thin's, even when I wanna ferget 'em.

SUZY. I c'n ferget anythin' I wanna.

SAMMY. I cain't.

SUZY. Them thin's—that folks been sayin'—'bout yuh paw. I don' pay no heed tuh them, Sammy. I sorta close m' ears an' don' lissen when folks starts talkin' bad.

[SAMMY *rises, moves up beside her, puts his arm about her. She smiles and lays her head on his shoulder.*]

SAMMY. [*Softly.*] Thin's gonna be diff'ren' some day. We're gonna get out a here.

SUZY. [*Dreamily.*] Where 'll we go, Sammy?

SAMMY. All ovah. See ev'rythin'.

SUZY. Like wha'?

SAMMY. Cally-for-nia.

SUZY. Where else'll we go?

SAMMY. Hell! We'll driff wit' th' win'. Mebbe East. I a'ways been wantin' tuh see Noo York. They says it's so big yuh c'n live right nex' door tuh a guy an' never know wha' he looks like. They says if yuh stan' on Times Square on a Sattiday night, yuh c'n see ev'rybody yuh know walk by.

SUZY. Aw, yuh kiddin' me.

SAMMY. Naw, I ain'. A guy tol' me that once. He said alla folks come tuh Times Square on Sattiday night, an' they all jus' stan' there, lookin' at alla folks passin' by. Sooner 'r later they sees somebody they know.

SUZY. [*Awed.*] Gee.

SAMMY. We'll go tuh lots a places. Then one day we'll fine a place we take tuh. We'll stay there. I'll get a job payin' good money. I don' care how hard th' wuk is. I c'n take tuh it. So lon' 's it pays good.

SUZY. [*Dreamily.*] I wouldn' wanna see yuh wuk too hard. That ain' good, neither.

SAMMY. Some time we'll buy a little place. A clean place wit' some grass aroun' it, mebbe some trees. Big trees that'll have branches reachin' up tuh Heaven.

SUZY. [*Happily.*] Mebbe a garden. We'll grow some vegetables in a little garden. Yuh'll do th' plantin' an' th' sowin' on Sundays—if yuh wanna.

SAMMY. Shore.

SUZY. We'll be happy.

SAMMY. Folks'll respeck us.

SUZY. Sattiday night we c'n go tuh see a show in town.

SAMMY. I'll get cha alla thin's I wan' cha tuh have. Nice clothes, mebbe a fox fur.

SUZY. [*Turning to him.*] Yuh'll be good tuh me, won' cha, Sammy?

SAMMY. Shore.

SUZY. No more drinkin'?

SAMMY. Jus' once in a while. Tuh be regular an' friendly like.

SUZY. [*Carefully.*] Yud never put a han' on me, wouldja? Even when yuh get real mad sometimes?

SAMMY. Naw.

SUZY. [*Hesitantly.*] M' paw—when they're havin' a fight— him an' Maw—times he gets Maw an' he hits her. She cries fer a while, says she's gonna leave 'im. But she never does. They kisses an' makes up—till th' nex' fight. . . . Sammy, I'll never nag yuh. I promise I'll never nag yuh. I'll love yuh a'ways— like a good wife. I love yuh, Sammy. [*She strokes his hair.*] If yuh ever leff me, I'd die. I'd jus' die. . . . Yuh know I ain' sayin' this 'cause I'm wit' th' baby. Yuh know that, Sammy, don' cha?

SAMMY. [*Quietly.*] I know.

SUZY. I ain' never had a boy fren b'fore. An' I ain' never gonna love nobody agin. Jus' you.

SAMMY. I'll be good tuh yuh, Suzy.

SUZY. [*After a pause.*] Yuh don' hafta marry me if yuh don' wanna. I don' care. Ain' no diff'rence tuh me.

SAMMY. [*Tenderly.*] I wanna marry yuh. I wan' th' baby tuh have a real maw an' paw. I don' wanna have folks sayin' nothin' 'bout 'im. 'Cept mebbe that he's a good, stron', honess boy who c'n hol' his own in any fight. I'm gonna teach 'im tuh perteck hisseff. Not tuh be afraid a no one. 'Cause a guy who's afraid tuh fight fer hisseff is a sissy, an' nobody has respeck fer a sissy. Ev'rybody hits 'im an' pushes 'im aroun'.

SUZY. I don' wanna let 'im fight alla time.

SAMMY. Naw. Jus' when he's picked on by other fellas.

SUZY. [*Slowly, dreamily.*] Sammy, when is alla this—alla thin's we been talkin' 'bout—when're they gonna happen?

SAMMY. I dunno. Some day. Soon, I hope.

SUZY. Yuh paw . . .

SAMMY. I cain't leave Paw. Paw wouldn' wan' me tuh go. He needs me. I cain't leave Paw alla lone.

SUZY. I ain' goin' home no more. I'm gonna stay here wit' yuh paw an' you.

SAMMY. Yuh cain't leave yuh folks so sudden. They won' know wha' happened tuh yuh.

SUZY. I don' care. I'm gonna stay here.

[*The voice of a man is heard, offstage, loud and drunkenly rambunctious.* SAMMY *jumps up quickly.*]

SAMMY. Paw!

[*The voice grows louder.* MR. BERRY *appears from back of the shack. He crosses around, and half walks, half stumbles to the front of the house. He is a cadaverous looking man, gaunt, greying, with the remnants of a once powerful physique. His eyes are deep set and lifeless; his face is sallow complexioned, his shoulders stooped. He is only fifty years old, but hard work, privation, the multiple miseries of life have aged him, and he appears much older than he actually is. At present, his sobriety could well be questioned, for he staggers about lamely, miserably. His clothes are torn, and his face is scratched in several places, a bruise perceptible near his chin. His eyes are half shut, and when he speaks he does so with obvious discomfort. Almost falling over a rock that appears in his path, he approaches them, smiling weakly.*]

MR. BERRY. [*Drunkenly.*] Hullo!

SAMMY. [*Miserably.*] Paw . . .

MR. BERRY. Ain' cha glad tuh see me?

SAMMY. [*Hurt.*] Watcha been doin' tuh yuhseff, Paw?

MR. BERRY. Nothin'. Nothin' atall.

SAMMY. Yuh clothes is all ripped, Paw. An' yuh face is scratched all ovah.

[MR. BERRY *touches his face.*]

MR. BERRY. [*Weakly.*] It ain' nothin'.

SAMMY. [*Crossing to him.*] Somebody beat yuh, Paw?

[*He tries to take his father's arm, but his father pulls it away.*]

MR. BERRY. [*Coldly.*] Nothin'. Ain' nothin' happened.

[*Seeing* SUZY *for perhaps the first time, he speaks warmly.*]

Hullo, Suzy. Watcha doin' here?

SUZY. [*Quietly.*] Jus' visitin', Mr. Berry.

MR. BERRY. [*Drunkenly.*] Visitin'? Tha's downright neighborly. Folks out visitin' their neighbors is good folks, I a'ways says. Ain' that right, Suzy?

SUZY. [*Shyly.*] Yes, Mr. Berry.

MR. BERRY. Thank yuh, Suzy girl, thank yuh.

SAMMY. Paw—tell me. Why did they hit yuh?

MR. BERRY. [*Roughly.*] Sammy, there's a lady here. Ain' I tol' yuh never tuh talk a ruff thin's when a lady's presen'?

SAMMY. Yuh look like yuh was beat up, like yuh got a beatin'.

MR. BERRY. Mine yuh own business!

[SAMMY *grabs his father by the arm.*]

SAMMY. Who hit yuh, Paw? Why did they hit yuh? I'm gonna kill 'em! I'm gonna kill 'em all!

MR. BERRY. [*Exhausted.*] I—I fell—near th'—mill. On a rock.

[*Looking at his clothes. A weak laugh.*]

Looka wha' I done tuh m'seff. Ain' it a shame? Nice suit a clothes, too. M' Sunday suit.

SAMMY. Yuh lyin'. Yuh lyin' tuh me. It ain' so; yuh didn' fall. They beat cha! They beat cha up, didn' they?

MR. BERRY. [*Slowly.*] Yeah. [*He averts his head.*] They beat me.

SAMMY. Who? Who done it?

MR. BERRY. I dunno who. [*Weakly.*] Some kids, I think.

SAMMY. Why? Why did they beat cha?

MR. BERRY. [*Slowly.*] Tuh rob me.

SAMMY. Rob yuh?

MR. BERRY. I was comin' down th' Drag. I was sorta—sorta dizzy. I seen 'em followin' me. One a them looked like Tommy Sims.

SAMMY. Preacher Sims' Tommy?

MR. BERRY. Yeah. They followed me pass th' mill. They come runnin'—an' they jumped me.

SAMMY. They ain' got no reason tuh . . .

MR. BERRY. [*With drunken fury.*] Yuh gonna let me finish? Be quiet! . . . One a them grabbed m' han's an' held 'em behin' m' back. Tommy said thin's—'bout me. He had a piece a iron, an' he hit me 'cross th' face. I tried tuh fight 'em, but there was too many fer me.

SAMMY. [*Enraged.*] Sons of bitches! I'm gonna fine 'em an' kill 'em. I'm gonna fix Tommy once an' fer all!

MR. BERRY. One a them [*He touches the bruise near his chin.*] one a them had a cigarette—an' he burned m' face. . . . Th' money yuh gimme, th' money fer rent an' grub an' fer a new suit—Tommy Sims—took it out a m' pocket. I couldn' stop 'em. They was too many. They took alla money, then they run away. [*He breaks down and sobs profusely. He covers his face with his hands to hide the tears.* SAMMY *looks compassionately at his father, then he turns and starts toward the back of the house.*]

SUZY. [*Afraid of what he might do.*] Sammy! Where yuh goin'?

SAMMY. [*Firmly.*] Tuh fine Tommy Sims.

MR. BERRY. Don'! Don' go, Sammy! They'll beat cha, like they done me. Those boys is tuff an' mean.

SAMMY. [*To* SUZY.] I'll be back soon. Wait here wit' Paw. [*He starts to go.*]

SUZY. [*As she runs to him.*] Sammy, please don' go!

SAMMY. [*Anger and fury in his eyes.*] I'm gonna fine Tommy Sims an' ass him jus' one thin'. I'm gonna ass him if he done it—if he beat Paw. I'll know if he's tellin' th' truth 'r not. [*Slowly, portentously.*] If he beat Paw, I'm goin' to fix 'im; fix 'im so's he'll never beat nobody no more.

SUZY. [*Grabbing his arm, excitedly.*] Don' go! Don' fight wit' 'im! Sammy, yuh gonna get in tuh trouble. They'll beat cha. Yuh gonna get hurt.

[*He pushes her away and strides off around the back of the shack. A look of utter dejection appears on her face; she turns slowly and stares blankly at* MR. BERRY.]

MR. BERRY. [*Crying out as if in pain.*] Don' let 'im go! Don' let 'im go, Suzy! I'm afraid . . .

[SUZY *starts to turn, stops suddenly and looks again at* MR. BERRY.]

SUZY. [*Quietly.*] Ain' no use, Mr. Berry. Ain' no use tryin' tuh stop 'im.

[*There is a repetition of* MR. BERRY'S *drunken, exhausted sobbing.*]

SUZY. Yuh better—come in—th' house, Mr. Berry. I'll he'p yuh. . . .

[*She starts to cross to him as the curtain falls.*]


## SCENE 2

*The scene is the same. It is several hours later. The stage is dark and deserted, an intense forlornness pervading the atmosphere. A glaring light inside the shack illuminates the rotting, broken porch. The sky above is black, brooding.* MR. BERRY *comes out of the house and stands near the porch stanchion. He is in a somewhat better condition than he was in the previous scene. His face is washed and his hair is combed neatly back. He is smoking a cigarette, his eyes searching the vastness of the barren, level land. He stands silently for a few moments, then he turns and calls into the house.*

MR. BERRY. C'm out here, Suzy. [*A pause. A moment later* SUZY *appears at the door.*] It's awful hot inside, ain' it?

SUZY. I was jus' fixin' up th' room a little.

MR. BERRY. [*Kindly.*] Yuh shouldn' be doin' wuk in this hot weather, Suzy.

SUZY. [*As she comes out.*] I wasn' doin' nothin'. Jus' cleanin' up a bit.

MR. BERRY. There ain' much tuh clean in there, is there? We ain' got much. Not much like a home. Yuh cain't speck much fer seven bucks a month. Nigger shack, 'bout all it is.

SUZY. M' folks ain' got much more.

MR. BERRY. Yuh folks live in town. [*Bitterly.*] They got us pushed alla way out here. [*With a laugh.*] We ain' lonely. We got th' MKT right by. Biggest railroad for alla Texas! Takes yuh ev'rywhere yuh wanna go. No stoppin' it. Man's bes' friend, th' railroad! Back a us is Carson's, largest jute mill b'tween here an' th' Panhandle. Wukin' day an' night tuh make rope fer alla th' country—enuff rope tuh string f'om here tuh China.

SUZY. M' paw's on th' night shiff at Carson's.

MR. BERRY. Mos' men wuk th' night shiff. They got a lotta wimmen wukin' in th' day.

SUZY. M' sis quit school las' year tuh go tuh wuk there.

MR. BERRY. [*Musing.*] Yuh know—yuh wuk in a place fer years an' years. Like I use tuh wuk at th' mill—till I hit th' bottle an' I got me canned. Day in, day out, yuh wuk tuh live; an' yuh live offen wha' yuh make. Mebbe yuh don' like it; mebbe yud much better fine a patch a lan'—clean, fine lan'— an' grow alla yuh need tuh live. Mebbe have a cow an' a few chicks, a clean little house on fine brown earth—God's Earth. God never meant men tuh own it—jus' live on it. He made it rich an' brown an' fertile, so's a man could raise hisseff all he needs tuh live. Wha' he don' need, he sells tuh buy wahm clothes fer winter. Man ain' doin' wha' God wanted him tuh do. Man don' tak care a th' lan'. He gets tuh wantin' too much, so's he c'n sell a lot an' make money. An' when he makes some money, he gets tuh cravin' fer more. Th' lan' gives all it c'n. Then it stops givin'; it ain' got no more tuh give. It dries up an' becomes hard an' dead. Alla th' life's been dragged out a it. It dies, an' comes tuh lookin' like this here lan'—fergotten; fergotten an' unwanted by no man. Machines, on'y machines wan' th' lan', 'cause it's dead now. Men don' live on it no more. They leff it, fergot it, an' wen' on tuh another place.

SUZY. [*Anxiously.*] Sammy shouldn' a gone tuh fine Tommy Sims.

[MR. BERRY *looks at* SUZY *carefully and thoughtfully.*]

MR. BERRY. [*Slowly.*] Yuh folks know yuh here, Suzy? [*She shakes her head negatively.*] Yuh been lovin' Sammy fer a lon' time now, ain' cha?

SUZY. [*Very sincerely.*] I been lovin' Sammy since th' fust day I ever seen 'im. I ain' never loved no one else.

MR. BERRY. He loves yuh, too. He ain' said nothin' tuh me, but I know he loves yuh.

SUZY. [*Dreamily.*] I ain' never loved no one b'fore. 'Cause I a'ways been waitin' fer Sammy, waitin' fer him tuh love me. [*Simply.*] I give m'seff tuh him th' fust time I seen 'im. I let 'im love me, 'cause I wanted tuh have 'im love me. I wanted Sammy tuh hol' me tight, tuh love me like husban' an' wife. [*Slowly and very passionately.*] When Sammy's nex' tuh me—his body nex' tuh mine—it's like I never lived till then, like I been dyin' alla m' life—an' somepin was tryin' tuh save me, tuh *make* me wanna live. [*Softly.*] I'm gettin' a baby, Mr. Berry.

[MR. BERRY *looks at her with eyes of deep understanding.*]

Sammy an' me—we was talkin' b'fore. I ain' never goin' home no more. I'm stayin' here wit' Sammy. It ain' no sin, 'cause now th' baby's comin' Sammy's like m' husban'. I'm stayin' here, takin' care a th' house, lookin' affer Sammy an' you. I ain' goin' back tuh school no more, an' when it's time fer th' baby tuh come, I'll go tuh th' charity hospital in town.

MR. BERRY. [*After a pause.*] Yuh folks don' like me, or Sammy, yuh know that, don' cha, Suzy?

SUZY. [*Coming down the porch steps.*] That don' make no diff'rence tuh me, Mr. Berry.

[*She seats herself on a large rock.*]

MR. BERRY. They got it in fer me. They been holdin' thin's agin me fer a lon' time now—this town. Sayin' thin's 'bout me, an' Sammy's maw. Bad thin's. [*Suddenly but gently.*] Yuh cain't stay here, Suzy. Not that I don' wan' cha. I like yuh very much. Yuh been kind tuh me—like b'fore, he'pin' me in tuh th' house; he'pin' tuh sober me up; washin' m' face. Yuh good, Suzy— tha's why yuh cain't stay here. 'Cause it ain' right. It's not like you an' Sammy was legal married. If yuh stay here, yuh folks gonna fine out an' have th' sheriff here tuh take yuh back; mebbe lock up Sammy. Then folks 'll start sayin' worse 'bout us. Yuh wouldn' wan' that, wouldja? It'd make thin's very bad— fer Sammy an' me, an' fer yuh, too. I'm gonna tell yuh somepin —somepin I ain' never even tol' Sammy. But I figger yuh c'n unnerstan'. I figger yuh love Sammy, an' mebbe yuh should know.

SUZY. [*Simply.*] Is it 'bout Sammy's maw, Mr. Berry?

MR. BERRY. [*Seating himself on a porch step.*] Sammy's maw an' me. Yuh see, Suzy, Sammy's maw never was wha' mos' folks ud call re-spectable. She was a good, kind woman, gentle an' lovin'. But b'fore we come t'gether, she done thin's that weren' right. . . . She run away f'om her maw an' paw when she was very young. They was a'ways fightin' an' carryin' on, an' it a'ways ended up that they was takin' ev'rythin' out on her. She tol' me once that her ol' man use tuh beat 'er an' keep 'er locked up so's she couldn' go out tuh play—'cause mebbe she'd wear out 'er shoes, an' he had no money tuh buy new ones fer 'er. Her folks was real mean tuh her. So one day she jus' run off.

SUZY. Gee. How ol' was she?

MR. BERRY. Mebbe fifteen.

SUZY. She jus' run off?

MR. BERRY. She come f'om near Tulsa. She was passin' through this town, wantin' tuh head fer Dallas, when she got picked up by Lily Granger.

SUZY. [*Uncomprehending.*] Lily Granger?

MR. BERRY. [*Carefully.*] She was a bad woman, Lily Granger; she had a house—where men ud go. [*Delicately.*] Yuh know wha' I mean? [SUZY *nods affirmatively.*]

She didn' know much 'bout livin'; they fooled 'er, took 'er tuh this place. They filled 'er wit' likker an' made 'er carry on. She tol' me once that they tol' her if she tried tuh run away, they'd get 'er an' kill 'er. So she stayed there. She got tuh bein' like th' other girls, got low an' dirty. I come tuh know 'er one day. I was wukin' at th' Big Bargain Grocery. M' maw an' paw was dead, an' I was livin' wit' another guy who come out of th' orphanage wit' me. She come in tuh buy grub fer Lily Granger.

I seen 'er an' wen' ovah tuh wait on 'er. She was purty, real purty. She didn' say nothin' 'bout Lily Granger. She'd been in town fer a year now, but it was th' fust time I seen 'er. Lily was real hard on alla girls. Never let 'em go out, 'cept mebbe once in a while, fer a walk, an' then she never let 'em come near th' main stem. [*Pause.*] I on'y saw 'er when she come in tuh buy grub fer Lily's table. She'd smile, sweet-like, an' I used tuh get all red an' blushin'. She was real tall fer 'er age, like Sammy, tall an' slender, an' her smile ud set m' heart beatin' fasser an' fasser, till I loved 'er more 'n life itseff. . . . Sammy's like his maw—wild, fulla passion an' cravin'. His maw had th' reddest lips I ever seen, an' her face was soff an' milky-white. She laffed at ev'rythin' [*Softly.*] laffed at alla silliness of livin'. I sure loved 'er. I a'ways loved 'er—till th' day she died.

SUZY. [*Hesitantly.*] Folks—say she run off.

MR. BERRY. Folks don' know. Folks jus' talks; they don' know. She died right here, in this house, an' I buried 'er out there, out near th' MKT tracks, where th' lan' is deep, an' where nobody ud ever bother 'er. I buried 'er m'seff, put 'er tuh res' near th' tracks. She was young, but there weren' much leff a her. She was bones, an' all hollows where her eyes shoulda been. It was more 'n that, too. She was sick, sick in th' head. Times she'd scream that she done alla rotten thin's a pusson c'n do. She'd cry an' say she gotta die—it was th' Lord's wish—so she could pay fer alla her sinnin'.

SUZY. She be-leeved in Jesus?

MR. BERRY. Shore. She loved Jesus. She use tuh speak tuh Him, tell Him alla her sinnin', then ass tuh be fo'given. She'd cry affer she spoke tuh Him, cry an' beg fo'giveness.

SUZY. [*Awed.*] Gee . . .

MR. BERRY. She come tuh live here wit' me when she run away f'om Lily Granger's house. She come here an' live wit' me like we was married. Yuh see, affer she'd been comin' in tuh th' Big Bargain fer a while steady, we use tuh meet in th' back a th' store. Her an' me, when it was slow, an' we use tuh talk. Fust she never said wha' she did, then she seen I been lovin' 'er alla lon', an' she come tuh love me. She loved me honess an' true—

meanin' it deep in 'er heart. Then she tol' me 'bout Lily Granger, an' I 'member how she was shiverin' when she tol' me, beggin' me tuh try an' unnerstan'. [*Pause.*] I unnerstood, an' I fergive 'er, an' then I wen' an' rented this place fer seven a month. I tol' 'er she could come an' stay wit' me. She was a good wife, kind an' dutiful. We lived here a'ways. She never wen' in tuh town.

SUZY. Didn' Lily Granger ever fine out she was livin' here?

MR. BERRY. One night I was wukin' at th' mill late; she was alone here. She was three months wit' Sammy, an' sick near ev'ry day. One a th' railroad men who use tuh come tuh Lily Granger's house come walkin' by, an' he sees 'er settin' on th' porch. He reco'nized 'er. She tried tuh fight 'im off, but he beat 'er. . . . When I come home nex' mornin', an' I seen 'er, I knowed she was clear out a her mine. Screamin', tearin' 'er hair, cryin'. Later she tried tuh kill herseff, tried tuh stab herself wit' a knife. Then on, she was out a her head mos' a th' time. I seen she was dyin'. . . . She had Sammy right here in this house. Was nobody here but me. Sammy come okay, but she died right affer. . . . Nex' day I buried 'er. Dug th' grave m'seff, an' buried 'er deep so's she'd rest an' never be bothered agin.

[*There is a long pause.*]

SUZY. Sammy ain' never had much love, has he?

MR. BERRY. Alla love I could give 'im. I had tuh be both his maw an' his paw. I raised 'im m'seff. Durin' th' day, or when I wuked at nights, I'd leave 'im wit' a nigger woman I knowed in town. She had six a her own, so one more didn' make much diff'rence. I use tuh pay 'er five bucks a month tuh look affer Sammy. She was good tuh him, like a real maw.

SUZY. Nigger wimmen is good maws.

MR. BERRY. Affer that I sorta took tuh drinkin'—tryin' tuh ferget ev'rythin'. . . . I ain' never made it—startin' new an' clean. A guy takes jus' so much f'om life, then he cain't swalla much more. He lets hisseff go, sinks lower an' lower inta th' mud, don' even try tuh save hisseff. He gets tuh figgerin' that mebbe he ain' worth savin', mebbe he c'n be happy rollin' in th' dirt an' slime. . . . There ain' no road back, neither. On'y down.

[*He lowers his head and there is silence, a melancholy silence, broken only by the shrill sounds of a lonely cricket. Then* SAMMY *appears from around back of the shack.* SUZY *sees him, jumps quickly to her feet and runs to him, throwing herself into his arms, kissing him tenderly and lovingly. He stands there impassively, coldly, unresponding to her kisses.*]

SUZY. Sammy, they didn' hurt cha, did they?

SAMMY. [*Coldly.*] I couldn' fine 'em.

SUZY. I was so afraid they'd hurt cha.

SAMMY. [*Stoical.*] I wen' all ovah town, but I couldn' fine Tommy Sims, or none a them.

SUZY. Yuh paw an' I was worried.

[SAMMY *slowly turns his head and looks fiercely at his father, eyes scowling and lips drawn in contemptuous hatred. He says nothing; he crosses over to where his father is standing and stares at him resentfully.* MR. BERRY *cringes slightly under the intensity of* SAMMY's *glaring eyes.*]

MR. BERRY. [*Weakly.*] Wha' cha lookin' at me like that . . . Sammy?

SAMMY. [*Flatly.*] Yuh lied tuh me, Paw. Yuh lied tuh me.

MR. BERRY. [*Drawing himself up.*] Lied? I ain' never lied tuh no one.

SAMMY. [*Stolidly.*] Yuh lyin' now, Paw.

MR. BERRY. What're yuh sayin'?

SAMMY. I'm sayin' that I c'n never be-leeve yuh agin, never trust yuh agin.

MR. BERRY. Yuh seem tuh ferget yuh talkin' tuh yuh paw.

SAMMY. [*Bursting out furiously.*] Yuh're a liar! A drunken, stinkin' liar! An' ol' whorin' liar! Tha's wha' cha are!

[MR. BERRY *reaches out and gives* SAMMY *a resounding smack across the face.* SUZY *cries out.* SAMMY *doesn't flinch; he remains rigid and motionless.*]

MR. BERRY. [*Turning and going toward the house.*] Embarrassin' me b'fore Suzy like that. Yuh oughta be ashamed a yuh-seff!

[*He starts to go up the stairs of the house.* SAMMY *doesn't move, but when he speaks his voice is brutal.*]

SAMMY. Tommy Sims is home, sick in bed. He ain' been out a th' house fer th' pas' week. Preacher Sims tol' me.

[MR. BERRY *stops in his tracks, his back to* SAMMY. *He stands quite still, saying nothing.*]

Where's th' money I give yuh, Paw? Yuh ain' got it, have yuh? M' money, Paw, wha' cha do wit' it?

MR. BERRY. [*Faintly.*] Since when yuh gotten tuh question me?

SAMMY. [*Flatly.*] Where's m' money I give yuh tuh hol'?

[*No answer. Suddenly* SAMMY *jumps forward and grabs his father's shirt. He seems to have lost all control over himself, all the pent-up fury of his anger finally being released.*]

Yuh bum! Yuh lousy bum! I trusted yuh. I trusted yuh wit' m' money. I let cha hol' it fer me. Yuh spen' it all. Yuh spen' it on likker an' whores. I foun' out. I know. Nobody robbed yuh; yuh lied tuh me. I was gonna kill Tommy Sims, an' he ain' done nothin'. He's home, sick in bed fer a week. I wuked like a dog an' give yuh alla m' money. Yuh ain' never been savin' it. Yuh been drinkin' it up, treatin' ev'rybody at th' Lucky Seven tuh drink, ev'ry time yuh wen' there.

MR. BERRY. [*Weakly.*] Who tol' yuh that?

SAMMY. [*Furiously.*] None a yuh business! I foun' out. I seen one a yuh whores. She tell me tuh give yuh a message: don' come botherin' 'er till yuh got more money! She ain' got time tuh play wit' guys tha's broke. Nex' time yuh come, she ain' gonna see yuh till yuh pay up.

MR. BERRY. [*Coldly.*] Yuh gone out a yuh head. Yuh stark ravin' crazy.

SAMMY. Then where's m' money?

MR. BERRY. I tol' yuh I was robbed.

SAMMY. Yuh lyin'! Sadie Jenks tol' me all 'bout cha.

MR. BERRY. Sadie Jenks is jealous 'cause I ain' never paid no heed tuh her.

SAMMY. M' eyes musta been closed alla this time. Yuh took m' money an' spen' it on likker. Yuh drunk ol' fool! Yuh ain' never wuked; yuh been livin' offen me. Eatin' m' grub; sleepin' in m' house, 'cause I pay th' rent. Yuh too lazy tuh wuk, yuh ol' bum!

SUZY. [*Frightened.*] Sammy, don' . . .

SAMMY. [*Violently.*] Keep out a this!

SUZY. [*Painfully.*] Sammy . . .

SAMMY. Keep out! It ain' none a yuh affair!

MR. BERRY. [*To* SUZY.] Don' pay no heed tuh him, Suzy. He's clear out a his mine.

[SAMMY *is enraged after these last words. His hand shoots out wildly, landing squarely on* MR. BERRY'S *jaw. The older man falls forward on his face, just missing the first step of the porch.* SAMMY *stands over him, his fists clenched, his arms moving nervously at his sides.* SUZY *screams. It is several moments before* MR. BERRY *recovers himself completely and is able to look up at the towering figure of his son before him. He gets to his feet slowly, carefully. Then he speaks in a hoarse, low voice to* SAMMY.]

Inside. I'll fight cha inside. Yuh jumped me, then. I still got enuff in me tuh lick th' life out a yuh.

SAMMY. [*Fiercely.*] Here! Out here I'll fight cha!

MR. BERRY. No. . . . Suzy don' hafta see nothin' like this.

SUZY. [*Nearly in tears.*] No, please! Don' fight!

[*She crosses to* SAMMY *and tries to take his arm.*]

SAMMY. [*to* SUZY, *savagely.*] This ain' none a yuh business. Go away! I give 'im alla m' money! I give it tuh him tuh hol'. He ain' been robbed. Th' whores an' likker been robbin' 'im alla lon'.

[MR. BERRY *starts up the stairs of the porch, turns and faces them.*]

MR. BERRY. [*Slowly.*] Shore!—I ain' got yuh money. I spen' it. I spen' it fer wha' I craved. A man needs tuh get wha' he craves, else he goes out a his mine.

SAMMY. [*With a sobbing fury.*] Yuh're an ol' man! Yuh don' need no wimmen. Yuh sick; yuh been dyin' fer a lon' time. . . . Yuh disgraced m' maw in her grave! Was jus' as good as throwin' rocks at her grave!

[*He breaks down and begins to sob.* SUZY *tries to embrace him, but he sobs "Go away." He turns to hide his eyes. When he sees his son crying, the expression on* MR. BERRY'S *face changes. His eyes seem to come alive for perhaps the first time, and a warmth spreads over his countenance. Slowly, tiredly, he comes down the steps and goes to his son. He puts his hand on the boy's shoulder; when he speaks, the words are loving and affectionate.*]

MR. BERRY. [*To* SAMMY.] Sammy . . .

SAMMY. [*Pulling away—through his tears.*] Lee me alone. Go away f'om me.

MR. BERRY. Fergive me—son. Fergive me—for wha' I done. Yuh ain' done nothin' wrong by hittin' me. Mebbe it was comin' tuh me. I been low—low 's dirt.

SAMMY. [*Bitterly.*] I trusted yuh. I be-leeved in yuh.

MR. BERRY. [*Desperately.*] I didn' wanna do it. I didn' wanna keep on spendin' yuh money. Somepin inside a me—drivin' me on. Makin' me do th' wust thin's a man c'n do. Torturin' m' soul till I had tuh roll in th' dirt! I been lonely, very lonely, fer a lon' time now. Son, some day mebbe yuh'll know, some day yuh'll unnerstan'.

SAMMY. Why didn' yuh tell me yuh spen' it all? Why didja hide it f'om me?—Alla while sayin' yuh been savin' it fer us. Why didn' yuh tell me yuh wanted it? I wouldn' a cared.

MR. BERRY. I couldn' a tol' yuh. It woulda made me feel—like I was beggin' f'om yuh.

[SAMMY *turns and faces his father.*]

SAMMY. [*Interrupting, passionately.*] Paw, Paw, wha's gonna happen tuh us? We gonna hafta go on livin' in this slop? We ain' got no money; we ain' got nothin'; th' town hates us. Wha's gonna happen, Paw? There ain' no future fer us.

MR. BERRY. [*Tired.*] There ain' nothin' fer me tuh do. A man lives in one place fer a lon' time, he sorta becomes part a th' place. He grows tuh thinkin' it's his—bad 'r good, it's his. This place is mine. Th' lan' is no good; dead—like alla th' dead mem'ries hauntin' this house, day in an' day out. . . . I ain' never gonna leave here. Mebbe soon I'll go meet yuh maw, out there in th' earth that ain' fit tuh hol' th' bones of a houn' dog. But I ain' never leavin' here. That don' mean yuh gotta stay.

There ain' nothin' fer both a yuh here. Yuh ain' got nothin' here. If yuh was smart, yud get out now, when yuh got a chance. 'Cause soon's Suzy don' come home, th' sheriff's gonna come lookin' fer 'er. An' when they fine out she's gonna have a baby, they'll sure as shootin' take 'er away, an' then yuh'll never see 'er again. [SAMMY *looks at* SUZY.]

If yuh was smart, yud go now—quick. Now's yuh chance tuh go. I ain' got nothin' tuh give yuh. Jus' m' bes' wishes.

SAMMY. [*To* SUZY.] We could hop th' seven-thirty freight. Be in Dallas t'morra mornin'. [*He looks at his father.*] Paw—yuh'll be all alone.

MR. BERRY. I ain' afraid a bein' alone.

SUZY. [*Haltingly.*] Sammy . . .

SAMMY. Yeah?

SUZY. If yuh wanna go now, I'll go. I ain' scared a nothin'.

SAMMY. [*To his father.*] Wha'll yuh do, Paw?

MR. BERRY. I'll git on okay.

SAMMY. Yuh ain' got a job.

MR. BERRY. Mebbe I'll fine one.

SAMMY. Who'll take care a yuh?

MR. BERRY. I'll git on.

SAMMY. Mebbe—affer Suzy an' me settles some place—yuh'll come tuh live wit' us. We'll sen' yuh th' train money.

SUZY. Yuh'll come an' stay wit' us, Mr. Berry.

[*In the distance, the whistle of the seven-thirty freight can be heard.*]

MR. BERRY. [*To both.*] Yuh better git goin'! It'll be here soon.

SAMMY. [*Hesitantly.*] Paw . . .

MR. BERRY. Yuh ain' got much in th' house I c'n give yuh tuh take alon'.

SAMMY. I don' wan' nothin'. We're gonna travel light.

SUZY. [*Softly.*] Mr. Berry, tell m' folks I wen' away wit' Sammy. Tell 'em not tuh worry 'r look fer me. Don' say nothin' 'bout th' baby. They mebbe won' unnerstan'.

[*The train whistle sounds again, this time nearer.*]

MR. BERRY. Yuh best start hoppin', if yuh wanna jump th' freight when she rounds th' bend.

SAMMY. [*Offering his hand.*] 'Bye, Paw.

[*They shake.*]

MR. BERRY. Take care a Suzy—yuh wife.

SAMMY. I will.

SUZY. [*Embracing* MR. BERRY.] Take care a yuhseff—Paw.

[*She kisses him. The train whistles again, nearer.*]

MR. BERRY. Yuh best run fer it.

[SAMMY *takes* SUZY'S *hand and they start off left, toward the tracks. At the extreme left,* SAMMY *stops and looks back at his father.*]

SAMMY. [*Calling.*] Take care, Paw!

[MR. BERRY *smiles. The boy and girl quickly disappear.* MR. BERRY *stands watching them go off. The train is very near now, and the noise of its approach is a plethora of sound. The train seems to slow down, then gradually pick up speed.* MR. BERRY *turns, walks wearily up the stairs of the porch, enters the house. The door closes silently behind him. In the near distance, the plaintive wail of the departing freight is heard in the night.*]

**CURTAIN**

# A WORD IN YOUR EAR

*A Study in Language, from the radio series,
"Ways of Mankind"*

By

WALTER GOLDSCHMIDT and LISTER SINCLAIR

*(Published here for the first time)*

# A WORD IN YOUR EAR

## CAST

*A Word in Your Ear* was originally produced in the studios of the Canadian Broadcasting Corporation, Toronto, by the National Association of Educational Broadcasters, under the terms of a grant from the Fund for Adult Education, established by the Ford Foundation. The following participated.

HERE ................................... Robert Christie
THERE ...................................... Lorne Green
HUMAN: COOK: FELLOW: HEADLINE: ........... Frank Perry
WIFE: SWEDISH MOTHER: NORWEGIAN MOTHER:
  NAVAHO MOTHER: ...................... Beth Lockerbie
HUSBAND: POLITICIAN: .................... Tommy Tweed
AMERICAN: SALESMAN: JIM: ................. Ed McNamara
ENGLISH: CHUCKCHEE: TROBRIANDER: ............. Alan King
WICLIF: PROFESSOR: MAC: .................. Godfrey Tudor
ANGLO-SAXON: QUEEN VICTORIA: FRENCH MOTHER:
  GERMAN MOTHER: ....................... Alice Mather
SAXON: ESKIMO: .......................... Larry McCance
NORMAN: AMIABLE: GUY: .................... Alan Pearce
INFANT: MOTHER: HOPI MOTHER: ................ Alice Hill
NAVAHO ............................... Paul Kligman
ANNOUNCER ............................. Bernard Cowan

This is one of twenty-six radio programs in the project supervised by Professor Walter Goldschmidt, of the Department of Anthropology and Sociology of the University of California in Los Angeles. Ruth Roreck assisted.

Written by Lister Sinclair.

Produced by Andrew Allan.

Original music by Lucio Agostini.

# WALTER GOLDSCHMIDT
# LISTER SINCLAIR

In the preface to this annual, I have called the attention of young writers to the necessity for some real thinking about the kind of language to be used in any American play. Here is a radio play, *A Word in Your Ear,* one of a series about "The Ways of Mankind," which tackles the problem of language through the understandings of modern social anthropology. As Dr. Goldschmidt says: "The language that a people speak has important influence upon the way they feel about and react to the world."

In connection with the study of language, there is a book just released by another Professor, Dr. Charlton Laird of the University of Nevada, "The Miracle of Language," (World Publishing, Cleveland and New York.) It is a book which serious student writers and earnest readers will find enjoyable as well as useful.

Dr. Walter Goldschmidt, Project Director of "The Ways of Mankind" series, is Professor of Anthropology and Sociology at the University of California in Los Angeles. He is responsible for the intellectual content of the plays, and their selection. More than seven of them were written by Lister Sinclair, of Toronto, and all were produced originally in the Toronto Studios of the Canadian Broadcasting Corporation. The plays are now being released over educational radio stations which are members of the National Association of Educational Broadcasters, and are available for rebroadcast from any commercial station desiring to have them.

# A WORD IN YOUR EAR

HERE. Watch your language! Remember whom you're speaking to! To the ladies, speak Italian; to the gentlemen, French; to the birds, English; to the dogs, German; and Spanish should be spoken only to God!

MUSIC.

ANNOUNCER. "A Word in your Ear," a study in Language.

HERE. All people have language with which to express their feelings.

THERE. But language is not the *same* as expressing your feelings. Some people think animals have language because they can often express their feelings; as when in the Arctic wilderness, we hear the wolf.

[*Sound of the wolf's howl.*]

HERE. But there is all the difference in the world between that wolf and this.

[*Sound of human wolf whistle!*]

THERE. The four-legged wolf howl expresses its feelings there and then, and so does the wolf whistle; but the whistler can back up his expression with language.

HUMAN. How about taking in a show on Saturday night?

HERE. And that is a communication about another time and another place. It is true language, not just expression of feeling. And all human beings have language, from the Eskimo by the Arctic Sea warm in his kayak with his suit of furs, to the Patagonian by the Antarctic Sea shivering in his canoe with a fire in it, because he wears almost no clothes at all. From one extreme to the other, all people have language.

MUSIC.

THERE. What's more, all these languages are adequate; they all do the job: communication.

HERE. But we often think that whatever we speak ourselves

169

is the proper thing; what the other fellow speaks is scarcely more than a string of grunts.

WIFE. [*Reading from the paper.*] I see by the paper there are over fifteen hundred different languages spoken in the world today.

HUSBAND. [*Not interested or listening.*] Oh.

WIFE. And it says there are more families of languages among the American Indians than in the whole of the Old World.

HUSBAND. [*Even less interested.*] Uh.

WIFE. Well, every one knows Indians don't talk properly. They just grunt.

HUSBAND. [*A negative.*] Uh-uh.

WIFE. [*With an edge.*] You aren't listening. [*Pause.*] Are you?

HUSBAND. [*Coming to.*] Hmm?

WIFE. Are you listening?

HUSBAND. [*With the false enthusiasm of one who hasn't been.*] M-hm!

WIFE. I say Indians don't talk properly. They just grunt.

HUSBAND. [*Not having quite caught it.*] Huh?

WIFE. *Grunt!*

HUSBAND. [*Having caught it.*] Uh!

WIFE. What do *you* think?

HUSBAND. [*Thinking.*] U-u-u-u-u-u-uh! [*Then he plunges.*] Language is language, and grunts are grunts.

MUSIC. [*Something hoggish.*]

HERE. One man's speech is another man's jargon, but all people have language, and these languages are highly diverse in form. But always, we begin by speaking as we think, and end by thinking as we speak. Our language is an expression of our culture, shaped by the way we are brought up; and on the other hand, the way we are brought up is shaped by our language.

THERE. For, as we know from our own language, English, language reflects place, time, age, sex, and circumstance. And this is true of other languages.

HERE. Language reflects place.

THERE. As everybody knows: very often the most foreign thing about a foreign country is the foreign language.

HERE. And English-speakers can't visit one another's country without meeting the great Trans-Atlantic Rift.

AMERICAN. Lookit, Jack: when you get off the street-car, get off the pavement, get on the sidewalk, go two blocks, turn right, there's a drug-store on the corner, take the elevator down to the gar*age:* you can't miss it.

ENGLISH. All right, chum: you mean, when I get off the tram, get off the road, get *on* the pavement, take the second turning to the right, there's a chemist's shop on the corner, take the lift down to the *gar*age: what do you mean, I can't miss it!

THERE. Language then, is a function of place.

HERE. And language is a function of time. Listen to the Lord's Prayer as it sounded nearly six hundred years ago.

WICLIF. Oure Fadir that art in heuenes, halwid be thi name;
Thi kyngdom cumme to; be thi wille don as in heuen and in erthe;
Gif to vs this day oure breed ouer other substaunce;
And forgeve to vs oure dettis, as we forgeve to oure dettours;
And leede vs nat in to temptacioun, but delyuere vs fro yuel. Amen.

THERE. Then, quite soon after the Norman Conquest, English had a tang of French to it. But let's jump back beyond ten sixty six, and listen to English in its hard Teutonic infancy as Anglo-Saxon: the Lord's Prayer in the year one thousand A. D.:

ANGLO-SAXON. Faeder ure thu the eart on heofonum; si thin name gehalgod.
To-becume thin rice. Gewurthe thin wille on eorthan swa swa on heofonum.
Urne gedaeghwamlican hlaf syle us to daeg.
And forgyf us ure gyltas swa swa we forgyfath urum gyltendum.
And ne gelaed thu us on costnunge ac alys us of yfele. Sothlice.

HERE. Language then is a function of time, and even modern English still keeps the record of that Norman Conquest. The Saxons became the servants, and looked after the beasts while they were alive, and their names are still the Saxon ones.

SAXON. Ox. Calf. Sheep. Swine.

THERE. Compare the German: *Ochs. Kalb. Schaf. Schwein.*

HERE. But when they were killed, their meat was served up to the Norman master; and on the table those animals' names are still the Norman ones.

NORMAN. Beef. Veal. Mutton. Pork.

THERE. Compare the French: *Boeuf. Veau. Mouton. Porc.* Language reflects culture.

MUSIC.

HERE. Language is a function of age. We don't expect a child to talk like a college professor.

INFANT. Simple harmonic motion can therefore be represented graphically by a sine or cosine curve.

THERE. Nor do we expect a college professor to talk like a child.

PROFESSOR. What's the matter, said the doctor,
What's the matter, said the nurse,
What's the matter, said the lady with the alligator purse?

MUSIC. [*"Says the lady with the aligator purse."*]

THERE. Language is also a function of sex. Among the Carayahi Indians of Brazil, the women and the men speak slightly different languages. For example, the word for girl is *yadokoma* in the women's language, but *yadoma* in the men's.

HERE. And in English: here's a traveler chewing his cigar in the smoking room of the Santa Fe Chief; but he's speaking the women's language.

SALESMAN.[*Very gruff and masculine in voice and manner.*] I don't want to be catty, but, my dear, it was simply too terrible. I really thought I should have died. I just wanted to sink right through the floor. My gracious me, I thought, if Bert and Charlie aren't wearing that same cunning Homburg hat.

HERE. Unfortunately, in our society the men's language is taboo to women: that is to say, they are supposed not to know it. So we don't dare give you an example of a lady speaking the men's language. Sailors present.

MUSIC. [*Hornpipe.*]

THERE. Language is a function of occasion. There is a time for one kind of speech, and a time for another. Sir James Frazer tells us that in Siam there is a special language to be used when discussing the Siamese King. When he eats or drinks or walks, a special word indicates that these acts are being performed by the sovereign, and such words cannot possibly be applied to the acts of any other person whatever.

HERE. We do not perhaps carry things quite so far as that, but none the less a fellow may be greeted when he comes into the office by:

AMIABLE. Hi, Charley boy, how's the kid; what've you got to say for yourself?

HERE. But a few minutes later when the board meeting convenes, he is asked:

AMIABLE. [*Now very solemn.*] And now, Charles, we trust you have overcome the hardships of your journey. Would you be so good as to present your report regarding market conditions in the West?

THERE. The Chinese, of course, are famous for their elaborate forms of greeting; but other languages are far more complicated. For example, the Nootka Indians of Vancouver Island not only distinguish by the choice of words, the sex of the person speaking, the sex of the person spoken to, and whether the speaker is more, or less important than the person spoken to, but also, on top of this, have a special way of talking to a man who is lefthanded; and a special way of talking to a man who is circumcised.

HERE. English cannot go this far; but even so, language must be suitable to the occasion. Queen Victoria certainly knew this when she expressed her dislike of Gladstone in the words:

QUEEN VICTORIA. "Mr. Gladstone always addresses me as if I were a public meeting."

HERE. And imagine a politician proposing in the language he uses on the platform!

POLITICIAN. Unaccustomed as I am to private proposals, I kneel before you today unwilling, nay reluctant, to assume the burdens of matrimonial office, but none the less prepared to bow to your opinion, and dedicate myself unselfishly if I receive an unmistakable draft.

MUSIC. [*Mendelssohn.*]

THERE. [*Summing it up.*] Language, therefore, by reflecting place, time, age, sex, and circumstance, is a function of society. Language reflects culture.

HERE. The easiest way to see this is through vocabulary. The Eskimos have no word for coconut, and the Samoans have no word for snow.

ESKIMO. And neither do the Eskimos.

HERE. I beg your pardon?

ESKIMO. We Eskimos have no word for snow. Ask me the word for snow, and I ask you, what kind of snow? Snow is to us Eskimos too important to be dismissed with one word; we have many words telling us, for instance, when it fell, and describing its exact condition to us; for the knowledge is vital, and our lives may depend on it.

THERE. Since language reflects society, whatever is important in society has many words in the language. The Arabs have a thousand words for sword; and the Siberian Chuckchee that live on the shores of the Arctic Ocean have thirty or so words describing the skins of the caribou: as, for example, this one:

CHUCKCHEE. *Cechenyaqilhm.*

THERE. This word means that the underleg of the caribou skin is greyish; also that it is light grey on the groins, but that the prevailing body color is brown. And there are innumerable similar examples. The Yurok Indians of California place a high value on woodpecker scalps and obsidian blades; and besides the ordinary set of numerals one, two, three and so forth, they have two extra sets: one for counting woodpecker scalps, and another one for counting obsidian blades.

HERE. English is full of relics of vocabulary that remind us that other days thought other things important. There was a time when English speaking men lived very much by hunting. They had special words for congregations of animals: a flock of sheep and a herd of cattle, but a pride of lions, a skulk of foxes, and a gaggle of geese. They also had special words for the carving of each of the animals and birds of the chase when they arrived on the table ready to eat. Nowadays, if we saw a pile of game birds and wanted them carved, the cook might say:

COOK. Hey, mac!

MAC. Yeah?

COOK. Cut up them birds, will you?

HERE. For nowadays one game bird is much like another—out of season.

THERE. But to the Elizabethans, game birds were the very meat of life, and their carving required a special and ornate vocabulary.

COOK. You, sirrah!

MAC. Anon?

COOK. Dismember that heron, unbrace that mallard, allay that pheasant, wing that partridge, display that quail, unjoint that bittern, thigh that woodcock, lift that swan, and rear that goose. As for that curlew . . . !

MAC. Aye, Sir?

COOK. Unlatch it!

MUSIC. [*Pompous.*]

HERE. A noble handful that has been replaced by other rich treasures of vocabulary as our language (like all other languages) has changed to reflect our culture.

ESKIMO. As we Eskimos found out, when I was sent down to study *your* culture. Your language is like ours, very often. Our Eskimo language, like many other North American Indian languages, is polysynthetic.

HERE. How's that, polysynthetic?

ESKIMO. Not Eskimo word; English word: polysynthetic. One word means a whole phrase, one word has in it the compressed wreckage of a phrase. Thus suppose we wish to say in Eskimo, this, "When they were about to go out they would take the boot-stretcher, using it to thrash the dogs because they usually stay in the entrance passage."

That is twenty eight words in English. In Eskimo it is

six words: *Anilerunik:* when-they-were-about-to-go-out; *kammiut:* the boot-stretcher; *tingussaat:* they-would-take-it; *anaataralongo:* using-it-to-thrash-with; *qimmit:* the-dogs; *torsooneetaommata:* because-they-usually-stay-in-the-entrance-passage.

HERE. But where does English contain words that are the compressed wreckage of a phrase, as you put it?

ESKIMO. In English, not exactly like Eskimo, but nearly like. The other day I saw a newspaper headline.

HEADLINE. UNRRA DP'S laud UNESCO.

ESKIMO. UNRRA DP'S laud UNESCO. Back to my dictionary I go. There I find the word *"laud,"* nothing else. The other words are missing. Then it is explained to me. These other words are not normal English; they are instead the compressed wreckage of phrases, and four words "UNRRA DP'S laud UNESCO," means:

HEADLINE. United Nations Relief and Rehabilitation Agency Displaced Persons laud the United Nations Educational, Scientific and Cultural Organization.

ESKIMO. Seventeen words compressed into four; well, that is about the average for Eskimo!

MUSIC. [*Eskimo triumphant.*]

THERE. Again, language reflects culture. As modern life sets up more elaborate agencies and organizations, modern language adapts itself, and forms words and builds polysynthetic forms almost like the Eskimo. Other languages besides English have been doing this. German, for example. *Gestapo* stands for *Geheime Staats Polizei*, Secret State Police. *Flak* is the compressed wreckage of *Flugzeugsabwehrkanone,* anti-aircraft cannon.

HERE. As we think, so we speak; as we speak, so we think. As we are taught reading, writing, and arithmetic, as we are taught our manners, and the way things are done in the world we live in, so we are taught our language. And as we learn our language from our mother's lips, we also learn the customs and attitudes of our society; for language reflects these customs and attitudes, that is, language reflects culture.

THERE. Over here, for instance.

[*Sound of child wailing and misbehaving.*]

Here's a child misbehaving; and here comes its mother. She's going to tell it to behave properly, but let us notice carefully what word she uses.

MOTHER. Johnny, be *good!*

[*Sound. Child subsides.*]

HERE. Be *good!* The English-speaking child that misbehaves is bad; it is naughty, it is wicked. So is the Italian-speaking child, or the Greek-speaking one.

THERE. But listen to what the French mother says to *her* child!

FRENCH MOTHER. *Jean, sois sage!*

THERE. *Sois sage,* be wise. The French-speaking child that misbehaves is not bad; it is foolish, it is imprudent, it is injudicious.

HERE. In the Scandinavian countries, things are different again. The Swedish mother says:

SWEDISH MOTHER. *Jan, var snell!*

HERE. And the Norwegian mother says:

NORWEGIAN MOTHER. *Jan, ble snil!*

HERE. Both mean the same thing: be friendly, be kind. So the misbehaving Scandinavian child is unfriendly, unkind, uncooperative.

THERE. Things are very different in Germany.

GERMAN MOTHER. *Hans, sei artig!*

THERE. Be in line! The misbehaving German child is not conforming; it is out of step, out of line. A mother of the Hopi Indians of the Southwest United States has the same idea, only in a more gentle spirit, when she tells her child:

HOPI MOTHER. [*Gentle.*] No, no, no, no; that is not the Hopi way.

THERE. *Hopi* is the right thing, the proper way to do things, the way the affairs of the tribe and indeed of the universe are managed. The Hopi child that misbehaves is not bad, nor imprudent, nor unfriendly, nor, quite, out of line. He is not on the Hopi way; he is not with the Hopi view of destiny and of life.

HERE. So even in the words a mother says to her misbehaving

child, we can detect again how language reflects culture.

MOTHER. Johnny, be good!

FRENCH. *Jean, sois sage;* be wise!

SWEDISH. *Jan, var snell;* be friendly!

GERMAN. *Hans, sei artig;* get back in step!

HOPI. No, no, no, no, that is not the Hopi way!

MUSIC. [*Rock-a-bye Baby.*]

THERE. East of New Guinea, in the Southern Pacific, lie the Trobriand Islands. The people who live there are great mariners, lively and active. But they take no interest in things changing. If a thing changes, then it becomes something else, and they call it something else.

HERE. Just as we do not introduce an old gentleman with a long white beard as "a bouncing baby boy, Jim Jones."

JIM. [*Aged 99.*] Very pleased to make your acquaintance.

THERE. [*Sotto voce, to here.*] Buster here isn't any more a bouncing baby boy than I am.

JIM. Ah, but you see, once upon a time, I was, in the long, long ago.

HERE. [*Dismissing him briskly.*] But he isn't now; and in fact, we don't think of him as a kind of modified infant, but as something else: an old gentleman, a different kind of animal.

THERE. Now the Trobriand Islanders think like this all the time. They raise a yam crop, and a first-rate yam is called:

TROBRIANDER. *Taytu.*

THERE. But an overripe yam is not overripe *taytu;* it's different. It's:

TROBRIANDER. *Yowana.*

THERE. And a *yowana* with underground shoots isn't *yowana* any more, but:

TROBRIANDER. *Silisata.*

THERE. Though with new tubers on the underground shoots, it isn't *silisata* of any kind, but rather:

TROBRIANDER. *Gadena.*

THERE. Among the Trobriand Islanders, in short, the name of a thing alone is all you need say about it.

HERE. How different with us! Consider the case of a fellow

being shown a new baby.

[*Sound of new baby bawling.*]

Red-faced, boiled-looking, dribbling, cross-eyed and squalling. The fond parents are watching you like hawks; you have to say something. But what? [*Speaking now into our ear.*]

FELLOW. [*To himself.*] How intelligent looking?

HERE. [*The devil's advocate.*] But it looks like a moron!

FELLOW. [*Trying another one.*] How beautiful?

HERE. Just look at the ugly little beast!

FELLOW. How small and tiny?

HERE. For that, they'll kill you; he's three thirty seconds of an ounce over-weight; he's a giant!

FELLOW. How exactly like his father?

HERE. Say that, and he'll punch you right on the nose. There's nothing you can say; all you can do is shuffle around from one foot to the other and look as foolish as the baby.

THERE. [*Loud and cheerful, like a breath of fresh air.*] But in the Trobriand Islands, the whole thing's simple. Show a Trobriand Islander the same messy, bellowing brat, and he says:

TROBRIANDER. How baby!

THERE. How baby! Which nobody can deny, and everyone's happy.

MUSIC. [*Everyone's happy.*]

HERE. Yet our language is like the Trobriand in some ways, just as our society is like theirs in some ways. They place a high value on yams and have an elaborate yam vocabulary. We place a high value on other things, and have an even more complicated and exact vocabulary to describe the special objects of our interest.

[*Sound of street-corner traffic.*]

Just look here! Standing on a down-town street-corner, we have a Trobriand Islander; he's come to study our society. He's talking to a guy and writing down the answers.

TROBRIANDER. What is the name of that thing on wheels going by now; the green one?

GUY. That's a *Plymouth*.

TROBRIANDER. *Plymouth.* There is another green one, also a *Plymouth.*

GUY. No, it's green, but it ain't a *Plymouth.* That's a *Studebaker.* Studie has a kind of turret in the middle.

TROBRIANDER. Then here is a great big *Studebaker.*

GUY. No, the big one with the kind of turret, that's a *Cadillac.*

TROBRIANDER. Here is another big one; that is a *Cadillac?*

GUY. No, no; look at the back! That's a *Lincoln.*

[*Traffic sounds fade.*]

HERE. And so it goes on. That Trobriander'll be there for a week. And then we'll break it to him that there's a difference between the fifty-three model and the fifty-four model. A week! He'll be there for a year.

THERE. But when he *does* go home, he'll talk to his friends, just as our travelers come home and talk to us.

TROBRIANDER. They are a very peculiar people, attaching fantastic importance to little differences of their automobiles, so that a certain kind of small automobile is called a *Plymouth;* but with a turret in the middle, it is not a Plymouth with a turret, but a *Studebaker.* Quite a different word. And a big thing like a sort of Studebaker with other differences here and there is not a big Studebaker, but a different word again, a *Cadillac;* and so it goes on. They are a very peculiar people.

THERE. How Trobriand! But now we end with the most striking and interesting example of language reflecting culture: the wonderful and varied language of the Navaho Indians.

MUSIC. [*Ethnographic recording of Navaho night way.*]

ANNOUNCER. Navaho Indians live in the great red desert of the Southwest United States, not very far from the Grand Canyon, in Arizona. Their nomadic life is filled with uncertainties, and they seek security and balance in ritual and ceremony, by which they find their place in the natural harmony of the universe, and health and a sense of belonging. Now life on this vast, unconsidering mountain desert is very much influenced by forces the Navaho do not command: the long drought, the sudden torrential rain, the sweep of epidemic disease. And the Navaho view of the universe seems to be connected with what they have learned from the country that is their home.

HERE. We try to control Nature.

NAVAHO. We seek to understand it, and our place within it.

HERE. To us, the world is made up of beings and things that act on other beings and things.

NAVAHO. To us Navaho, the world is one of actions and events associated with things, among which our own acts are only a few among many.

HERE. Our outlook is centered on things; our language is centered on nouns, which are the names of things. The first words our children learn might well be the names of things.

MOTHER. Man. Ball. Boat. Bird.

NAVAHO. Our Navaho outlook is focused on actions and events, our language on verbs; the first words our children learn may well be those expressive of actions.

NAVAHO MOTHER. Standing. Rolling. Sailing. Flying.

HERE. Navaho words, like those of Eskimo, are often polysynthetic, the compressed wreckage of phrases. Take this single word:

[*Recording of the one word: ná sh'ááh.*]

And it means: I am causing a round object to turn over.

THERE. Navaho has many words for what we speak of as moving: a word for a round object moving, a fabric moving, and many more. And pronouns and adverbs are only parts of the verb, for the verb is central in Navaho speech, just as actions are central in Navaho thinking.

HERE. We have a few verbs that are perhaps similar: the word *shrug* must carry with it the idea of shoulder: you can't shrug your stomach. In English, we say "John is dying," just as we say "John is walking" or "John is working," for we speak even of death as though it were an act performed. But the Navaho, translated, says something like:

NAVAHO. Dying is taking place with John.

HERE. We are active towards Nature; we think of our world as full of objects doing things to other objects; our language is centered on nouns, the names of things.

NAVAHO. We Navaho see ourselves as part of Nature, in harmony with it; our world is one of actions to which we, and other things, are linked; our language centers on the verb, expressive of acting.

THERE. Finally, here is an editorial in a Navaho newspaper. The writer is angry. He wants to know why a school is not built at Kayenta, though other places have schools. But he expressed his indignation in the Navaho way.

[*Recording of speech in Navaho.*]

NAVAHO. The school at Kayenta, in vain we are hoping for it. Many children here have no school to attend. To one who comes to see, there are three hundred or more children who are in this state, who have no school. Therefore, let a school become a reality here at Kayenta. Long ago this matter was brought up. Why is this so, please?

MUSIC. [*Finale.*]

ANNOUNCER. Our program is about man's unique gift, language. Only human beings are able to communicate intricate thoughts and feelings, and it is this ability that makes culture possible, and in turn, the form of language influences the culture of its speakers. A Word in *your* Ear:

We have tried to translate the Navaho words to show how they emphasize the occurrence, the event; but English forces us to use nouns. Despite this trouble, we can see that the speaker talks about happenings, whereas we would blame somebody—the administrators, the whites, the opposition. No question about it, the way we talk and the way we see the world influence one another.

Man is different from animals, above all in his capacity to speak. A few animals can imitate our words, several follow our commands, and many are able to communicate feeling, but animals do not talk. That is, they do not re-create experiences and knowledge in sound. Therefore, they cannot have culture, they cannot accumulate knowledge, they cannot create art.

On the other hand, all peoples have language. We learn, when we travel, that languages differ in sound, in vocabulary, and in grammar. But all languages are adequate to communicate experiences. The form of each language tends to set for its speakers certain modes of observation and interpretation, and to define the nature of reality. Modern physics has had to develop special language to get rid of some of the notions that our grammar imposes on our thinking. The linguist and anthropologist, Edward Sapir, put it this way: "The worlds in which different societies live are distinct worlds, not merely the same world with different labels attached." These different worlds that different people see make it possible to fail to communicate—to misunderstand—any language. It is this possibility of misunderstanding, and the different worlds that our languages imply, that we must appreciate if we are to fight the implications of our own speaking, and learn to understand those of our neighbors who speak and live differently from ourselves.

MUSIC. [*Closing theme.*]

# ANOTHER SUMMER

## By

## WILLIAM HARTWELL SNYDER, JR.

*(Published here for the first time)*

For my parents

# ANOTHER SUMMER

## CAST

*Another Summer* was originally presented at Yale University, New Haven, Conn., on November 4, 1953, with the following cast:

PAPA BEAUFORD ...................... Wallace W. Briggs
PETER BEAUFORD, JR. ..................... Edward Cantor
NORMA JEAN .............................. Lisa Davidson
LONNIE DEAR ....................... Wylma Lynn White
BELLE MAE BEAUFORD ................ Betty Jane Dawson
GRANDMOTHER BEAUFORD .............. J. Jewett Langdon
AUNT JANNOLAH ...................... Sue Ann Gilfillan
MELINDA BEAUFORD ..................... Dorothy Chace
PETER BEAUFORD, SR. .................. Romulus Linney

Philip Wiseman directed.
Settings by Don Tyrl.
Lighting by George Hersey.

TIME: The present.
PLACE: Holly Springs, Miss., and Memphis, Tenn.

# WILLIAM HARTWELL SNYDER, JR.

WILLIAM HARTWELL SNYDER, JR. is a newcomer to these pages. He is now working at the Yale Drama School for the degree of Master of Fine Arts.

Mr. Snyder was born in Memphis, Tennessee, and educated there, until he went to Stamford, Connecticut, to prepare for college at the Daycroft School. From there, he went to Principia College, Elsah, Illinois, where he wrote some pantomimes, and had one short play produced before he was graduated in 1952.

*Another Summer* is Mr. Snyder's fourth play.

# ANOTHER SUMMER

*The stage shows two houses. On one side, we see the porch and the kitchen of* PETEY'S *grandparents' home in Holly Springs, Mississippi. On the other side, we see a portion of the living room and bedroom in* PETEY'S *house in Memphis, Tennessee. The front porch of the Beauford house in Holly Springs is the only portion that is visible. It is late afternoon of a late summer day. A part of one end of the porch is blocked off by a sheet strung on a wire.* PETEY (PETER BEAUFORD, JR.) *a little boy of seven, is standing in front of this sheet mouthing the words of "Moonlight and Roses," while a record of the song is playing somewhere behind.* NORMA JEAN, *a little girl of six, is sitting in one of the wicker chairs, watching the performance. She seems almost terrified. When the song is finished,* PETEY *bows and goes behind the sheet. There is a moment of silence, and then* PAPA BEAUFORD, *the boy's grandfather, peeks out and speaks.*

PAPA. Now's the time to clap, Norma Jean. Remember how I told you.

[NORMA JEAN *only stares at him. We hear* PETEY.]

PETEY. Why doesn't she clap?

PAPA. I don't know.

PETEY. [*Calling.*] Clap, Norma Jean! Clap!

[NORMA JEAN *still does not respond, so* PAPA *and* PETEY *begin clapping and shouting, "Hooray!" "Bravo!" "Encore!"* PETEY *comes out and takes another bow, then disappears again.*]

NORMA JEAN. I got to go home, Petey.

PETEY. Not right this minute, Norma Jean. There's only one more act. Wait until the act's over.

NORMA JEAN. I rilly got to go, Petey.

PAPA. Go on out and announce the act.

[NORMA JEAN *is beginning to edge out of her chair, when* PETEY *reappears—this time as the Master of Ceremonies.*]

189

PETEY. And now, Ladies and Gentlemen, for the first time on this or any stage, the Great Theodore Lester Beauford, who in his private life is my grandfather, and who has played many times before the crowned heads of Europe, will do his miraculous, marvelous, and stupendous trick of removing his very own teeth from out of his mouth. He will pass same among the members of the audience for your inspection, an' then he will put same back into his mouth and chew a stick of Chewing Gum. Are you ready, Mr. Beauford?

PAPA. [*From behind the curtain.*] I am ready, sir.

PETEY. The trick shall be revealed!

NORMA JEAN. I rilly got to go; I'll get a whippin'.

[PETEY *pulls back the sheet, and there sits* PAPA *in the porch swing. He sits rigidly, with his eyes staring into space, and his arms stretched out stiffly on each side of him. Suddenly his face broadens into an enormous grin, which reveals two rows of beautiful, store-bought teeth. He raises one of his hands mechanically to his lower jaw and pulls it open. He is preparing to remove his lower plate. When* NORMA JEAN *sees what he is about to do, she rushes off the porch, and off the stage with a terrified scream.*]

PETEY. Norma Jean! Norma Jean, come on back! The show's not over yet, Norma Jean.

PAPA. It looks like Norma Jean had another engagement.

PETEY. Darn it, I wanted to pull the curtain for your curtain call.

PAPA. Well, we'll give another show tomorrow. We'll call up Sara Lees Mason, and ask her to come watch.

PETEY. Sometimes I think I'd rather pull the curtains than be on the stage. They won't let me have any curtains at home. I push my cedar chest up to my bedroom door for the stage, but I never have any curtains. Remember those curtains down at the Orpheum? They were the most beautiful ones I've ever seen. Remember those ripples in them? They looked like beautiful silk waterfalls. Beautiful yellow silk waterfalls. And they made such a beautiful—uh—uh . . .

PAPA. Breath-taking?

PETEY. Beautiful, breath-taking sound when they were opened up. [*He indicates the sound of the curtains opening.*] Shh-h click!

PAPA. They're beautiful curtains, all right. I don't believe I've seen any to beat 'em anywhere in the South.

PETEY. What do you want to play now, Papa?

PAPA. Whew! I don't know. I'm still out of breath from the show just now.

PETEY. Well, you can sit down and rest until I count up to five hundred by fives, and then we'll play something.

PAPA. [*Laughs.*] We've really been having a good time this summer, haven't we?

PETEY. Yeah, now come on, Papa. We can play Chinese school, if you're all tired out.

PAPA. Remember your birthday party and the green birthday cake I bought you?

PETEY. Yes, and Grandmother and Belle Mae wouldn't eat any of it. Belle Mae said it made her sick to look at it. Do you want to tell ghost stories?

PAPA. You wanted a green birthday cake. Mrs. Bone said, "A green birthday cake? Why, Mr. Beauford, I've never heard of a green birthday cake. I've never heard of a *green* cake at all." But she made it.

PETEY. I still have the letters that came on it. "Happy Birthday to Petey."

PAPA. It was a beautiful cake. [*He laughs.*] And remember how Betty Jane Acheson blew out the candles before you had a chance to? Oh, I was so mad at her, I like to have died. [*He laughs again.*]

PETEY. Papa, I'm tired of remembering. Let's play a game.

PAPA. But there're so many funny things to remember.

PETEY. Do you want to play Rook?

[*The scene quiets down.*]

PAPA. Whew, I'm tired.

PETEY. Papa.

PAPA. If I was to sit here and go to sleep, I'd probably never wake up. I'd just drift away.

PETEY. Papa.

PAPA. Whew—whew!

PETEY. Would you like me to do the savage volcano dance?

PAPA. Yes, sir, there're about a million funny things to remember.

[PETEY *begins, half singing with a far-away voice. It is a jazz song, but he sings "Nasty Man" (Movietone Music Corp.) very slowly. As he sings,* PAPA *gets up and walks slowly off around the right stage side of the house.* PETEY *turns and sees that* PAPA *has gone.*]

PETEY. Papa! Papa!

[*There is a moment of silence. Then we hear* LONNIE DEAR'S *voice calling from inside the house.*]

LONNIE DEAR. Lord God! Lord God! Miss Belle Mae's hand-mirror is broken up into pieces. Mmm! Save us, sweet Jesus! Petey! Petey! Did you break up Miss Belle Mae's hand-mirror? Petey? Where you at?

[LONNIE DEAR *appears at the door. She is a skinny, aged negro woman.*]

PETEY. [*He is frightened.*] Here I am, Lonnie Dear.

LONNIE DEAR. Why you don't answer me when I call? Did you break up Miss Belle Mae's hand-mirror?

PETEY. I guess so.

LONNIE DEAR. Child! Child! It's a terrible thing to break up a hand-mirror.

PETEY. I'm sorry, Lonnie Dear. I was having an ice skating show on it with Papa's chess men, and when I went to put it back, it fell offa the chiffarobe. I'm sorry.

LONNIE DEAR. Ain't no use to tellin' me you sorry. You bes' tell the Lord. He the one send you seven years of bad luck. I just thank my sweet Jesus it wasn't me knocked it offa the chiffarobe.

PETEY. You mean God will send seven years of bad luck on me for breaking a hand-mirror?

LONNIE DEAR. Smarter heads than mine say he will.

PETEY. But I didn't mean to, Lonnie Dear. The Lord'll believe me when I tell Him I didn't mean to.

LONNIE DEAR. You best pray, child. How do the Lord know what your intentions was, when you slip off leavin' them crystal shivvers lyin' all over the floor without even tellin' nobody?

PETEY. I forgot about it, Lonnie. I'll run right now and sweep it up.

LONNIE DEAR. Run in there in your bare feet with all that glass? If you cut your feet up, and get lockjaw—then your bad luck will start for sure. [*She goes back into the house.*] I thank my sweet Jesus it wasn't me broke up a hand-mirror. [PETEY *begins crying. In a moment* PAPA *comes back.*]

PAPA. Now hold the phone! What's going on here?

PETEY. Papa, I broke Belle Mae's hand-mirror, and Lonnie Dear said that the Lord was going to send seven year's bad luck on me. Is that true?

PAPA. I should say not!

PETEY. Will I get lockjaw if I run a piece of glass up into my foot?

PAPA. Do my jaws look locked?

PETEY. No.

PAPA. Well, I've run about five thousand pieces of glass up into my foot.

PETEY. She scared me.

PAPA. Well, there's certainly nothing to be scared of.

PETEY. I got scared that time we went to the show, and we came out through the glass doors and it was so hot, and I got dizzy and sick and I was lost.

PAPA. We just got separated from each other for about a minute.

PETEY. Whenever I get scared, I think of that time.

PAPA. Well, I'm right here, now. I couldn't get any closer than I am now. I'm right here. [*They sit quietly together for a few minutes.*] I think it's about time for us to do something. How about an excursion to the Dixie Castle Cafe for a cup of coffee?

PETEY. Will we stop to admire points of interest in the route?

PAPA. We certainly will. And since the day is as hot as a fire-cracker, we will probably treat ourselves to a popsickle on the way back.

PETEY. Let's have a real round trip.

PAPA. Train style?

PETEY. Yes.

PAPA. Okay. All aboard the Rock Island train—The Southerner—leaving for Gatesville, Hazlehurst, Beauregard, Brookhaven, Johnson's Station, Magnolia, Tangina, Arcola, and all points South!

[PETEY *grabs on to* PAPA's *waist, and they form a train. They begin chugging around the yard. At this moment, we hear* BELLE MAE's *voice calling,* "Papa! Petey!" *from inside the house. Then she appears in the door, carrying a suitcase and a color book.*]

BELLE MAE. Petey! It's time to go to the station. Here's your suitcase and your coloring book. Now run on in like a good little boy and tell Grandmother and Lonnie Dear, "Good-bye."

PETEY. I don't have to go home today, do I? I don't have to go home today, do I, Papa?

BELLE MAE. It's the end of the summer, Petey; and the train leaves in twenty minutes.

PETEY. We were on our way to the Dixie Castle, Belle Mae. Papa, let's go on down to the Dixie Castle.

BELLE MAE. [*Calling.*] Mama! Lonnie Dear! We're leavin' for the station. Come tell Petey, "Good-bye"!

PETEY. Please, Belle Mae, don't make me leave! Let me stay until tomorrow. Please, Belle Mae!

BELLE MAE. Now, Petey, don't start acting up. It's the end of the summer, and you have to go home. If you're a good boy, you can come again next summer.

PETEY. [*Almost desperate.*] Papa, let's go to the Dixie Castle!

[GRANDMOTHER BEAUFORD *comes out of the house.*]

GRANDMOTHER. Is Petey starting to act bad on his last day?

BELLE MAE. I guess he wants us to think that he hasn't had a good time.

PETEY. I have had a good time. I have!

GRANDMOTHER. You ought to act nice, Petey.

BELLE MAE. If you keep on acting bad like this, Grandmother

and I won't ask you to come back next summer. We'll find us another little boy, who won't cut up when it's time to go home. [LONNIE DEAR *comes out with* PETEY'S *shoes and socks.*]

LONNIE DEAR. Heah his shoes and socksies. I better look round and see if he done leff anything else. He done strewed things from one end of the house to the other.

[*She exits.*]

BELLE MAE. I'll back the car out of the garage.

[*She starts to go off-stage.*]

GRANDMOTHER. [*Calling after her.*] We need some milk and sliced ham for supper, Belle Mae.

BELLE MAE. I'll stop by the store after I put Petey on the train.

PETEY. Let me stay for supper, Grandmother. Please let me stay for supper.

GRANDMOTHER. Petey, don't make Grandmother nervous. You know how nervous I get in hot weather.

PAPA. Did you pack Tiny and Sandy and the victrola records I bought him?

GRANDMOTHER. I don't know. Lonnie Dear! Lonnie Dear! Did you pack Petey's dolls? [*She goes into the house.*] There's no tellin' where they're liable to be.

PETEY. They're not dolls.

[*The horn honks.*]

BELLE MAE. Come on, Petey! Come on! The train's gonna leave.

PAPA. We just have a minute, Petey, so listen to me. This summer's flown by quicker than you can say "Jack Robinson," hasn't it? Well, the winter's going to fly by even quicker than that. It won't be any time until you're right back here with me. And we'll be putting on bigger and better shows than ever before, and we'll be going to the Dixie Castle, and having watermelon parties, and taking rides after supper, and generally raising cain just like we always do. You know I've had some new ideas about our shows for next summer. Now first of all, I'm gonna get us a real curtain instead of a sheet. And then I thought I'd make us some footlights, so we can give shows at night as well as in the day time.

PETEY. Like the real shows down at the Orpheum?

PAPA. That's right.

PETEY. And we can give the day time show for the little children, and the night time one for the daddys and mothers.

PAPA. We'll really be big-time producers, won't we? And listen, you've got a few things to do between now and then, too. You've got to learn lots of new songs and really work hard at dancing, so you can do new routines, hear?

PETEY. Okay.

[*The car horn blows again.*]

BELLE MAE. [*Calling.*] Petey! Come on! The train leaves in fifteen minutes.

PAPA. Petey, you know how we were talking about remembering all the funny things that happened this summer?

PETEY. Yes.

PAPA. Well, you'll remember those things, won't you?

PETEY. Sure I will. [*He closes his eyes.*] Want to know what I'm remembering right now?

PAPA. What?

PETEY. The time you dressed up in Grandmother's clothes and I pretended to be your little boy, and we went into all the stores downtown and fooled everybody. Do you remember that?

PAPA. [*He laughs.*] Do I! Everybody said, "What's that pretty little boy doing with that ugly old woman?"

[GRANDMOTHER *comes out on the porch holding Tiny in one hand and Sandy in the other. Tiny is a figure of one of the Three Wise Men from a manger set, and Sandy is a stuffed dog.*]

GRANDMOTHER. Here are the dolls. We couldn't find the victrola records.

PETEY. Papa!

PAPA. We'll find them and mail them to you, Petey. But wait a minute! We've got our favorite right out here.

GRANDMOTHER. I hope you learn to be more neat and orderly before next summer, Petey.

[BELLE MAE *enters.*]

BELLE MAE. You all don't seem to realize that Petey has to catch a train. [*She picks up his suitcase.* PAPA *hands her the victrola record.*] Say, "Good-bye," Petey.

PETEY. [*He hugs* PAPA.] See you next summer, Papa.

PAPA. Good-bye, Petey.

GRANDMOTHER. [*Patting* PETEY's *head.*] You be a sweet boy, Petey.

PETEY. See you next summer, Lonnie Dear.

LONNIE DEAR. If the Lord's willin'.

[PETEY *comes down the steps and looks at* PAPA. *He and* BELLE MAE *exit.* PAPA *waves good bye, then sits on the steps.* GRAND-MOTHER *and* LONNIE DEAR *are on the porch. There is a pause.*]

GRANDMOTHER. That child has just about worn me out this time. It's just too hard on me to have to look out for a child in all this hot weather.

LONNIE DEAR. He broke up Miss Belle Mae's hand-mirror this afternoon.

GRANDMOTHER. Her silver hand-mirror to her dresser set?

LONNIE DEAR. Yes, ma'am. I swep' up the glass myself.

GRANDMOTHER. Isn't that too bad!

LONNIE DEAR. I just thank my sweet Jesus it wasn't me broke up a hand-mirror.

[*She goes back into the house.*]

GRANDMOTHER. Isn't that too bad! [*Pause.*] Papa, I hope you're not going to get into one of your moods.

[*She goes into the house, leaving* PAPA *alone on the steps. The scene fades.*]

*When the lights come up again, we are in the living room of* PETEY's *home in Memphis. The important set piece in this area is a large French window with draw curtains. It is October, and we can see through the window that it is raining.* AUNT JAN-NOLAH *stands looking out of the window.* PETEY *calls from the bedroom.*

PETEY. Mother! Daddy! Mother!

[PETEY *enters.*]

JANNOLAH. Your mother and daddy have gone off, Petey.

PETEY. What are you doing here, Aunt Jannolah?

JANNOLAH. I came last night.

PETEY. I don't remember.

JANNOLAH. I came after you were asleep.

PETEY. Where're Mother and Daddy?

JANNOLAH. They've gone to Holly Springs.

PETEY. Why didn't they take me?

JANNOLAH. Because, honey—because you've got to go to school.

PETEY. They didn't even tell me they were going.

JANNOLAH. Your grandfather isn't feeling very well. Look at that rain! It's really pouring cats and dogs, isn't it?

[AUNT JANNOLAH *walks away.* PETEY *stands looking out the window. He closes and opens the curtains slowly, and begins to hum* "Oh, You Nasty Man." *Then he walks back into his room, picks up Tiny and Sandy and sits in his chair by his bed as the lights go down.*

*When they come up again,* PETEY *is still sitting in his chair, and has fallen asleep.* MELINDA *and* PETER SR. *enter the living room.* MELINDA *helps* PETER SR. *off with his coat.*]

MELINDA. The house is so quiet, isn't it? . . . We're supposed to have dinner with Eleanor and Ben tomorrow night. I'll call her in the morning and tell her we can't come.

PETER SR. No, it's all right.

MELINDA. Why don't you go to bed, Pete? I'll go see if Petey's kicked all his covers off. . . . When should we tell him?

PETER SR. I don't know.

MELINDA. I don't know, either.

[*The light on* MELINDA *and* PETER SR. *fades.* MELINDA *enters* PETEY's *room and see hims asleep in the chair. She wakes him up.*] Petey! Petey!

PETEY. [*Waking up.*] Hey, Mother! It's about time.

MELINDA. What in the world are you doing up?

PETEY. I been waiting for you all. I was going to scare you.

MELINDA. Where are your bedroom slippers? Aren't your feet cold?

PETEY. Tiny and Sandy and I just about wore ourselves out waiting for you all to come home. Tiny said, "When are they gonna come home?", and I said, "Don't you all worry. They'll be here before you can say, 'Jack Robinson.' " How's Papa?

MELINDA. We'll talk about all that in the morning, honey.

PETEY. Talk about it now!

MELINDA. Petey, it's too late to talk about anything.

PETEY. I made up a song about Papa. Want to hear it? I was gonna put on a show for you and Daddy.

MELINDA. It's awfully late.

PETEY. It'll just be a minute. I just have to put on my costume. [*He takes his spread off the bed, and wraps it around him, and puts his pillow on his head for a hat.*]

MELINDA. Don't mess up your bed, Petey!

PETEY. It's my costume. Aren't you gonna clap?

MELINDA. We can't make any noise, Petey. Daddy's gone to bed.

PETEY. Tiny and Sandy really got a kick out of my costume. Tiny said I looked like the king of the Devil Dogs. Please, Mother, talk about Papa. Did he send me some victrola records?

MELINDA. No, honey.

PETEY. Why?

MELINDA. Papa was very seriously sick, Petey.

PETEY. Didn't he have an ear ache?

MELINDA. No, honey.

PETEY. What was the matter with him?

MELINDA. Now give me your bed-spread and pillow.

PETEY. Talk about Papa!

MELINDA. That's enough, Petey. Mother said she'd talk about it in the morning.

PETEY. Please, Mother.

MELINDA. Petey, I said . . .

PETEY. Is Papa still sick?

MELINDA. Petey . . .

PETEY. Why don't you talk about him?

MELINDA. Papa—passed away, Petey.

[*There is a pause, as* MELINDA *gropes for a way to explain it.*]

Petey, when everybody gets to be old like Papa, they—all get tired, and they need to rest—do you see? And they deserve to rest, too, because they've worked so hard for so many years.

And so—God gives them a chance to rest—and He comes along and puts them to sleep—and then they pass away. And then there's a funeral. And that's what happened to Papa. Do you see, Petey?

[PETEY *crosses to his chair, and sits in it with Tiny and Sandy. After looking at him for a long moment,* MELINDA *fixes his bed.*]

Come on, Petey. Your bed's all ready.

[PETEY *gets into bed.*]

PETEY. Mother, what was Papa's funeral like?

MELINDA. It was beautiful, Petey. I don't believe I've ever seen so many flowers. There were rows and rows and rows of them. And the family sent a whole blanket of white gardenias.

PETEY. Were there lilies-of-the-valley and pansies?

MELINDA. I don't believe so.

PETEY. You know those lilies-of-the-valley and pansies that grow in Grandmother's garden? Papa and I always make corsages out of them for Lonnie Dear and Belle Mae and Grandmother.

MELINDA. You do?

PETEY. Did Papa pass away to heaven?

MELINDA. Yes, darling.

PETEY. When you say "pass away," I always think of somebody walking off down a road in the country some place.

MELINDA. You do?

PETEY. Yes. Does God look like an owl?

MELINDA. I don't know what He looks like. Now, quiet down, Petey!

PETEY. That's what I always think He looks like when I think about Him. Mother?

MELINDA. Yes, darling.

PETEY. May I tell everybody at school tomorrow that Papa passed away?

MELINDA. If you want to. Now quiet down, Petey, you're so sleepy you don't know what to do.

PETEY. My head feels like it's winking.

MELINDA. I know it. The Sandman's right here and waiting for you.

PETEY. Mother, will you play show with me tomorrow after school?

MELINDA. We'll see, honey, but you know I'm not very good at playing show. Now go to sleep, and dream beautiful dreams, and I'll see you in the morning.

PETEY. We're going to have footlights and a curtain next summer.

MELINDA. That's wonderful, Petey.

[*He is asleep.* MELINDA *stands beside his bed for several moments, then* PETER SR. *enters.*]

PETER SR. How is he?

MELINDA. All right, I think. I told him. He wanted to know if he could tell everybody at school tomorrow.

[MELINDA *and* PETER SR. *stand together looking at* PETEY.]

PETER SR. He certainly is sound asleep, isn't he?

MELINDA. It's so hard to tell what's going on in his mind.

PETER SR. I wish I could sleep like that.

MELINDA. I'm never really sure just what he's thinking about.

*The lights fade. When they come up again, we are in* PETEY'S *room. It is a day in early summer.* MELINDA *is packing* PETEY'S *suitcase.*

MELINDA. Well, this time tomorrow you'll be on your way to Holly Springs, and Daddy and I'll be on our way to New York, isn't that right?

PETEY. Uh-huh. How long are y'all going to stay in New York?

MELINDA. Two weeks. And then Daddy and I'll come home, and then you'll come home.

PETEY. Can't I stay any longer than two weeks?

MELINDA. Now, we've been through all that, honey. You know Grandmother hasn't been feeling too well since Papa Beauford passed away. It's awfully nice that she's invited you even for two weeks.

PETEY. That means I won't get to spend my birthday over there.

MELINDA. Well, we'll see if we can't have some sort of party for you here.

PETEY. I wanted to spend my birthday in Holly Springs.

MELINDA. Why are you so restless today, honey? You've been pacing the floor like a caged lion all day long.

PETEY. I'm not restless. I wanted to spend my birthday in Holly Springs.

MELINDA. [*Sits on bed.*] Why don't you come sit in my lap for a minute and let me comb your hair.

PETEY. I don't want to, Mother.

MELINDA. You said once that you were going to sit in my lap until your knees touched the ceiling.

PETEY. I don't want to right now, Mother. [*He talks to himself.*] I'm gonna call up Norma Jean and Betty Jane Acheson as soon as I get to Holly Springs, and we'll start practisin' for a show right away.

MELINDA. Were you talkin' to me, darlin'?

PETEY. Uh—uh.

MELINDA. How would you like to help me finish packing, and we can pretend that we're going to Paris or to London. Why don't we play a game?

PETEY. I don't want to, Mother. You know we don't ever play games.

MELINDA. But it might be a lot of fun if we did once in a while, don't you think?

PETEY. I guess maybe I'll go outdoors for a while.

MELINDA. Maybe that would be a good idea. You've been pacing the floor like a caged lion all day long. Is anything the matter, Petey?

PETEY. [*Almost shouting at her.*] No! [*He goes out of the bed room.*] Don't forget I'm gonna take my bull frog costume. [*He exits, but in a moment reappears. His mood has changed.*] Mother?

MELINDA. What, honey?

PETEY. I'm gonna have a real good time at Holly Springs this summer.

MELINDA. I know you are, darling.

PETEY. Would you like to comb my hair now?

MELINDA. Sure. Come on over and sit down.

[*He sits in her lap.*]

PETEY. I'd rather be going to Holly Springs than to New York with you and Daddy.

MELINDA. You certainly are excited about going, aren't you?

PETEY. Yes, I am.

[*The lights black out.*]

*When the lights come up again, we see the Beauford house in Holly Springs. It is the same, except that the curtain is no longer there. Two bent nails, one in the house and one in a porch column, mark its place. It is dusk, a windy and luminous dusk. Leaves are blowing. Everything on the stage stands out sharply in the fading light that seems to come from all directions. When sounds begin to come from the house as the scene progresses, they are isolated sounds, a screen door slamming shut, a pan banging on the kitchen sink, the clatter of silverware. They are isolated and intense sounds that almost seem to have an echo. When the people begin to speak from the house, their voices also seem to echo. They grow loud, fade away and then grow loud again, like a radio whose volume is turned up and down. The house is dark, and the stage is empty when the scene opens.* GRANDMOTHER, BELLE MAE, *and* PETEY *enter.* PETEY *holds Tiny and Sandy.* BELLE MAE *carries his suitcase.*

GRANDMOTHER. I'll tell Lonnie Dear we're home, so she can start supper. Lonnie Dear! Lonnie Dear!

BELLE MAE. [*On porch.*] I'm just starved; aren't you, Petey? I bet little old Petey's about starved.

[*She goes up on the porch and into the house.* PETEY *is left alone. There is silence, then the wind blows through the trees.* PETEY *walks up to the porch. The screen door slams shut. During the following conversation,* PETEY *listens to all of it. Lights go on in the house.*]

LONNIE DEAR. How you feel, M's Beauford?

GRANDMOTHER. I feel some better, Lonnie Dear.

LONNIE DEAR. You say Petey's momma and daddy done gone up to New York City?

GRANDMOTHER. Yes, they left Memphis this afternoon, soon

after we did.

LONNIE DEAR. I certainly would not want to go to no New York City.

GRANDMOTHER. I wouldn't either, Lonnie Dear.

LONNIE DEAR. Too many trains and airplanes and automobiles. I'd be struck down sure as I was born, the first day I set foot up there. [*Pause.*] M's Laird died.

GRANDMOTHER. Maud Laird? When?

LONNIE DEAR. This afternoon. Jessie come over here d'reckly after it happen. Jessie was right wit' her. One minute M's Laird was eatin' a dish of orange sherbert. She say, "My, Jessie, this were good." The next minute she stretched plumb out on the floor. She didn't say nothin' else. She just sighed and breathed a little bit, and then passed right on out.

GRANDMOTHER. Hmm! That's a shame. I'll have to get Belle Mae to drive me over to the funeral home after supper. Maud's suffered with angina for years.

LONNIE DEAR. It don't make no diffunce what you sufferin' with. When the Lord decide to take you, he take you then and there.

[*The sound of the locusts begins. It is a shrill and intense one-note sound that begins suddenly with full force.*]

PETEY. [*Screaming.*] Belle Mae! Belle Mae!

BELLE MAE. [*From deep inside the house.*] What is it, Petey?

PETEY. Come here a minute, will you please? Quick, Belle Mae!

BELLE MAE. What is it, Petey?

PETEY. Quick, Belle Mae! Quick!

BELLE MAE. [*She comes out on the porch.*] What in the world is going on out here?

PETEY. I don't know. It seemed like something was going to happen.

BELLE MAE. It seemed like what was going to happen?

PETEY. I don't know.

BELLE MAE. Well, my goodness gracious, I thought the sky had fallen in on you.

PETEY. It was getting dark.

BELLE MAE. Of course it is, Petey-boy. Looks like we might get a little rain later on. Now, why don't you come on into the house and wash your hands and face and clean your fingernails, and get ready for the nice supper that Lonnie Dear is fixing for us. I bet this little fella's hungry after that long trip. And I wouldn't be a bit surprised if he was ready for bed a little bit early tonight.

PETEY. No, Belle Mae, I'm not tired at all. Can't we go to the show? I wish we could go to the show tonight.

BELLE MAE. The show! My goodness, sugar, Belle Mae's too tired herself to go to the show. There'll be lots of other nights we can go to the show—lots of other nights. We're gonna have a good time this summer, Petey-boy, a real good time. You know, Petey, Belle Mae's never had a little boy of her own—so while you're here this summer, you'll be my little boy and I'll be your second mother. Because you see, honey, I know what goes on in little children's minds. I can still remember how I used to feel when I was a little child. I'm not so old that I've forgotten that.

GRANDMOTHER. [*Calls from the kitchen.*] Belle Mae! Belle Mae! You and Petey come on! Supper's ready.

BELLE MAE. There now, you see? Supper's on the table, and I know one little boy who hasn't even washed his hands. [*She takes him by the hand and leads him into the house. There is lightning in the distance and the sound of thunder. The interior of the kitchen becomes visible.* GRANDMOTHER *is there.* LONNIE DEAR *stands over the stove.* BELLE MAE *and* PETEY *enter.*]

GRANDMOTHER. You don't mind staying here with Petey for a little bit while we go to the funeral home, do you, Lonnie Dear?

LONNIE DEAR. No'm. Church don't start fo' nine.

GRANDMOTHER. Oh, we'll be back long before that. And then Miss Belle Mae can drive you over to the service. You wouldn't mind driving Lonnie Dear over to her church service, would you, Belle Mae?

BELLE MAE. Why, I'd be glad to.

LONNIE DEAR. I'm much beholden to you.

[BELLE MAE, PETEY, *and* GRANDMOTHER *sit down to supper.*]

BELLE MAE. My goodness, isn't this a wonderful supper! We certainly do thank Lonnie Dear for this, don't we, Mama?

GRANDMOTHER. We certainly do.

BELLE MAE. Ham and eggs certainly hit the spot. And corn dodgers, too! This is really a feast.

GRANDMOTHER. Yes, isn't it nice? May I have my hot water and lemon, Lonnie Dear?

LONNIE DEAR. You betta eat you suppah, Petey. If you thin down any more than you is, you gonna get sick, sure as the world.

BELLE MAE. Why, what's the matter? Isn't Petey-boy eating his supper? This wonderful supper that Lonnie Dear fixed especially for him?

GRANDMOTHER. Ye-es, you have to eat this nice supper, Petey.

PETEY. Listen, Belle Mae. There's something very important I need to tell Mother and Daddy. I think I'd better call them long distance. Will you please call them on the telephone for me?

BELLE MAE. Long distance? You can't get them on the long distance, Petey. They're on a train headed for New York City.

PETEY. But maybe they haven't left yet. You can get them on long distance, Belle Mae. Please do it, because it's an emergency.

BELLE MAE. Petey-boy, that train pulled away a little after four this afternoon. They're up in Tennessee somewhere by now. What's wrong, Petey, what's this emergency? You can tell me. After all, I'm gonna be your second mother.

PETEY. [*He is about to cry.*] Belle Mae, it's an emergency and I really ought to call now.

GRANDMOTHER. What is it he wants to do, Belle Mae?

BELLE MAE. I don't know, Mama. It looks like Petey doesn't enjoy being with us at all. He keeps talking about calling his mother and daddy.

GRANDMOTHER. Well, he can't do that.

PETEY. [*He is crying now.*] Please, you all! Please!

GRANDMOTHER. What in the world is wrong with you, Petey?

PETEY. I need—I need to tell Mother and Daddy—I need to tell Mother and Daddy—something. I can't tell you.

GRANDMOTHER. But your mother and daddy are on their way to New York.

BELLE MAE. I've told him that, Mama. But he just wants to be ugly, I guess.

GRANDMOTHER. Don't be ugly, Petey.

BELLE MAE. I guess he doesn't want me to be his second mother. I guess he doesn't want to do any of the nice things we've planned for him. See, Petey, I even had it arranged so that you could sleep in Papa's room.

PETEY. I can't!

BELLE MAE. You mean to say you don't want to sleep in Papa's room?

PETEY. Don't talk about Papa!

BELLE MAE. Petey!

[PETEY *suddenly jumps up and rushes for the telephone, which is the wall type.* BELLE MAE *rises.*] Petey!

PETEY. [*He grabs the phone off the hook and shouts into it.*] Long distance! Long distance!

BELLE MAE. [*Wrenches the phone from his hand.*] You put that telephone down, Petey! You're bad! You're just bad! [PETEY *runs out.*] Petey!

GRANDMOTHER. I told them I wasn't up to having him come this summer.

PETEY. [*He is in the yard, standing under the tree.*] It's a trick! It's a trick! Please, God, don't let me die! Help me! Don't make me sleep in the bed that Papa died in.

[*There is a pause. Lightning flashes again, and there is a distant sound of thunder. The sky is getting darker.* BELLE MAE *and* GRANDMOTHER *come out on the front porch.*]

BELLE MAE. We'll be back before too long, Lonnie Dear. And if Petey doesn't behave himself, you just tell us.

GRANDMOTHER. We're only going to the funeral home, Lonnie Dear.

[LONNIE DEAR *enters on porch.*]

LONNIE DEAR. Yas'm.

PETEY. [*Trying to control his crying.*] Belle Mae, please take me with y'all. Don't leave me by myself.

BELLE MAE. If some little boys learned how to behave, they might find they'd get to go to a lot more places, wouldn't they, Mama?

PETEY. I'll be good, Belle Mae. I promise.

BELLE MAE. Come on, Mama! Some little boys have to learn their lessons the hard way.

[*They start to walk off stage.*]

PETEY. Belle Mae! Grandmother!

GRANDMOTHER. [*As they leave.*] Children have no respect for older people's nerves.

[LONNIE DEAR *goes back into the house, singing, leaving* PETEY *alone. The lights in the house are dim. Again there is lightning and thunder. This time the thunder is closer.* LONNIE DEAR *can be heard singing, "Without a mother—without a father— You've got to make that journey by yourself."* PETEY *sits on the porch steps with Tiny and Sandy. Then* LONNIE DEAR *comes out, looks up at the sky, and sits down.*]

LONNIE DEAR. Oh, my sweet Jesus, there's going to be a thunderstorm for sure.

PETEY. Lonnie Dear, would you read to me for a little while?

LONNIE DEAR. Chile, I got to get up from heah, and wash them deeshes. I only set down for to rest myself.

PETEY. Have you seen my family? This is Tiny and Sandy. Say, "Hello," to Lonnie Dear, Tiny and Sandy. [*He pretends they are speaking.*] "Hello, Lonnie Dear."

LONNIE DEAR. If it start in to bein' a thunderstorm, I'm not washin' no deeshes for nobody.

PETEY. Why can't you wash dishes in a thunderstorm?

LONNIE DEAR. Because lightning will strike you, if your hands is in water.

PETEY. It will?

LONNIE DEAR. I say it will. Lightnin' take to water, to mirrors, and anything what's metal.

PETEY. But you can keep yourself from getting struck by lightning, can't you?

LONNIE DEAR. When lightnin' come, you best close all the doors and windows. Lightnin' come through an open window quicker'n anything. And then you turn out the 'lectric, and you pray, chile, you pray.

PETEY. Lonnie Dear, don't talk about the lightning any more. Talk about the times when you were a little girl, and what all you used to do.

LONNIE DEAR. I did then like I does now. I worked hard and kept faith with the Lord.

PETEY. But didn't you use to have funny things happen to you?

LONNIE DEAR. Let me get up from here and get at them deeshes before it come up to stormin'. M's Beauford and M's Belle Mae will be comin' back, an' I ain't even commenced to clean up my kitchen.

PETEY. I wish you'd talk to me a little bit.

LONNIE DEAR. Chile, I ain't got no time for talk. You play wit' your dolls and behave yourself.

[*She goes into the house.*]

PETEY. They're not dolls. You're not dolls, are you, Tiny and Sandy?

[*The wind blows in the trees, and it is getting darker.*]

Would you like to hear a story?

[*The lightning flashes and the thunder begins.*]

God, please don't let a thunderstorm come up! Once upon a time there was a very happy family. There was a mother and a father and a little child. The mother and father were the king and queen, and the child was the prince. And they lived in a huge stone castle.

[*The lightning flashes again.*]

There's not going to be a storm, so don't you all worry! There were silver candlesticks and crystal chandeliers in every room, and there were pianos in every room, and all the family could play them, and nobody had to worry about sitting at an old coffee table and pretending it was a piano.

[*The thunder and lightning again.* PETEY *is almost crying.*]

And they had a beautiful time together. And at night when they would go to bed, they'd leave the light globes burning all over the castle. Every light globe was left burning all night long.

[*The sky is very dark, and the wind is blowing.*]

And they would pull the sheets up over their heads, and the soft white light would shine through, and they would be warm and go to sleep.

[*The wind blows the front door closed. The storm begins in earnest.* PETEY *runs to the door, but he can't get it open. He bangs on it with his fists and cries.*]

Lonnie Dear! Lonnie Dear! The thunderstorm's come up! Lonnie Dear! Mother! Daddy!

[*The scene fades to a blackout.*]

*When lights come up, we are in the kitchen of the Beauford house in Holly Springs. It is morning, two weeks later.* BELLE MAE *and* GRANDMOTHER BEAUFORD *are sitting at the table, eating breakfast.* PETEY *sits in the yard, and overhears their conversation.*

BELLE MAE. Petey'll be going home tomorrow.

GRANDMOTHER. Well. Who's going to take him?

BELLE MAE. Eleanor Simpson. She's a friend of Melinda's. She's gonna be driving through here on her way home from New Orleans, and she's gonna pick him up.

GRANDMOTHER. Isn't that nice?

BELLE MAE. If I have anything to say about it, these will be the last two weeks Petey will ever spend in this house. You can do and do and do for somebody, Mama, but there comes a time when you can't do any more.

GRANDMOTHER. You're absolutely right, Belle Mae.

BELLE MAE. I had such nice plans for this summer. I thought Petey and I were going to become real pals. I understand children. You know I do, Mama. You know what they all said when I did practice teaching in college.

GRANDMOTHER. I know it, Belle Mae. You would have been a wonderful teacher.

BELLE MAE. But what can you do with a child like Petey? He wanders around the house and yard like a chicken with his head cut off. He didn't want to play with Norma Jean or Betty Jane Acheson.

GRANDMOTHER. I know it.

BELLE MAE. And look at the nice things Lonnie Dear has cooked for him. Why, he's barely touched his food.

GRANDMOTHER. We have had delicious meals.

BELLE MAE. But to me the most scandalous thing I've ever heard of, is the way he's behaved about Papa. Why, you'd think Papa was his very worst enemy. He won't talk about him; he won't mention his name. Why, to me, some of my most precious memories are of the times we had with Papa, and I love to go back over them.

GRANDMOTHER. So do I, Belle Mae.

BELLE MAE. I haven't written Melinda and Pete about all this, because I didn't want to spoil their trip. I said he was a little homesick, and that was all. But believe you me, I'm going to write them about it after tomorrow. They are really going to get a report from me.

GRANDMOTHER. Have they been writing to Petey all along?

BELLE MAE. Every three or four days. And he carries those letters around with him from daylight until dark. And he sleeps with them! Have you ever heard of anything like it?

GRANDMOTHER. No, I haven't, Belle Mae.

BELLE MAE. Would you like another piece of coffee cake, Mama?

GRANDMOTHER. I believe I would. It certainly is delicious.

BELLE MAE. How do you feel this morning?

GRANDMOTHER. I feel some better.

BELLE MAE. That's good. Yes, sir, he sleeps with those letters!

GRANDMOTHER. Well.

BELLE MAE. He's the most ungrateful child I've ever seen. All he talks about is going home.

GRANDMOTHER. Well!

BELLE MAE. Lila wants me to play bingo at her house tonight, Mama. Is it all right?

GRANDMOTHER. It is if you don't stay out too late, Belle Mae. You know I get frightened when I stay here in the house late at night.

BELLE MAE. Oh, it won't be late.

GRANDMOTHER. Well.

BELLE MAE. Yes, sir, he sleeps with those letters! I've never heard of anything like it. Anyway, tomorrow he'll be going home, and if I have anything to say about it, these will be the last two weeks he'll ever spend in this house.

*The scene fades. When the lights come up, we are in the living room of* PETEY's *house in Memphis. It is late afternoon of the following day. In a moment,* PETEY *comes through the door and into the room. He carries his suitcase in one hand, and Tiny and Sandy in the other. He is very excited. His mother,* MELINDA, *runs into the room from another part of the house. She is dressed for a summer evening party.*

MELINDA. Look who's here! Look who's here! Hello, darling! Oh-oh, you're holding on so tight! Look who's here, Daddy! Look who's here!

[PETER SR. *enters.*]

PETER SR. Hey there, Petey! What's this about your getting homesick?

[*He hugs* PETEY.]

MELINDA. Didn't you have a good time, Petey? Belle Mae wrote us that you were a little bit homesick. Did you miss us?

PETEY. I'm so glad to be home, I don't know what to do.

MELINDA. Oh, and I can't wait to tell you about all the stage shows we saw in New York. We certainly did wish for you. But we brought you all the programs, and about a thousand and one postcards. Oh, Daddy and I had a whirl all right. We were high steppin' it mornin', noon and night. We really had a whirl, didn't we, Daddy?

PETER SR. We really did. Mother just about wore me out.

MELINDA. And now, what about you, honey? Did you get all those letters I sent you?

PETEY. Yes.

MELINDA. Yes? I know you. I bet you were so busy puttin' on shows that you didn't even read them.

PETEY. I did read them. I promise I did, Mother. Don't you believe that I read them?

MELINDA. Of course I do, honey. I was just fooling.

PETEY. Is Leona still here?

MELINDA. Leona's right in the kitchen with her uniform on, getting you something to eat. And your victrola and your records and your toys—everything's just exactly the same, just waiting for you.

PETEY. [*Very intensely.*] Listen, you all! I'm gonna turn over a new leaf, hear? I'm gonna eat what's put before me, and I'm gonna play outdoors more, and you won't have to tell me to do something twice. I'll do it the first time you tell me. And when you want me to go to bed, I'll go, and I won't disturb you before ten o'clock on Sunday morning.

PETER SR. What does all this mean?

MELINDA. Sounds like a pretty big new leaf to me.

PETEY. Mother, let's us go to the picture show tonight. How about it?

PETER SR. Oh, now I see why you're going to turn over that new leaf.

MELINDA. Darling, Daddy and I have been invited out to a dinner party at Frieda and David Norfleet's house. I've asked Leona to stay on with you.

PETER SR. And we'd better start getting ready to leave.

PETEY. [*Stunned.*] Are you all gonna go out?

MELINDA. It looks like we'll have to, honey.

PETEY. Oh.

MELINDA. I hate to run off and leave you on your first day home.

PETER SR. Well, let's go if we're going, Mother.

MELINDA. Listen, you! I was ready fifteen minutes before you were. I just have to get my stole. I'll be back downstairs in a minute to say, "Good-bye, Petey."

[MELINDA *exits. There is a pause.*]

PETER SR. You look like you've lost some weight. Mother and I really wished for you in New York. There was one show in particular that I know you would have gotten a kick out of.

PETEY. What was the name of it?

PETER SR. Now, let's see. I can't even remember, but it sure had a lot of singing and dancing.

PETEY. Was the curtain pretty?

PETER SR. Beautiful.

PETEY. What did it look like?

PETER SR. I don't remember, Petey. It was made out of some kind of colored stuff.

PETEY. Was it satin or velvet?

PETER SR. I don't remember.

PETEY. Who took the starring parts?

PETER SR. They were all good actors and actresses. I don't know any of the names.

PETEY. Was Ruby Keeler in it?

PETER SR. I don't know, Petey.

PETEY. Was Dolores Del Rio in it?

.. PETER SR. [*Sharply.*] Petey, I said I didn't remember who was in it. Now you better take your suitcase to your bedroom and get ready for dinner.

PETEY. Daddy, please talk some more about the plays!

PETER SR. I've got to go, Petey; we're going to be late as it is. Melinda!

MELINDA. [*Off-stage.*] Coming!

[PETER SR. *exits.* PETEY *crosses into the bedroom and sets down the suitcase, putting Tiny and Sandy on it. Then he sits on the bed.* MELINDA *enters with her stole.*]

MELINDA. I hate so much to run off and leave you. Is there anything I can do for you before we go? Do you want me to put on some music? [*She goes to the phonograph and puts on a record.*] I'll bet you'll remember this one.

[*"Moonlight and Roses" begins playing.*]

PETEY. You can't play that, Mother!

MELINDA. But this is your favorite.

PETEY. Take it off quick!

MELINDA. Why?

PETEY. Please, Mother. I can't touch it!

MELINDA. But why?

[*She stops the record.*]

PETEY. I can't tell you.

MELINDA. What is it, Petey?

PETEY. Nothing! [*There is a pause.*] Mother, will you tell me what Mrs. Norfleet's phone number is, so that I can call you all in case there's an emergency?

MELINDA. What kind of emergency?

PETEY. I don't know. Just in case.

MELINDA. I will certainly give you the phone number, darling, but there surely won't be any emergency while we're having dinner with Brooks and Burnham.

[*She gets her purse, and a pad and pencil on which she writes the number.*]

PETEY. Will you all be home before midnight?

MELINDA. I certainly hope so.

PETEY. Will you promise?

MELINDA. Well, honey, I feel pretty sure that we'll be home by midnight—but you know, something might come up.

PETEY. Please promise, Mother, will you?

MELINDA. But what difference can it make? You'll be sound asleep by then.

PETEY. [*Intensely.*] It's very important, Mother. Please promise!

MELINDA. What's wrong, Petey? Is anything wrong?

PETER SR. [*Calls.*] Melinda!

PETEY. Nothing's wrong, Mother. But please promise.

PETER SR. Melinda!

MELINDA. All right. I promise. Night-night, my precious.

[*She kisses him.*]

PETEY. I'll see you in the morning.

MELINDA. See you in the morning, Petey!

PETEY. I'll see you in the morning.

MELINDA. I've got to run, honey. I can't keep Daddy waiting any longer.

PETEY. I'll see you in the morning.

MELINDA. I've got to run, honey.

PETEY. Mother, you have to say, "I'll see you in the morning."

MELINDA. I've said it.

PETEY. Please, Mother, say it again.

MELINDA. I'll see you in the morning, darling.

PETEY. I'll see you in the morning. Just say it one more time.

MELINDA. [*She is really concerned now.*] Petey, what is it?

PETEY. Say it, Mother! Please say it!

MELINDA. Can't you tell me what's the matter? I'd give anything in the world if you'd tell me.

PETEY. Mother!

MELINDA. I'll see you in the morning. Petey, you're so flushed. You don't have any fever, do you?

PETEY. I don't know. Do I have any fever, Mother? Do I have any fever?

MELINDA. [*Realizing she has said the wrong thing.*] Of course you don't, darling. I don't know what made me say that. Of course you don't.

PETEY. I don't believe it. I do have a fever! You're telling me a story because you don't want me to get worked up.

MELINDA. I'm not telling you a story, Petey. I wouldn't tell you a story for anything. Your forehead's cooler than mine.

PETEY. Is it? Do you promise?

MELINDA. Yes, Petey. I promise. Your face is as cool as can be.

PETEY. Will the Lord be your witness?

MELINDA. Petey!

PETEY. Will He?

MELINDA. Yes. The Lord is my witness.

PETEY. All right, Mother. You can leave for the party now. [*There is a pause.*]

MELINDA. Petey, would you like Daddy and me to stay home with you tonight?

PETEY. No.

PETER SR. [*Calling.*] Melinda!

MELINDA. Are you sure?

PETEY. Yes, we're all right.

[MELINDA *looks at him for a moment. He sits calmly in his chair.*]

MELINDA. All right, darling. [*She starts to leave, then turns and smiles at him.*] Good night, Petey.

[*She exits.* PETEY *follows her into the living room and stands looking after her. Then he quickly closes the draperies on the*

*French window, and returns to his bedroom. He puts a new record on his phonograph. It is "The Good Ship Lollipop." As the record begins to sing,* PETEY *sits on the floor beside his bed with Tiny and Sandy and talks to them.*]

PETEY. Listen, you all, did you know something? Christmas is coming very soon. And we're all gonna be alive and happy at Christmas, and we're all gonna get so many toys we won't know what to do. Santa Claus is coming, and God won't let us die before Christmas. And we won't drink out of any glasses that have been chipped at the top, and we won't swallow any broken glass, and we won't drink any unpasteurized milk and get undulant fever, the way Lonnie Dear's little baby nephew did, and we won't take a bath right after we eat lunch and get a heart attack, and we won't get angina. And we'll keep the closet door shut every night, and we'll say, "I'll see you in the morning," once for Mother and once for Daddy and once for me, and we will see each other in the morning. And when we commit a sin, God will forgive us because he'll forgive us seventy times seven and we've only been forgiven fifteen times. Christmas will be here before you know it, and Santa Claus will come and say, "God bless us, every one," and he will bring tidings of comfort and joy unto everyone in the world, and he will . . .

[*The scene fades.*]

CURTAIN

# KARMA

By

## ERIC KOCHER

*A drama with dance*
*(Published here for the first time)*

# KARMA

## CAST

DENIS
MERNA, *his wife*
KARMA
PUNDAR
REVELLERS

TIME: The present.
PLACE: A West Indian island: Trinidad.

# ERIC KOCHER

*Karma* is the second play by Eric Kocher to appear in these annuals. The first, *The Shadow of the Cathedral*, was included in the 1951–1952 volume.

Mr. Kocher was born in the British West Indies, in 1912, and became an American citizen through his father's naturalization in 1925. He received his B.A. at Princeton, his M.B.A. at Harvard, and his training in playwriting at the Yale Drama School.

His occupations have ranged from Analyst with the Federal Housing Administration and Social Security Board, Washington, D.C., to a three-year assignment with the army, beginning as a private and ending as a captain, with duties in England, France, Germany, Belgium, and Austria. He then became director of three displaced persons' camps (Polish, Yugoslav, Jewish) in Braunau, Austria, and New England organizer for the Citizens' Committee for Displaced Persons. After that, he was appointed First Secretary and Labor Attaché at Embassy Brussels, the Department of State; and he recently completed a year of study at the National War College, Washington, D.C. He is now stationed at The American Consulate, Kuala Lampur, Malayan Union.

# KARMA

*On the West Indian island of Trinidad, in February or March,
it is* Coolie hosein *time, that annual festival of the native
coolies when poverty, illness, and oppression are forgotten
for one glorious evening of freedom and revelry. The rise of
the curtain reveals the living room and patio of a rich sugar
plantation owner. The indescribably lovely purple of tropical
moonlight can be seen in the background.* DENIS *is sprawled
out on a long bamboo chair when* PUNDAR *enters.*

PUNDAR. Massy want fan?

DENIS. [*Sipping a whiskey.*] Too hot.

PUNDAR. I wave fan. I brush out the flies.

DENIS. [*Without looking at him.*] Brush *away* the flies. You
must learn to speak correctly, Pundar.

[PUNDAR *takes a fan and vigorously waves it over* DENIS.]
I'm not a potentate. Thanks, Pundar, but I've had enough.

PUNDAR. [*Cutting a grotesque caper around the master.*] Then
you want I lay out the boots? Yes, Pundar lay out the boots.

DENIS. [*Without moving.*] February heat! The dry sun rotting
bananas on the trees—and you have the stupidity to mention
my rainy season boots. [*Sighing.*] What the devil, Pundar?

PUNDAR. [*Obviously disappointed—a childish pleading.*] You
want something—you must want something. [*Brightening.*] Ah,
the juice from the cocoanut—fresh—white like milk goat!

DENIS. [*Helplessly.*] Pundar, Pundar—no fan, no boots, no
juice! [*Getting up suddenly.*] Now what is it? Out with it, you
drunken coolie!

PUNDAR. [*Standing his ground.*] Pundar no drink.

DENIS. Miscreant—stupid revolting miscreant!

PUNDAR. [*Smiling.*] That word. Miscry—I was looking and
wanting that word. Thank you.

DENIS. [*His mock fury increasing.*] You son of a whore—filth of the gutter—scum from the earth belly!

PUNDAR. You very kind. I kiss you for it.

[*He takes* DENIS' *hand and puts it to his lips.*]

DENIS. [*Smiling in defeat; quietly again.*] All right, Pundar. Would you—could you please tell me what's going on today? Why are you so damned servile?

PUNDAR. The *Coolie hosein.* [*More slowly, significantly.*] The *Coolie hosein.*

[*He looks at* DENIS, *his forced childish smile trying to entice an answering warmth from the master.*]

DENIS. [*Softly again.*] Ah—the *Coolie hosein.* How could I have forgotten? [*A sympathetic paternal laugh comes from him.*] All right, Pundar. Here's something you can do for me. Get me another whisky.

[MERNA *enters.*]

PUNDAR. Pundar thank you for letting him serve you. He prays for you tonight.

[*He speeds out with the empty glass.*]

MERNA. Talk about chameleons! Pundar must have seen the smile of God.

DENIS. Merna, darling. [*She leans over and gives him a long kiss.*] More! [*She gives him another.*] No more.

MERNA. Easily satisfied.

DENIS. If I were Pundar, I'd explain it this way. The first and second kiss—cool as the ocean. Then the third starts burning with the noonday sun.

MERNA. Is that the only reason?

DENIS. Don't you remember that Circe once tried to kiss a man?

MERNA. [*Smiling.*] And why should you be frightened?

DENIS. She turned his married life into a hell, didn't she?

MERNA. But if Circe and the wife are the same . . .

DENIS. Then God help the peace and calm of marriage.

MERNA. Calm? [*Laughing.*] After only two weeks of marriage? [*Shaking her head.*] Denis—Denis! Life at our finger tips! A private coral beach around an island paradise—plantations—sugar overflowing on the land—hundreds of coolies in one big feudal estate . . .

DENIS You sound like a travel circular.

MERNA. Life *is* a travel circular. Yet you'd like to put a cage around it. The world's free, Denis—and yours.

DENIS. Ours.

MERNA. Thank you, darling.

DENIS. What shall we do with the fortune? Swimming pools— tennis courts—a palace of jade and gold shading into the palms of the jungle?

MERNA. [*A note of seriousness.*] Too selfish. Let's be generous.

DENIS. [*Looking out of the window.*] You can just see it across the moonlight—the Denis bridge. And over on the left, the Denis waterworks.

MERNA. Monuments to your ego. That isn't what I meant.

DENIS. And beyond them, the Denis hospital. Sixty-five beds. A dispensary. Why, we save a hundred lives every month.

MERNA. *Noblesse oblige.* But kings and titles belong to a past generation. Denis, why not free the coolies?

DENIS. [*Astonished.*] What!

MERNA. Denis, we have everything. Can't we afford to be generous?

DENIS. With the coolies?

MERNA. Give them a chance to be human.

DENIS. They get their wages.

MERNA. A few pennies a day.

DENIS. They can quit work, if it isn't enough.

MERNA. And starve? They've got to work somewhere.

DENIS. [*Sighing.*] Women are such sentimentalists. Unfortunately, the reality on this island has provided for two distinct classes, the master and the servant. The masters are outnumbered twenty to one. Treat the servants like humans and you'll find them taking over the island—and the cane won't get picked.

MERNA. At least you could . . . [*Then suddenly.*] Let me look at your hands! [*He extends them.*] No, the palms. [*She turns them over.*] Denis, you have been using the whip. Haven't you?

DENIS. Yes.

MERNA. Today?

DENIS. I had to.

MERNA. Oh, Denis, and I asked you not to.

DENIS. It was necessary.

MERNA. It's degrading—a human . . .

DENIS. [*Annoyed.*] Merna!

MERNA. Who was it this time?

DENIS. A lazy fellow. Calls himself Karma.

MERNA. But why?

DENIS. He's lazy and dirty and sullen.

MERNA. Human traits. They're not reasons. Did he steal, murder, rape a virgin?

DENIS. Your standards are too scrupulous.

MERNA. What did he do, then?

DENIS. Refused to work. Just sat down and bowed his little black head between his knees—a motionless black lump in a ditch beside the waving fields of gray sugar cane.

MERNA. He might have been tired.

DENIS. Five hundred *other* blacks could drip with sweat.

MERNA. So you whipped him? Denis . . .

DENIS. I had to. Power—force—show your fist and they respect you. Open your hand and five hundred niggers despise you.

MERNA. And Karma?

DENIS. [*Slowly.*] He bled—and looked—the strangest look, really. Almost a smile of love—and went back to work on the cane. [*A pause.*] I don't think I'll ever forget that smile.

[PUNDAR *returns with the whisky.*]

PUNDAR. For you.

DENIS. On the table, Pundar. Thanks.

PUNDAR. Missus want something?

MERNA. Nothing.

PUNDAR. [*Pleadingly.*] Something. Please, something!

MERNA. Can't think of a thing, really.

PUNDAR. The juice of the cocoanut? A flower from the jungle . . .

MERNA. No, thanks, Pundar. I . . . [*Then in slight exasperation.*] There is something, Pundar. Swim over to the next island

and bring me back a mango. I haven't had a swamp mango in days.

PUNDAR. Oh, yes. Pundar go now.

[*He is about to go.*]

MERNA. You're really . . . ? But Denis, this is incredible. Silly Pundar, you can't swim over to the next island. It must be at least a mile. You'd drown.

PUNDAR. But you want me to go. I go.

MERNA. No, you won't go at all! You'll stay right here. Denis, can't you think of something?

DENIS. The whisky, Pundar, isn't it enough?

PUNDAR. Very little. [*Sorrowfully.*] Very much little.

DENIS. Never mind! Your soul will be at rest soon enough—deep in the valley of nothingness.

PUNDAR. One more. I like to do one more big service. I die sooner, and my life of pain dies, too. I am happy then.

DENIS. No more! Your happy death will come soon enough.

PUNDAR. Please . . .

DENIS. [*In mock fury.*] Son of a pig's snout—sucker of scum and slime—get out—get out!

PUNDAR. Thank you. Thank you much.

[*He goes out, smiling.*]

MERNA. Pundar—how strange! All day he's been annoyingly servile.

DENIS. *Coolie hosein.*

MERNA. What's that? Sounds like a new kind of drug.

DENIS. A yearly festival of the natives.

MERNA. What festival?

DENIS. A celebration of reincarnation—tonight—the one night of the year.

MERNA. Reincarnation? You mean . . . ?

DENIS. The soul leaving a dying life and entering into some other life that is being born.

MERNA. Does that apply to whites, too?

DENIS. Of course.

MERNA. Then I might have been anything in my former lives —a queen, a slave, perhaps a prostitute?

DENIS. Why not? Interesting possibility, eh?

MERNA. This fascinates me. How long does the soul continue its career, passing from one life to another?

DENIS. Just long enough to cleanse itself of all sin.

MERNA. Strange superstition!

DENIS. And by the same token, a revelation of a future life— if any.

MERNA. By what token?

DENIS. Every sin leads to pain and suffering in future lives, until the sin is wiped out. So when the person has suffered and served again and again and the sin is quite gone, then the soul reaches a state of blessed happiness and forgetfulness similar to nothingness.

MERNA. I can't imagine—nothing—being very attractive.

DENIS. At least it's more peaceful than angels—or harps.

MERNA. Anyway, it explains Pundar. He must have been a vile fiend at one time or another.

DENIS. With lots to repent for. Every sin is punished by [*Slowly.*] by—Karma. . . . It's amazing!

MERNA. What?

DENIS. Karma, the moral law that requires compensation— and Karma, the beaten coolie.

MERNA. There's strange coolie symbolism in that. But this festival—it's been so quiet all day. Isn't there a celebration? Fireworks, tom toms, something?

DENIS. The music and dancing start a little before midnight.

MERNA. [*Looking at her watch.*] And it's after eleven. Only a few more minutes before the miracle. Do you think Pundar will just sink into—nothingness—right before our very eyes?

DENIS. I doubt whether *his* sins are cleansed so quickly. Not Pundar!

MERNA. I'm half believing all this, you know. Only two weeks on the island and I'm feeling slightly—coolie already.

DENIS. [*Laughing.*] They cater to tourists. They'll stage a good show for you.

[PUNDAR *enters.*]

PUNDAR. A note.

DENIS. From whom?

PUNDAR. Slipped under the door. Like a snake on the belly.

DENIS. [*Taking it.*] Thanks.

[*As* DENIS *reads the note, the music of* Coolie hosein *begins in the background. It is strange, sinister music, outwardly gay in the primitivism and frankness of sensuality, but with a beating undertone of background voices like a chant of the oppressed. The music becomes clearer and clearer as the following scene progresses.*]

PUNDAR. [*In suppressed excitement.*] Hear music? Music high —music low. Music tell story of soul.

[*He starts out.*]

DENIS. Where are you going?

PUNDAR. Pundar go to music. Coolies come soon to tell white man secrets.

[*He leaves.*]

MERNA. Denis, what does the note say?

DENIS. [*Laughing.*] The voice of prophecy—conscience made conscious—the veil of the future rent by a thousand primitive superstitions.

MERNA. What in heaven's name . . .

DENIS. I told you they'd stage a good show. The curtain rises on a note from Karma.

MERNA. Karma!

DENIS. Listen to this. [*Reading.*] You have made a wretched tortured soul more happy than he has been in generations. I come to thank you for your precious gift, and I come before midnight. In my visit, perhaps you may find meaning to yourself. It is too late to repent. The future is as fixed as the mountains. But there is meaning in knowledge—the knowledge that someday someone may bring the happiness to your lost soul that you have brought to mine today.

MERNA. He's literate, at any rate.

DENIS. [*Chuckling.*] A good show—for a two-weeks-old bride.

MERNA. But what do you suppose he means by happiness? You whipped him, didn't you?

DENIS. Yes.

MERNA. [*A pause, then uneasily.*] Denis—the music. It's coming nearer. It must be right outside the gate.

DENIS. They'll burst in any moment.

MERNA. In here?

DENIS. Everywhere. They'll dance and sing till dawn.

MERNA. But what will we do with them, in here?

DENIS. Give them what they ask for. Then they'll go on somewhere else.

MERNA. And Karma will be with them?

DENIS. Perhaps.

MERNA. [*Another pause, listening to the music.*] It sounds evil and horrible, but somehow fascinating.

DENIS. Like the natives, pagan, sensual, but childlike. Here they come.

[*The* REVELLERS *enter, dressed in grotesque animal costumes.*]

REVELLERS. *Coolie hosein. Coolie hosein. Coolie hosein.*

[*They are pleading and wailing and threatening at the same time.*]

DENIS. *Coolie hosein.* Greetings.

MERNA. [*Uncertainly.*] *Coolie hosein.*

[*The* REVELLERS *dance a grotesque dance around* DENIS *and* MERNA, *then put out their hands pleadingly.* MERNA *looks at* DENIS.] Money?

DENIS. Food.

MERNA. Good Lord!

DENIS. Like Halloween.

MERNA. [*Beckoning them.*] Come, everybody, come to the pantry.

ALL. [*In wild glee.*] Ah—ah . . .

MERNA. We haven't very many leftovers, but come . . .

[*Then, over her shoulder, reproachfully, as she leaves.*]

Why didn't you tell me, Denis?

[*The* REVELLERS *follow her out of the room.* DENIS *remains alone for a moment, then suddenly sees one* REVELLER *returning.*]

DENIS. So soon? You have the belly of a bird.

REVELLER. I am a bird.

[*He is right. His costume is that of a huge fantastic bird of red and purple, with white wings.*]

DENIS. And a miscreant.

REVELLER. [*Slowly.*] A stupid revolting—miscreant.

[*They look at each other.*]

DENIS. [*With rising anger.*] Pundar—you low abomination!

REVELLER. Pundar? I did not say that. I have only heard you talk many times.

DENIS. Who are you?

REVELLER. [*Casually.*] One who has heard you talk many times.

DENIS. And drunk too much. It is obvious.

REVELLER. That would make it simple—and palatable.

DENIS. Make what simple?

REVELLER. What I have to say.

DENIS. [*Not knowing whether to laugh or to be angry.*] So you are sick of hearing me talk, and you will talk instead?

REVELLER. Out of the gladness of my soul, the words will talk to you. My body now speaks.

[*He dances mockingly, with light movements about the room.* DENIS *stands amazed, then manages to seize him by the neck and shoulders. But the* REVELLER, *with a sharp gesture, escapes, his costume disarranged and hanging from one shoulder. The skin is bare, revealing ugly welts. He pats them lovingly.*]

I thank the white man. He is very good.

DENIS. [*Startled.*] Karma!

KARMA. That is my name this journey.

DENIS. What journey?

KARMA. This trip—this journey on earth. Some call it life.

DENIS. [*Now laughing.*] *Coolie hosein,* of course.

KARMA. I would not laugh. It is for the white man, too.

DENIS. Yes. For the white man, too.

[*He continues laughing.*]

KARMA. Aah—aah . . .

[*He now begins to laugh a mumbling, mirthless laugh.*]

DENIS. You are humorous, too.

KARMA. Only this journey; it is the last. [*Smiling.*] I am happy because I prepare for the last great happiness.

DENIS. [*Suddenly.*] Why did you smile today, a great beautiful child-like smile? You loved me for one moment.

KARMA. I love my suffering.

DENIS. Why did you smile?

KARMA. You do not believe. I smile when I am about to be happy. Your whip made me happy.

[*He caresses his welts again.*]

DENIS. [*Laughing uneasily.*] You are mad.

KARMA. And drunk. . . . It is the nature of man to suffer. That is reality. [*Sighing.*] I should have known that many generations ago.

DENIS. You're an old fool; but not that old!

KARMA. Even older. This morning when I arose from my mat, I surprised myself.

DENIS. This morning?

KARMA. *Coolie hosein.* Our eyes are dark other days.

DENIS. How old are you, then?

KARMA. Thirteen or fourteen generations. It is near the end of the day, and the mind is not as clear as it was at noon.

DENIS. And at midnight?

KARMA. At midnight, Karma is satisfied. I have suffered; my sins have melted like the snow and my soul is clean with a clean dampness.

DENIS. Because you were whipped? You old fool . . .

KARMA. The crime and the punishment are the same. I carry the marks of my sin with me.

DENIS. From womb to womb, I suppose.

KARMA. The bodies die and are eaten by rats, but each new body has that one mark. No, I have never forgotten.

DENIS. What mark?

KARMA. Look. [*He uncovers his palms and shows it to* DENIS.] This mark comes from only one instrument of the devil—a whip.

DENIS. [*A pause, laughing uneasily.*] You once owned a whip?

KARMA. And used it in the fields. Every day. Feel it. Feel my palms. [DENIS *softly runs his fingers over the palms of* KARMA.] Now, close your eyes. [*In fascination,* DENIS *closes his eyes.*] Let your mind drift. Run your fingers over my palm. My hands are your hands. Our paths will be the same. Only mine is at the end—and yours just at the beginning.

DENIS. [*Attempting to laugh.*] Ha—ha! That's good. Is that why you came tonight, to tell me such nonsense?

KARMA. It is the end of all my life tonight. I come to thank you before the end.

DENIS. Your palms—I can explain that. Hard work for forty years, picking the cane. [*Derisively.*] Your calluses don't come from a whip.

KARMA. You will believe me later, when I have gone.

[*He turns, and is about to leave.*]

DENIS. Wait! Please wait.

KARMA. The minutes are going.

DENIS. You once were rich?

KARMA. As rich as yourself.

DENIS. Supposing you are telling the truth—you're not—but supposing you are. What did you do with your money? Let it rot in the bank? Buy girls and opium dreams?

KARMA. I did at first. Afterwards, I tried to buy my peace.

DENIS. [*Triumphantly.*] But the waterways and bridges—yes, and the hospital. You forgot them!

KARMA. And you didn't, did you? But do you think that excuses you? A lash of a whip justified by a piece of stone or metal?

DENIS. But I built them, and you can see them across the moonlight and . . .

KARMA. I also *paid* for approval from my neighbors. You see! [*He takes off his mask, revealing a bloated pock-marked face. He smiles contemptuously.*]

DENIS. Horrible . . .

KARMA. You see the horror, but you cannot feel it. You cannot know the empty loneliness at night—the spitting, the laughing—the sighting of females walking down dark streets, and you trembling in the gutter—your whole body one tortured desire burning day after day. You cannot know this aching, but you will know it some day. [*The clock begins to strike twelve.*] Ah, it is coming . . .

DENIS. But the meaning—what meaning can there be?

KARMA. Must everything have a meaning?

DENIS. Rich—then poor, miserable, tortured. There must be a reason—more than compensation, more than punishment.

KARMA. The balance in nature. The unwinding of the universe. The circle repeating itself. The arc of the rainbow losing itself over the hills.

[*He starts out.*]

DENIS. And where are you going now?

KARMA. [*Smiling.*] Across the field of the universe, to stand on tiptoe and to touch the starlight, to lose myself in the mist, to melt in the air, and be scattered by the winds like seed . . .

[*Standing on the threshold and looking tenderly at* DENIS.]

Farewell, my friend who is starting his journey through the ages. You are like my child. You are so young I want to weep for your youth. But one day you will follow me, and we will be together in the air, in the wind, in the grass—part of all life, with billions of other specks that once were men. [*In final exaltation.*] Farewell, my friend.

[*He walks out at the last stroke of twelve.*]

DENIS. Karma.

[*The other* REVELLERS *return, carrying* MERNA *on their shoulders.*]

Go after—Karma . . . ?

[*But he is whirled around by the* REVELLERS. DENIS *tries to free himself, but he is passed from one to another, a pawn in a nightmare, unable to extricate himself. Suddenly the* REVELLERS *take* MERNA *from their shoulders, dance a short grotesque dance, and start to file out.*]

MERNA. Denis, what fun! What heavenly fun! But Denis, you're not listening.

DENIS. [*A pause—softly.*] It—it's so quiet. One less tick in the universe. Do you hear it, one less . . . ?

MERNA. [*Mimicking the song of the* REVELLERS.] *Coolie hosein. Coolie hosein.*

DENIS. [*With a pang.*] You're like a child again, Merna. Somebody's child.

MERNA. I feel clean and new, like the beginning of the world.

Why is it, Denis?

DENIS. The beginning and the end. The balance in nature. [*A pause, suddenly shouting.*] Pundar—Pundar—where is that nigger? [PUNDAR *comes in, dragging one leg after another.*]

Pundar, get me some whisky! A full bottle.

MERNA. But Pundar, you didn't just sink into—nothingness —after all, did you?

PUNDAR. This year my last year. For sure. Next year, I disappear.

MERNA. Of course you will.

DENIS. The bottle, Pundar. Quickly!

MERNA. Poor Pundar. He's so disappointed. He just didn't fade away.

DENIS. Quickly, miscreant! Vile, stupid miscreant!

PUNDAR. [*A big unconcerned yawn.*] Um.

DENIS. [*Bellowing.*] Pundar!

PUNDAR, [*Jumping a little, then yawning again.*] Pundar get bottle.

[*He leaves.*]

MERNA. The world's normal again.

DENIS. Until a year from today.

MERNA. [*Walking to the window and looking out wistfully.*] It's been lovely. How could I have been afraid of anything so really exciting? [*A pause.*] A year from today.

[PUNDAR *returns with a bottle, which he places on the table next to* DENIS.]

PUNDAR. Pundar almost forget. There is dead body outside.

MERNA. Dead—body?

PUNDAR. Yes, on grass under trees.

MERNA. But surely—who is it, Pundar? What happened?

PUNDAR. Coolie just disappear. *Coolie hosein*—so he just disappear. Next year, my turn.

MERNA. But who is it? Denis, do you believe that?

DENIS. [*Uneasily.*] Who is it, Pundar?

PUNDAR. One of dancers. I do not know.

MERNA. But maybe he's not dead. Maybe—bring him in, Pundar. Maybe there's something we can do.

PUNDAR. [*Unconcernedly.*] Coolie dead.

DENIS. [*A nervous laugh rising in his throat.*] I'm going to ask you something—strange. Pundar, go to the dead man. I want you to tell me something.

[PUNDAR *walks out unemotionally into the moonlight.* DENIS *sits motionless facing the audience.*]

Stay there, Merna. Keep looking out of the window. Tell me what happens.

MERNA. [*Uncertainly.*] Pundar's on the lawn, walking over to the clump of trees. There is something dark, an object. Pundar is kneeling down. He's touching it and now he's turned it over. It is a—body. My God, Denis!

DENIS. Ask him to feel his palms.

MERNA. But Denis, what for?

DENIS. [*His voice tightening.*] Ask him to feel—his palms!

MERNA. All right, but— Pundar, feel his palms. Do you hear? Feel his palms! Denis, he's felt his palms—and now he's coming back to the house. Who can it be, Denis? What happened to him, and why did you make that strange request. You're keeping something from me. Why did you ask me to tell Pundar to do that—to feel the hands of a dead man?

[PUNDAR *comes back.*]

DENIS. You did feel them, Pundar? You felt—the hands of the dead man?

PUNDAR. Yes.

DENIS. And how did they feel—his palms?

PUNDAR. Like no other palms in the world—soft, smooth like baby, as if he never hold something in hand, not even pencil. [*His voice trails off, and he slouches out after a moment.*]

MERNA. What does that mean, Denis? Who is the dead man? I'm not a child. You really must tell me.

DENIS. Karma. Just Karma.

MERNA. Karma? What happened? Why is he dead?

DENIS. He isn't dead. He's gone across the field of the universe —to stand on tiptoes and touch the starlight.

MERNA. And his palms. Answer me, Denis! You look so white.

DENIS. [*He lets out a short, feverish laugh.*] Tomorrow, Merna.

Tomorrow. Right now [*He quickly pours two drinks.*] drink!
Come drink, Merna! COOLIE HOSEIN!
[*They look at each other, a vast nameless gulf between them.*
DENIS *is on the verge of hysteria.*]

MERNA. [*Uncertainly.*] Coolie hosein.
[*They drink deeply.*]

CURTAIN

# THE WISHFUL TAW

By

## ELIZABETH WILSON HUGHES

*A folk play with original libretto and musical arrangements*

*(Published here for the first time)*

> This play, with its music, was originally
> granted the major award in drama in the
> Avery and Jule Hopwood Awards Contests
> at the University of Michigan.

# THE WISHFUL TAW

## CASTS

*The Wishful Taw* was originally produced as a full-length folk opera at the Lydia Mendelssohn Theatre at the University of Michigan, under the direction of Valentine Windt, with the following participating: Blanche Holpar, Marjorie Leete, Barbara White, Nathan Bryant, John Babington, Harold Cooper, Maxmilian Bryer, Phyllis Wheatley, Clarence Foster.

Television production as folk opera, over WMAL-TV, Washington, D.C., with the following participating: Irving Chandler, Grace Mehl, Anita Beasy, Ann Gould, Richard Baxter, Leonard Holmes, Arnold Thierry, George Reinhardt, a chorus of ten children, and a dance group of eight.

Produced by the same cast for five nights by the United States Department of Agriculture Opera Workshop, under the musical direction of G. Orville Trondson, staged by Frank and Ionia Zelenka, with choreography by Evelyn de la Tour.

Produced in short musical form (plus Estes Kevaufer's coonskin cap and squirrel rifle, borrowed from the museum of the University of Maryland) at the National Press Club, for the Missouri State Society.

# ELIZABETH WILSON HUGHES

*The Wishful Taw* is the fifth play with music, written by Elizabeth Wilson Hughes, to appear in these annuals. Previously, she has been represented by an opera, *Rise of her Bloom,* and three plays with music, *The Lord and Hawksaw Sadie, Frankie and Albert,* and *Wantin' Fever. Frankie and Albert,* translated into Italian as *Paradiso Bar,* has been produced twice during 1953 by Radio Rome.

*The Wishful Taw,* like most of Mrs. Hughes' plays, is set in the Missouri Ozarks. It is a complete musical play with original libretto and musical arrangements throughout, but it is not possible to give here more than a brief suggestion of the melodies included. First written and produced as a full-length folk opera, it has now been done into short form for stage and television use.

The author is well acquainted with the hill country that she portrays. She was born in Springfield, Missouri, and from childhood was accustomed to long vacations in the Ozarks, where she was treated by the natives as one of their own children. Her family still retains the Ozark cabin where Elizabeth grew to know the speech and the tunes of the people. She has recorded many of their songs for the Folk Song Archive of the Library of Congress, and has sung them at concerts, accompanying herself on the dulcimer.

Elizabeth Wilson Hughes graduated from Drury College in Springfield, and received her Master of Arts degree in Musicology at the University of Michigan. Then she studied voice and folk music at the Juillard School. She is now married to a navy officer, and is the mother of two sons.

# CAST FOR MUSICAL

### as published

GAMP LANKLE ....................... *an old mountaineer*
TESS LANKLE ................. *his younger grand-daughter*
GRANNY LANKLE ................... *an old granny woman*
LORNY LANKLE .................. *her older grand-daughter*
JOHN VINCENT ............................. *an outsider*
GOOBER WHITTY ........................... *an old crone*
JAPE WHITTY ....................... *her no-account son*
MARRYIN BURYIN SI ...................... *a hill preacher*
BIG DUKE ................................... *a farmer*
EB TURNER ................................ *his friend*
NELLIE TURNER .............................. *Eb's wife*
GROUND HOG KIDS .......................... *four children*
JESSE ........................... *an old fiddler*
BLIND OLD DAISY ........................ *a ballad singer*
MAYOLA HEMIE ......................... *a single woman*
DODIE FAIRCHILD .......................... *a young girl*
TIBO BASORE ................................. *her beau*

Other mountain people and wedding guests, if desired.

The parts of Tess, Granny, Lorny, John, Jape and Blind Old Daisy require singing actors. Other parts are choral.

TIME: During the first quarter of the twentieth century.
PLACE: A hillside in the Ozark mountains.

# THE WISHFUL TAW

## ACT ONE

*The scene is the hillside yard by the Lankle cabin. The Lankles
live just above the ridge road to Oto, Missouri, a very small vil-
lage in the Ozark mountains.*

*On stage, right, is a small cabin made of rough, split cedar logs
patched with clay. The roof is corrugated iron and has been
patched here and there with tin "ad" signs telling the merits of
Bull Durham and Peachy-Plug Tobaccos. On the visible side of
the cabin, some large tomato cans have been nailed to the wall.
Out of them grow large and trailing pink and red geraniums.*

*The cabin porch and steps slant off toward the front. One can
see where several of the flat, brown river bottom rocks that form
the foundation have been dislodged. The porch roof is sup-
ported by scaley cedar saplings, but the porch rail, also of cedar
saplings, has had the bark smoothed away. There are nails in
the posts, from which hang a fly swatter, a granite-ware dipper
and a clean rag. On the porch is a home-made bench. There is
one little window, and at center, a practical door to the interior
of the cabin. The door is open and unscreened.*

*To each side of the cabin are exits: upper right to the spring,
lower right to the back yard.*

*Upstage, just left of center, is the trunk of a great tree. From the
tree to the exit, down left, extends a split rail fence, and beyond
the fence is a view of the mountains and the sky.*

GAMP LANKLE *lies asleep in a narrow iron bed, center. He is
swathed in two flannel sheets, a fur blanket and a patchwork
quilt. It is sun-up of an autumn day; the mists are beginning to
rise from the river valley, and a few bright leaves blow to the
ground.*

TESS, *carrying a water bucket and garbed in a short flour-sack
print dress and a sweater with the elbows worn out, enters from*

*the cabin. She is fourteen and has an air of thin, wildflower pret-*
*tiness about her. Barefooted, she hops up and down on the cold*
*ground.*

TESS.    Wow, Granny! Best put on Gamp's brogans.
         It's a powerful cold mornin for bare feet!
[GRANNY *pokes her head out of the cabin door.*]
GRANNY.    Get along with ye, gran'child!
           I was strikin fire outer flint rocks
           Wi' these bare feet afore ye was borned.
           Fetch the water!
[GRANNY *disappears from the cabin door.* TESS *stubs her toe.*]
TESS.    Yessum! Ow!
         Stump your toe, kiss your thumb,
         Ye'll see your beau afore night come.
[TESS *exits up right.* GRANNY *enters from the cabin. She wears a*
*cotton dress with three-quarter length sleeves and a long full*
*skirt, an apron and small knitted shawl. She is barefooted. She*
*hops down the steps with her twig broom, and touches her foot*
*to the ground, then dashes to* GAMP's *bedside, picks up his heavy*
*shoes and dons them. She then returns to the porch and sweeps*
*down the steps. She sings.*]
GRANNY.    Rooster crowin on yonder mountain,
           Hay mee low riddle raddle dee dye dee!
           Sweep me a space for to turn around in,
           Hay mee low riddle raddle dye dee!
[TESS *echoes* GRANNY's *singing from offstage.*]
TESS.    Dye dee, a day!
GRANNY.    Menfolk wake! Crawl outer that buntin,
           Hay mee low riddle raddle dee dye dee!
           Load your shootin irons, get to huntin,
           Hay mee low riddle raddle dye dee!
TESS.    It's a day, a day!
         It's a day!
GRANNY.    Dye dee!
GRANNY. ⎫
TESS.   ⎭ Dye day!

# IT'S A DAY

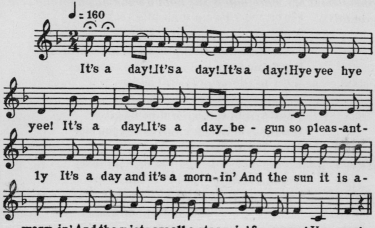

It's a day! It's a day! It's a day! Hye yee hye yee! It's a day! It's a day—be-gun so pleas-ant-ly It's a day and it's a morn-in' And the sun it is a-warm-in' And the mists are all a-storm-in' far a-way! Hye yay!

[TESS *enters from up right with the half-full water bucket. She sets down the bucket, sings and claps as* GRANNY *dances with her twig broom.*]

TESS.      It's a day! It's a day!
            It's a day! Hye yee hye yee!
            It's a day! It's a day
            Begun so pleasantly!

            It's a day and it's a mornin
            And the sun it is awarmin,
            And the mists are all a-stormin
            Far away! Hye yay!

            Rooster crowin on yonder mountain . . .
GRANNY.    Tessie, I'll thank ye
            Not to use that word.
TESS.      What, Granny?
[GRANNY *sinks to the steps to rest. Between puffings, she explains.*]
GRANNY.    Rooster ain't a polite word.

TESS.        Ye sang it.

[TESS *runs to the fence and kisses the middle rail.*]

GRANNY.      I been married up nigh fifty year
             And a Granny-woman besides.
             The propter word for a young gal
             Is boy-chicken.

TESS.        Boy-chicken crowin on yonder . . .
             It don't sound.

GRANNY.      But it's respectable. And goose-grease
             Is more practical for curin chapped lips
             Than kissin that rail fence.

[TESS *turns and points to a spot on the hill beyond.*]

TESS.        There, Granny, yonder on the slope,
             I see Aunt Sadie's chimney smoke.

GRANNY.      Sadie's fire is allers the first one lit.

TESS.        There's another smoke-finger
             Pointin right up to the mornin moon!
             The Turners are up and about.
             The mists are arisin now. Look!
             They come bubblin over the crest.
             Look out, valley, your kettle's boilin over!

GRANNY.      Hush! Ye'll wake Lorny.
             It *is* afumin up.

TESS.        That a sign of rain?

GRANNY.      A drop or two won't hurt.
             It'll be bright again by noon.
             "Happy the bride the sun shines on!"

TESS.        There's Big Duke's fire!
             Tomorrow this time, Granny,
             You and I can stand together
             Watchin for his fire,
             Knowin Lorny's there
             To light it.

[LORNY *enters from the cabin and stands on the porch. She is
nineteen, sad in repose and with a way of avoiding the aspects of
life that seem harsh to her. She wears a simple cotton dress, a
shoulder shawl drawn closely around her. She is barefooted, and*

*like* TESS, *her hair is unbound.*]

GRANNY. Lorny's new hearth-fire.
Will climb its quiet, pretty way
To heaven from a brand new farmhouse:
All paid for.

LORNY. Good mornin.

[GRANNY *and* TESS *turn to her.* LORNY *comes down.*]

TESS. Mornin, Lorny! It's goin to be
A fine day for your marryin.

GRANNY. Gal, ye're white as the weddin sheets.

LORNY. I didn't sleep.

TESS. No gal's supposed to
The night afore she's wed.

GRANNY. I hope ye don't know
Whereof ye speak.

[TESS *grins, turns and kisses the fence rail again.*]

Goose grease, Tessie!
Kissin that fence
Is plum foolish.
See to the stove, now,
Your Gamp'll want
His feed afore long.

[TESS *primps her hair as she crosses to the porch. She picks up the water bucket and goes up the steps.*]

TESS. Marry in blue, your love will be true;
Marry in green, not fit to be seen,
Yellow's jealous and black is death.

[TESS *exits into the cabin.* GRANNY *turns to* LORNY.]

GRANNY. So pale! I never should've agreed
To your takin no warm bath!

LORNY. Granny, can't we wait?

GRANNY. Ye want settlin.

LORNY. Please, Granny, can't we postpone?

GRANNY. He's not comin back. Ye know it well.
John Vincent was a fancy stranger
With a fancy name. His were sweet words
On a flatterin tongue, and you,

Dear summer sighin fool, you hung
On his rhymes like a bee o'er honeysuckle.

LORNY.          Warn't ye moughty set on him also?
The first to brief his name to "John"?

GRANNY.          He was born beyond these hills,
From far off and away, a foreigner
With ways of thinkin and actin strange to ourn.
How do we know he come by his money honestly?
We never did see him do no kind of work.

LORNY.          I've seen him work harder'n a man
Plowin a rock field, to write
Just one of these!
It's a song for me, last spring,
When the dogwood was in bloom.

[LORNY *takes a folded piece of paper from her bosom. She gives
it to* GRANNY, *who turns it this way and that, then hands it back
to* LORNY.]

GRANNY.          Here. I can't read them chicken-tracks.

[LORNY *sings the first lines of the poem, then the song is taken
up by the voice of* JOHN VINCENT, *singing offstage.*]

LORNY.          My love is like the dogwood tree
So slender, light, so sweet, so free.

JOHN.          Shivering,
New and shy withal.
Pale-flowered,
Silken, green and tall.
Pink showered,
And so fraily fair,
Quivering
In the fragrant air.

O love so light, O love so free,
O sweet love like the dogwood tree!

GRANNY.          There's only one dogwood near here:
On the way to the blue hole. Were ye
In that lonely place with him?

LORNY.          It are soft-like, it are dark,

# DOGWOOD TREE

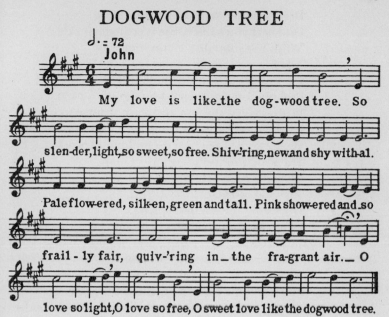

♩. = 72
John

My love is like the dog-wood tree. So

slen-der, light, so sweet, so free. Shiv-ring, new and shy with-al.

Pale flow-ered, silk-en, green and tall. Pink show-ered and so

frail - ly fair, quiv-'ring in the fra-grant air.— O

love so light, O love so free, O sweet love like the dogwood tree.

It are blue, blue, blue,
Down in the depths o' that ol' blue hole.
It are quiet-like and calm,
It are warm, warm, warm,
Standin in the sun by that ol' blue hole.

There's a wizened ol' tree
Right on the ridge
With its ol' roots a-draggin the water's edge.
Down by that ol' blue hole
Is where I dreamt to be
In the shadow o' that ol' tree,
And I glanced o'er so peacefully
To see my face in that ol' blue hole.

But the water wavered in circles runnin,
Some pebble-thrower was a-funnin.

And I turned round for to see
What one it was was a-watchin me
And it were he! Were he!

So we stood by the tree, right on the ridge,
With its ol' roots a-draggin the water's edge.
Its leaves was green, and its shade was cool,
We three just stood by that deep blue pool!

Granny, let me wait a spell,
Mayhap he will return.

GRANNY.    Have you give any thought
To Big Duke's feelins?

LORNY.    Better he should find
A willin wife.

GRANNY.    John is a flowerin of brightness:
Witch-fire ye can't not live by.
Best not change a weddin day
Oncet it's set.

LORNY.    That's just a ol' saw.

GRANNY.    Missy! We live by ol' saws.
It's proved out time and again:
Postpone a weddin date
And either the bride or the groom
Dies afore the year is out.

LORNY.    I don't believe it's so.

GRANNY.    What's so is so.

[TESS *enters from the cabin and puts two mugs of coffee on the* steps.]

TESS.    Here's you some coffee.

[TESS *exits into the cabin.* GRANNY *goes to* GAMP. *She pokes him here and there with her broom handle.*]

GRANNY.    Gamp! Ol' ground-hog, get up!
Stir your stumps, ol' man.
Aha! Drawin fire?
Get outer that truckle-bed, y'ol' mule!

[GAMP *pops his head out from under the covers.*]

# BLUE HOLE

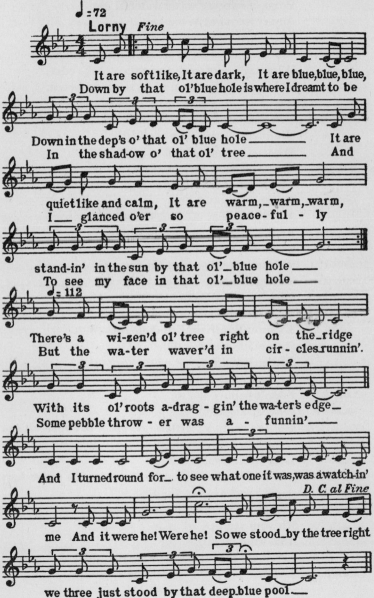

It are soft like, It are dark,    It are blue, blue, blue,
Down by    that    ol' blue hole is where I dreamt to be

Down in the dep's o' that ol' blue hole _____    It are
In    the shad-ow o' that ol' tree _____    And

quiet like and calm, It are    warm, _ warm, _ warm,
I __ glanced o'er    so    peace-ful - ly

stand-in' in the sun by that ol' _ blue hole ___
To see    my    face in that ol' _ blue hole ___

There's a    wi-zen'd ol' tree    right    on    the _ ridge
But the    wa-ter    waver'd in    cir - cles runnin'.

With its    ol' roots a-drag - gin' the wa-ter's edge _
Some pebble throw - er was    a - funnin' _____

And    I turned round for _ to see what one it was, was a watch-in'

*D. C. al Fine*

me    And it were he! Were he! So we stood _ by the tree right

we three just stood  by that deep _ blue pool __

GAMP.  Ol' woman, ye're askin for killin.
I need a mite more restfulness.

GRANNY.  Ye've had nothin but rest for the past fifty year.
Peer's like ye've been doin all the restin
For bothen us since we was jined man and wife.

GAMP.  That are right and propter.

[GRANNY *jerks the quilts off* GAMP. *He stands clothed in dignity and a suit of red flannels. Descending from the bed, he puts on his hat first, then flaps his overalls to shake off the frost.*]

GAMP.  Aw, it ain't even pure daylight.
It's cold as January. Iffen ye
Was a propter lovin woman,
Ye'd have warmed my clothes
Inside at the fire.

GRANNY.  It's September, goin on October,
And there won't be fire twill ye
Chop up more kindlin.

[GAMP *clutches his back while bending to hunt his shoes.*]

GAMP.  I'd sooner sleep in a gum-stump
Than this here again.

GRANNY.  Ye took it into your head . . .

GAMP.  I should ha' chose the table top.
I could ha' set off it all
The weddin finery. Or the floor,
By the fire, that would ha' been
The bestest.

GRANNY.  Poor ol' ground-hog.

[GRANNY *sits down on the bed by* GAMP; *she takes off the brogans and puts the shoes on his feet, then drapes a quilt around his shoulders.* TESS *enters from the cabin with food for all.* GRANNY *serves* GAMP *before she and* LORNY *eat.* TESS *goes to the rail fence.*]

TESS.  Look yonder! The Whittys
Have lighted their fire.

GAMP.  Lit it or set it?

TESS.  Lit! Most days Goober Whitty
Don't get it goin afore ten.

GAMP.  Iffen ye waited on Jape Whitty Junior

To rustle in your firewood,
Ten'd be the earliest.

GRANNY. He'll ne'er bring in the wood
For Tessie.

TESS. That's right.
I already got me a beau.

GAMP. Who's that?

GRANNY. Don't add to her foolishment.

TESS. Ever' mornin sice the first of May,
I've washed my face in dew.
And when my true love I wish to see,
I place my shoes in the form of a T.

LORNY. That's the truth. Ever' mornin
I fall over them. But that's a charm
For a distant man.

TESS. Iffen ye don't want that crust,
I'll eat it. Crusts and carrots
Is what keep my hair curly.
I even made love-medicine in a bottle.

GRANNY. Lordy, child!

TESS. And I've saved all our turkey bones
To hide about the cabin, when he
Comes back again.

LORNY. Comes back again?

TESS. And I have a powerful cunjer!

[TESS *lifts her skirt and reveals a man's hatband tied below her left knee.*]

There!

[GRANNY *yanks down her skirt.*]

GRANNY. There's a man-person present.

TESS. If I wore stockins,
It'd be my garter.

LORNY. That band?

GRANNY. It was John's.
Why, I'll tan your hide!
He's gone away for to stay.

GAMP. We put him up here for a year,

|        | Made him our friend . . . |
|--------|---------------------------|
| TESS.  | Ye allers hark back<br>To his not sayin good-bye. |
| GRANNY. | Don't sass your Gamp.<br>May be he did have his reasons<br>But nary a word did he say.<br>Weren't right. |
| TESS.  | There's a man far below, by the bend.<br>Lorny, are it Big Duke? |
| LORNY. | I don't know. |
| TESS.  | Crossin the road, now, see? |
| LORNY. | No, that's not Big Duke.<br>But see the maples yonder<br>On the curve of Haver's hill:<br>Their leaves is like tears fallin. |
| TESS.  | Tears ain't red and gold and green;<br>They's more like kisses. Yes!<br>That's the way kisses should rain down. |
| LORNY. | Don't let Granny hear ye. |
| TESS.  | Lorny! By the bridge, now! |
| TESS.<br>LORNY. | }John! |

[GRANNY *goes to the fence, looks down, then returns to* GAMP *and nods an answer.*]

|        |                          |
|--------|--------------------------|
| GAMP.  | You gals, go into the cabin . . . |
| LORNY. | Gamp! |
| TESS.  | No, Gamp. |
| GRANNY. | Ye've heard your Gamp speak. |

[TESS *and* LORNY *walk toward the cabin.*]

|        |                          |
|--------|--------------------------|
|        | And stay twill ye hear<br>Your names called. Lorny! |
| LORNY. | Yes, Granny? |
| GRANNY. | Don't set foot in that kitchen.<br>We don't want bad luck<br>On your weddin day. Let Tess<br>Do the chores; you keep<br>To your packin. |

[TESS *and* LORNY *exit into the cabin.* TESS *peeks through the doorway.*]

TESS.      I reckon we mought
Give him a bite to eat?

GAMP.     Can't starve a man.

GRANNY.    Lordy! I don't want nothin
Should go awry today.

GAMP.     Won't. We'll see to that.

GRANNY.    Tessie!

TESS.      Yessum?

GRANNY.    Bring fire for Gamp's pipe.

TESS.      Yessum.

GAMP.     We'll send him on his way
Soon as is decent.

[TESS *enters with a tiny brand held in a small scuttle.* GAMP *lights his pipe.*]

TESS.      Ain't it a fine thing to follow
Writin instead of fishin and farmin?

GRANNY.    All right for outsiders, I reckon.

TESS.      May be he roamed off a-walkin
For days come days, to write?

GRANNY.    All I know was he paid Gamp
To pitch his tent in the side patch,
Didn't never get full, nor act
Like a tourist.

GAMP.     Now, get!

[TESS *dashes to the fence to look for* JOHN, *then she returns to the porch steps.* JOHN *enters from down left. He carries a pack, slung over his shoulder, and wears good but worn hunting clothes. His features are sensitive and attractive, and although obviously he is not from the mountains, he escapes looking and acting "citified." He calls to* TESS.]

JOHN.     Hello, Tessie, how have you been?

TESS.      Oh, Mister Vincent, ye did come back!
I could say I'm fine and dandy
But I've missed ye somethin fierce.

JOHN.     Why, that's nice of you

            To say so, Tessie.
            Is it true Lorny is to be married?

TESS.     Today. Will ye dance with me
            At the wedding supper tonight?
            Is Lorny why ye came back?

JOHN.    Where is she?

TESS.     Inside.

GAMP.    Just where a bride orter be.

GRANNY.  Makin ready for her weddin.

[LORNY *apears in the doorway.*]

JOHN.    Lorny!

GRANNY.  No, Lorny. Go back in!

GAMP.    Tessie, go heat up some vittles
            For our guest.

TESS.     Yes, Gamp.

[TESS *exits into the cabin.*]

GAMP.    I'm moughty glad ye came back.
            It gives us a better chance
            To say good-bye.

GRANNY.  There be somethin I do
            Got to say.

JOHN.    Lorny . . . You must know . . .

GRANNY.  Lorny and Tessie are my onliest two
            Grand-babies. I don't intend neither
            Of them should come to harm. Tess is young
            As a new-hatched chick . . .

GAMP.    And just about as much sense.
            Lorny is spoke for. She's content.

GRANNY.  Or will be, in time.

JOHN.    You want me to go!

[GAMP *and* GRANNY *seem easier.* TESS *enters with a plate of food for* JOHN, *coffee and biscuits for the others.*]

GAMP.    Bag any more chickens?

JOHN.    What's that?

GAMP.    Thought ye mought be
            The chicken-thief we're arter.

TESS.   Don't feel they's a door
        Closed in your face.
        He's funnin ye, that's all.

JOHN.   Someone's been stealing chickens?

GAMP.   Y'ain't heard tell?

JOHN.   I went home to St. Louis
        To settle some matters there.

TESS.   All the way to St. Louis!

GAMP.   Like I say, right soon arter ye took out—
        Went home I mean—this country-side
        Is been plagued somethin fierce
        By this here hen-snatcher.

JOHN.   Why up in arms about one?

GAMP.   Dag nab and toot! Chickens is keepin
        Most families alive this year:
        Drought got the corn and the grain.
        Weed-fever took most of the cow-beasts.
        Lordy! Then the storms come and rolled
        All the tomatoes plum down off the hills.
        Chickens is all we got left.

[GAMP *and* GRANNY *sing.*]

GAMP.    ⎫ Ten cent tomatoes, forty cent meat;
GRANNY.  ⎭ How the hayshant can poor folks eat?

GRANNY. Down in the back, fingers sore,
        Hardly worth the trial to try once more.

GAMP.   Livin body to body in a ol' lean-to,
        Lordy knows what next to do.
        Corn crib's empty and the cow's gone dry;
        Can't conserve and nothin laid by.

GRANNY. Babies bornin every year,
        Poor folks're poorer 'round here.
        Nobody dared to die this year,
        Cost of the buryin's got too dear.

GAMP.   If we had a hog to sell in town,
        All we'd get'd be forty cents a pound.

GRANNY. Lordy, sure! Go ahead and try it:
        Dollar a pound when ye go back to buy it.

GAMP.     ⎱ Ten cent tomatoes, forty cent meat;
GRANNY.  ⎰ How the hayshant can poor folks eat?

JOHN.     I'm sorry to hear.
          What can we do?
GAMP.     I don't know about you,
          But we intend to take action!
JOHN.     Will you have
          This last biscuit, Tessie?
TESS.     No thank 'e, Mister Vincent.
          Y'orter know that who e'er takes
          The last one'll stay single. Not me!
JOHN.     I remember now. I'll kiss the cook.

[JOHN *takes the biscuit and kisses* GRANNY's *cheek.*]

GAMP.     Once we know who 'tis,
          God help him! 'Cause *we* won't.
JOHN.     No one can make better biscuits
          Than you, Granny.
GRANNY.                          Aw, John-boy!
GAMP.     We'll kill him!
          We'll string him up by the . . .
GRANNY.   Gamp!
GAMP.     . . . Ears and flay his hide!
JOHN.     When I said "we," I meant it.
          I've come back to settle here.
GAMP.     Too many in these parts now.
GRANNY.   Nary a parcel o' land for sale.
JOHN.     Not even after
          The hard summer you've had?
GAMP.     No.
GRANNY.   That's right.
JOHN.                  You mean
          There's no room for me here?

[GAMP *and* GRANNY *are silent.* JOHN *rises.*]

          Let us say good-bye, then.
GAMP.     That's allowable. Lorny,
          Come and jine us.

# TEN CENT TOMATOES

Ten cent to-ma-toes, for-ty cent meat.

How the hay-shant can poor folks eat? Down in the back,

fin-gers sore. Hard-ly worth the trial to try once more.

# THREE CROW BIRDS

There was three crow birds sat on a tree, They

was as black as they could be. The one of them said to his

mate: where shall we our feed-in' take?

# HYMN OF M.B.S.

Adam and Eve
Canaan Happy Land
Lord Jesus Took 'em

The bi-ble has re-la-ted that Ad-am lived a-

lone Then Eve she was cre-a-ted out

of his ve-ry bone Hal-le-lu-ja!

Hal-le-lu-ja! Hal-le-lu-ja! A-men.

[LORNY *comes forward from the cabin.*]

LORNY. Mornin.

JOHN. A fine one.

LORNY. For my weddin.

[GAMP *and* GRANNY, *carrying the bedding, move toward the cabin.* GRANNY *motions* TESS *inside.*]

TESS Don't leave here, Mister Vincent.
No matter what, please stay!

GAMP. Leave 'em get on with their
Farewells. Go along.

[TESS *exits into the cabin.* GAMP *and* GRANNY *exit down right.*]

JOHN. The summer has changed you.

LORNY. A hard one for all of us.
I have your poem still.
Shall I give it back?

JOHN. Keep it for a wedding gift.

LORNY. Should I have idled all my days
At Granny's hearthside? Could I know
Ye'd come again? Still there's no need
To fault each other now.

JOHN. I was wrong to give you
No word of my leaving.
Are you listening?
I had to go quickly, not knowing
Whether or not I should try to return.
After these hills, the city was unbearable,
And after this springtime of willow overhead,
May apple underfoot, of red-bud firing the hills
At Easter,
After I bent your back to the slender bole
Of the dogwood and kissed you, I had to return.
I shall never leave these hills, never leave you,
Lorny.

LORNY. Oh, ye can still charm birds
Down off the trees, and the heart
Out of my breast!

[*As* LORNY *and* JOHN *are about to embrace,* GOOBER WHITTY *and*
JAPE WHITTY *enter from down left.* GOOBER, *a whiny old crone
in a half-clean dress, carries her snuff can in one hand and a
small tin of fruit in the other.* JAPE, *a stringy, shifty-eyed fellow,
carries his new guitar, with its neck sticking out of a gunny sack.*]

GOOBER.  Well! Mister John Vincent come back.
For a spell, I thought ye was Big Duke.

JOHN.  It's Mrs. Whitty, isn't it?

GOOBER.  T'ain't none other. Y' knowed that
Lorny's marryin-up today? Why,
All to oncet she tol' Big Duke
She'd take him. Lord knows he'd been
Courtin her unsuccessfull till then.

I brung ye a present, Lorny,
They's pears. I was goin to give ye
My best coffee pot to set up housekeepin with,
But it's too shiny yet. The pears was a sudden
Good idy. The can's swole out a mite
At the top edge, so ye'd best use 'em up soon.

LORNY.  Thank 'e.

GOOBER.  Where's your gra'maw?
In the house, I reckon.

LORNY.  Out back, airin the beddin.

GOOBER.  I'll just go say how-do.

[GOOBER *exits down right.*]

JAPE.  Howdy, Lorny, I'd ha' said so sooner
Iffen maw'd button her lip.

LORNY.  Mornin, Jape.

JOHN.               Hello.

JAPE.  Ye come back to tom-cat 'round here
Again? Hah! I brung my guitar
For the weddin supper. I'll have it
At the Infare supper tomorrow
Likewise. What ye gonter feed us
At the Infare, Lorny?

LORNY.                              Don't know.

JAPE.         Ye'd best think on it. Ain't like ye
              Got nothin else to do.

[JAPE *laughs raucously as* LORNY *picks up the water bucket and exits right.*]

              Brides is sure tetchy, ain't they?

[JAPE *flinches, as* JOHN *walks over to him and picks a chicken feather off the sleeve of his jacket.* JAPE *laughs nervously.*]

JOHN.         Have you any reason to be here?

JAPE.         Have ye?

[JOHN *turns and walks up right.*]

              Gonter pester the bride some more?

[JOHN *returns and picks up his knapsack.*]

              Leavin?

JOHN.         Not for a while.

[JOHN *exits down right.* JAPE *pulls his guitar out of the gunny sack. He twangs it and begins to sing.*]

JAPE.         There was three crow-birds sat on a tree;
              They was as black as they could be.
              The one of them said to his mate:
              "Where shall we our feedin take?"

              "Down in yonder pasture lies
              A man what ne'er again will rise . . ."

[TESS *and* GOOBER *enter from the cabin doorway.*]

GOOBER.       Tessie, honey, somethin's riled Jape.
              Go sweet-talk him, honey. He'll quit
              Snarlin for ye in no time.

TESS.         No, Mrs. Whitty, I . . .

GOOBER.       Go on, honey!

[GOOBER *gives* TESS *a little push.* TESS *walks down to* JAPE. GOOBER *exits into the cabin.*]

JAPE.         "His huntin houn's lie at his feet
              So well do they their master keep."

              Hye, Tessie! Got me a new ballat:
              Blood and gore!

| | |
|---|---|
| TESS. | Some old-timey song, I reckon. |
| JAPE. | "His hawks they circle so eagerly<br>They's no other bird that dare come nigh." |

Now listen to this blood and gore!

"But we will sit on his breast bone<br>And pick his eyes out, one by one!"

| | |
|---|---|
| TESS. | That's a terrible ballat. Iffen ye<br>Had the heart of a cold-blood lizard<br>Ye'd not sing it. |
| JAPE. | Ye're gettin too brash for a gal<br>Your size. |
| TESS. | Leave me be. |
| JAPE. | I ain't never gonter leave ye be.<br>Ye know it well. For one whole year<br>I been settin up to ye, courtin ye<br>Serious. |
| TESS. | Huh. |
| JAPE. | Ye've put me off long enough. |
| TESS. | I've told ye a hun'erd times<br>I don't want ye a-courtin me.<br>Granny and Gamp don't, neither. |
| JAPE. | I don't care what they want or don't;<br>I reckon I can change your mind. |
| TESS. | I told ye to let me be. |
| JAPE. | I ain't never kissed ye,<br>Have I? |
| TESS. | Ain't give ye a chancet. |
| JAPE. | I noticed it. I reckon nobody<br>At all at all has kissed ye yet. |
| TESS. | Let me go. |
| JAPE. | Y' scart? What ye scart of? |
| TESS. | Ain't scart. |
| JAPE. | Good. I'll partner ye tonight. |
| TESS. | I may be partnered already. |
| JAPE. | Wi' me. Y' hear me? |

TESS.          Y'ain't learnin me.

[JAPE *tries to embrace* TESS. *She breaks from him.* JOHN *enters from down right. He carries a single fishing line.*]

JOHN.          Tessie, would you help me
               With this?

TESS.          Sure thing, Mister Vincent.
               Ye've got the line all tangled,
               H'ain't ye?

JOHN.                          Certainly have.

[TESS *and* JOHN *unsnarl the fishing line.*]

JAPE.          Ain't much of a line.

TESS.          Pretty cork!

JAPE.          Only town-folk what can't tell
               A bitin fish when they hook one
               Use corks.

JOHN.          That has it. Thanks.

[LORNY *enters from up right. She carries the half-full water bucket.* JOHN *goes to her and takes the water bucket to set it on the steps.*]

TESS.          Lorny has no call to carry on
               With Mister Vincent like that.

JAPE.          Nah! Ye're plum grain-tetchy!

[TESS *goes to* LORNY *and* JOHN. JAPE *fingers his guitar.*]

TESS.          Best go inside, Lorny. Granny
               Was askin where ye be and when
               Ye'd put on your dress.

LORNY.         I'm just goin now.

[JAPE *strikes a chord and sings.*]

JAPE.          The one of them said to his mate:
               "Where shall we our feedin take?"

[TESS *runs to* JAPE.]

TESS.          Cease it!

[GOOBER *enters from the cabin and stands on the porch.*]

JAPE.          Grain-tetchy for sure! Your nose
               Outer j'int? So that's it.
               I ain't as good as Mister Vincent
               In your eyes. Ye fancy him

Moren me. I ain't as good.

TESS.   Ye're not much bettern an ol'
Chicken-thief.

GOOBER.   I'll wager Tessie'll save a dance
For ye at the weddin supper.

JAPE.   I don't need nobody to ask
My partners for me.

TESS.   Iffen ye fault your own ma like that,
How bad would a wife o' yourn fare?

GOOBER.   Don't pay him no mind, honey,
He don't mean nothin by it.

[GOOBER *comes down the steps and stops by* LORNY *and* JOHN.
*She looks* LORNY *over, as if examining her for some taint.*]

Well, now, ye're gonter be
A right pretty bride.

We'd best be gettin along.
It's a far piece to church
When ye have to walk.

JAPE.   And ye don't know the road
Too good.

GOOBER.                 Don't fault me, boy.
I was to church oncet, just
Last year before.

[GOOBER *and* JAPE *exit down left.* LORNY *stands on the porch
steps and sings to herself. From offstage,* GAMP'S *voice is heard
calling.*]

GAMP.   Tessie!

LORNY.   I wish I had known
Before I courted
That love . . .

JOHN.                       Lorny,
Listen to me.

LORNY.   . . . Was such a killin crime.

GAMP.   Tessie! Come round
To the side patch
And help me.

LORNY.        I'd have locked my heart . . .
JOHN.         Come down to me here,
              If only for a moment.
LORNY.        With a key of golden . . .
GAMP.         Tessie!

[*Slowly,* TESS *exits down right.*]

LORNY.        And tied it down
              With a silver line.

              I would I were your love to be,
              All slender, light, so sweet, so free!
JOHN.         In the spring new and shy withal,
              Pale-flowered, silken, green and tall.

              Pink showered and so fair to see . . .

JOHN.   ⎫
        ⎬    I would offer my love to thee.
LORNY.  ⎭

[JOHN *and* LORNY *embrace.*]

JOHN          We must say to them all
              You cannot marry Big Duke.
LORNY.        It's too late now. Granny
              And Gamp did truly tell ye.
              Would ye have me cause his death,
              Or mine?
JOHN.                        Superstition.
LORNY.        Another of your big words.
              I allow I said much the same
              To Granny when she minded me
              Of the saw. I fear to go
              Again' it.
JOHN.                        You must grow
              Out of such notions.
LORNY.        Ye are from the outside.
              Would ye deny me to comb
              My hair outdoors at night,
              Not by lamplight and a mirror?
JOHN.         Such a foolish question!

LORNY. Deny that I should plant
    My yarbs by the four signs
    Of the moon?

JOHN. May I garden for you?

LORNY. Deny me the axe
    Beneath my child-bed?

JOHN. That I would deny.
    You should have a doctor,
    Not a granny-woman.

LORNY. Such could not be my way;
    I must have my axe.

JOHN.         Have it, then.
    But will you chew the baby's food,
    And pop the mess into its mouth
    The way your cousin does?

LORNY. Most likely, yes. I've been taught so.
    Best that I marry Big Duke.

JOHN. Lorny, these are only
    Little things.

LORNY. We're sundered by them.

[LORNY *exits into the cabin.* GAMP *enters from the right. He is
dressed in his Sunday best and is carrying a wicker fern stand.
He nearly runs into* JOHN, *on his way to place the stand in the
center of the yard.*]

GAMP. Whoa! Out of the way, John-boy!
    I aim for to set this
    Right smack dab in the middle.
    I messed up Granny's fern
    A mite, gettin it offen the stand.
    She won't pay it no mind,
    Not today, anyhow. Old woman!

[GRANNY *enters from the cabin. She wears her best dress, hat,
shoes and stockings, and an apron to protect her dress. She carries a flat box and lays it on the porch railing.*]

GRANNY. Yep?

GAMP. This where?

GRANNY. Yep. I'll get the Bible.

[GAMP *plunks down the stand.* GRANNY *exits into the cabin.* GAMP *dusts the fern stand with his bright handkerchief.* GRANNY *re-enters carrying a large family Bible.* TESS *enters behind* GRANNY. *She, too, is dressed in her best.* GRANNY *places the Bible on the stand, turns and speaks to* JOHN.]

               We done asked ye to go.

JOHN.     How can I?

[JOHN *goes to the rail fence, away from the others.*]

TESS.     Granny, please! Gamp,
          Ask Mister Vincent to stay
          For the weddin supper.

GRANNY.   Nope.

GAMP.           He's departin.

GRANNY.   What's 'at on your cheeks, gal?

TESS.     Nothin. Honest to goodness, Granny,
          I just pinched a mite to turn 'em pink.
          Granny, best to think how Goober Whitty
          Can make a good deal of his goin,
          With most folks.

GAMP.                 Her tongue's
          Tied in the middle and clacks
          At both ends. Nobody pays her
          Mind.

GRANNY.         They's been no talk.

TESS.     It's true none's come back
          To us. Ye've been wantin
          For Lorny a fine start. . . .
          Couldn't he stay just tonight,
          And partner me for the dancin?

GRANNY.   I don't know as there's need . . .

GAMP.     Best he go. But he
          Can hang 'round iffen
          He wants.

TESS.             Ye'll stay, Mister Vincent?

JOHN.     I don't know. Look, there they are!

[TESS *goes to* JOHN. *He points to the road below.*]

TESS.     So they be! Granny! Gamp!

Big Duke and Marryin-Buryin Si
Are comin! Big Duke's wagon
Has a fresh coat of paint.
And there's the Turners with 'em!

[TESS *goes to the porch steps.* GRANNY *unties her apron and hands it to* TESS.]

Lorny! Lorny!

GRANNY. Take in my apron, and all softly
Tell Lorny Big Duke and Brother Silas
Are nearin.

TESS. Yessum. Yessum.

[TESS *exits into the cabin.* JOHN *stays by the fence. Off stage left, can be heard the voice of* MARRYIN-BURYIN SI *booming out the verses of the hymn, with the voices of* BIG DUKE, EB *and* NELLIE TURNER *adding the lively refrain, as they come nearer.*]

M.B. SI. The Bible has related that Adam lived alone,
Then Eve she was created out of his very bone.

BIG DUKE.
EB. } Halleluja, Amen!
NELLIE. } Halleluja! Halleluja!

M.B. SI. The woman was not taken from Adam's head,
we know,
Therefore she'll not rule o'er him; that never
could be so.

BIG DUKE.
EB. } Halleluja! Halleluja!
NELLIE. } Halleluja, Amen!

M.B. SI. The woman was taken from under Adam's arm,
Therefore she'll be protected and never come to
harm.

GRANNY.
GAMP.
BIG DUKE. } Halleluja! Halleluja!
EB. } Halleluja, Amen!
NELLIE.

[MARRYIN-BURYIN SI, BIG DUKE, EB *and* NELLIE TURNER *enter. The preacher wears coat and trousers of black, a white shirt and long black tie. His hat is black felt, with a dented crown and a floppy brim. He carries his Bible.* BIG DUKE *has on a new tweed jacket and new tan shoes with his blue shirt and pants.* EB *and* NELLIE *have on their Sunday clothes.* BIG DUKE *and* EB *are hatless.* NELLIE *wears a hat and a jacket, and carries a few pink roses rolled in a newspaper.* GRANNY *and* GAMP *go to meet them. All but* JOHN *join in the last verse and refrain of the hymn.*]

ALL. The woman was taken from near to Adam's heart,
Therefore they're bound together never to part.
Halleluja! Halleluja!
Halleluja, Amen!

M.B. SI. Bless ye all!

GRANNY. Welcome, Brother Silas!

GAMP. How do! How do!

M.B. SI. How do!

GRANNY. A happy mornin to ye,
Big Duke!

BIG DUKE. It is that, Granny.

GRANNY. Howdy, Nellie!

GAMP. Howdy, Eb!

EB.
NELLIE. } How do! How do!

GAMP. Ye recollect John Vincent?

GRANNY. He come by to wish us luck.

M.B. SI. Why, how do!

[BIG DUKE, EB *and* NELLIE *nod a greeting to* JOHN.]

JOHN. Good morning.

[LORNY *enters from the cabin. She wears a long, pale blue dress and a wide-brimmed hat of straw.* TESS, *with crimson cheeks and her bonnet on the back of her head, enters behind* LORNY. *Both girls wear their little shawls.*]

M.B. SI. Come down here, child.

[LORNY *and* TESS *come down the steps.* LORNY *glances at* JOHN, *then looks down.* LORNY *and* BIG DUKE *join* M.B. SI, *who opens the family Bible.*]

Here we be: Proverbs,
The man's chapter, number twenty-one.

What's your birthday number, Big Duke?

BIG DUKE. Three. I was born on a
March third.

M.B. SI. "To do justice and judgment
Is more acceptable to the Lord
Than sacrifice." That sure
Fits ye, Big Duke.
Now you, Lorny?

LORNY. I was borned
The twelfth of May.

M.B. SI. Women's chapter: Chapter
Thirty-one, verse twelve:
"She does him good and not evil,
All the days of her life."
Why! With them prophecies
And the sunshine of a day
Like this one, the future
Looks mighty bright for ye.
Now, boy, got the ring?

BIG DUKE. Here 'tis.

[BIG DUKE *places a little white ring box on the open page of the Bible.*]

M.B. SI. Still in the wrappins.
Brand new?

BIG DUKE. Ordered it by mail. Not
A finger's touched it.

M.B. SI. Fine! Here, keep it, Eb,
Till I ask ye for it in church.
The signin of the Book
Better wait till we come back.

[EB *pockets the ring.* BIG DUKE *notices* LORNY *is crying. When he can't find his handkerchief, he wipes her eyes with his fingers.*]

NELLIE. Here's your flowers, Lorny,
The last of the little pink roses.

TESS. Ye can borrow my new hanky.

[GRANNY *takes a square of white veiling from the flat box.*]

GRANNY. This is your ma's bride-veil

From twenty years ago.

[GRANNY *settles the veil down over* LORNY'S *hat. It shadows but does not obscure her face.*]

How I wish she mought
Could see you today.

[GAMP *wipes his face with his handkerchief and gives* GRANNY *a comforting hug.* M.B. SI *is affected by these sentiments, and blows his nose into his silk handkerchief.*]

M.B. SI.     God bless us, let's get goin.
             Let's walk down to a tune.
             Shall it be "Adam and Eve" again,
             Or "Canaan, Happy Land"?

GAMP.        Pitch the tune and call the words,
             Si, we'll follow along.

M.B. SI.     "Canaan" then. It walks good.
             Ye comin, Mister Vincent?

JOHN.        Thank you, no. Later.

[M.B. SI *sings out the first line of "Canaan" and is promptly echoed by the wedding party.* M.B. SI *leads the procession out. He is followed by* EB *and* NELLIE TURNER, GAMP *and* GRANNY, TESS, *and finally* LORNY *and* BIG DUKE. *Because this is a special occasion, the women walk beside their men instead of behind them.*]

M.B. SI.     On Jordan's stormy banks I stand . . .

ALL.         On Jordan's stormy banks I stand . . .

M.B. SI.     And cast a sorry tearful eye . . .

ALL.         And cast a sorry tearful eye . . .

M.B. SI.     To Canaan's green and happy land . . .

ALL.         To Canaan's green and happy land . . .

M.B. SI.     Where all my hopes do lie . . .

ALL.         Where all my hopes do lie.

[M.B. SI *and the* WEDDING PARTY *have made their exits down left.* JOHN *remains alone by the fence. He watches their progress down the road. In the distance, their voices come back to him. He turns from the fence and begins to sing.*]

JOHN.        It was quiet, it was calm,
             It was blue, blue, blue—

Warm in the sun
By the old blue hole.

I turned round for to see
Who it was was watching me. . . .
Lorny! Lorny!

[*A last echo of "Canaan, Happy Land" is heard. Far away the
single note of a church bell sounds.* TESS *enters from down left.
Silently, she approaches* JOHN, *who has turned again to the fence
and watches the valley below. Feeling her eyes upon him,* JOHN
*turns to* TESS.]

TESS.    I was near down the hill with them
But each step was a weight on my foot.
All at once it was just like
I heard ye call. Did ye?

JOHN.    No.

TESS.    I don't know what's goin on
Inside me.
There's a way the mists break
From the valley along noon
Makes me cry for how pretty it is.
Did ye know I turned fourteen
Come last July? And now I
Slip outen the cabin at full moon
To bend the mullein.

JOHN.    You do that?

TESS.    All gals is young do.
It's to see iffen he loves you
Most truly. Bend down the mullein stalk
Unto your lover. Iffen the woody stem
Keeps to grow, he loves ye!

Are ye pleasured I made it
For ye to stay on here?

JOHN.    After tonight, I leave.

TESS.    It will be like
All the light gone outen

The sky.

JOHN.        You know I must go. . . .

Little Tessie, what can you know
Of love? Love, the torment,
Love, the killin crime?

TESS.        I do know. But
Just tonight, between the time
Of the colored lights strung up,
And the white moon wheelin away
Over the hills,
Couldn't ye partner me?

[JAPE *enters left. Quietly, he lays down his guitar and comes closer.*]

JOHN.        It's no use, Tessie.

TESS.        I'm moughty wishful
To be your taw.

JOHN.        You must leave me alone,
You'd best go along
To the others.

TESS.        Ye been cotched by Lorny!
She's past nineteen years,
Most nearly a ol' woman,
And marryin to another.

Ye'd rather have her;
I knowed that ye would.
Ye been cotched by Lorny
Just like she allers
Is a-cotchin unwary men-folk.

JOHN.        Don't be a little fool!

[JOHN *sees* JAPE.]

TESS.        I are not a fool. It's you!
Ye'll be sorry, what with all
Your roamin off. It's moren
Chickens bein stolt
F'om Big Duke!

JOHN.     Tessie, be quiet!

TESS.     I hate ye! And I hate her, too,—
          With all the hatin I can store up
          Inside me.

JAPE.     Tessie, your Gran'maw set me
          Back arter ye. Come along.

TESS.     Y'ain't learnin me!

JAPE.     I are, whether ye rightly
          Know it or not.

[TESS *bursts into tears.* JAPE *walks over to* JOHN.]
          Ye spell trouble to ever'body here.
          Why'n't ye get out afore ye're druv out?

[JAPE *takes* TESS *by the arm and leads her away. They exit left. Again the church bell rings.* JOHN *turns and watches the valley below, as the curtain falls.*]


# ACT TWO

*It is after sunset of the same day. The scene is the same as Act One, save for addition of the wedding supper arrangements and decorations. From one of the cedar posts of the cabin, across to the big tree, is strung a line of light bulbs on their wires. Their variegated colors brighten up the whole yard and send the moonlight back beyond the fence, where it shines upon the mountains.*

*At center is a table set with the cold covered dishes, and the fern stand now holds several earthenware, clay and glass jugs.* GAMP'S *bed has disappeared, but the strange assortment of chairs borrowed from the neighbors, along with stools, barrel kegs and boxes, provide enough seating space for the guests.*

*Near the cabin steps is a melodeon. Leaning against it, is* JAPE'S *guitar in its gunny sack. Over the porch rail hangs a blue knitted shawl. There are lights within the cabin.*

GAMP *is asleep on the porch steps; his feet are propped up on an orange crate. In front of the table are four children, who are skipping and singing.*

GROUND
HOG KIDS. } Cotch me a ground hog when I grow;
Cotch me a ground hog 'fore it snow.
Kay kay kitty kitty kay dee doe,
Kay kay kitty kitty kimeo!

Cotch me a pa'tridge, cotch me a quail;
Iffen I get cotched I'll land in jail.
Kay kay kitty kitty kay dee doe,
Kay kay kitty kitty kimeo!

[*The* GROUND HOG KIDS *gather around one little boy, who has a sling shot. The group sneaks up on* GAMP. *The pebble flies through the air, and* GAMP *wakes with a start. One child lifts a pie from the table.*]

GAMP. Hailstones! Lordy!
That's the sweet potato pie!
Ye lil hayshants, I'll get
My tater-pie iffen it's
My last act!

[*The* GROUND HOG KIDS *dash off wildly, with* GAMP *in pursuit. They exit down left.* BIG DUKE *and* LORNY *enter from the cabin.* LORNY *sighs, and lifts her hair from her neck.*]

BIG DUKE. Ye'll look fine with one of them
Lil bird-nest knots to the top
Of your head.

LORNY. I weren't thinkin on that.
It were so hot inside.

[BIG DUKE *takes a worn cardboard box from his pocket.* LORNY *takes it from him, opens and closes it.*]

BIG DUKE. There's been no fittin time
For this afore now.
I want ye to have it.

Here be the gifts I brung:
Bone hairpins ma wore,
"It's best to bind your hair
Up wet and clean, first time," she said,

# GROUND HOG

Don't like him.
Tell me about him tomorrow.

[GRANNY *picks up the box of hairpins and pockets it.* GRANNY *and* GAMP *exit into the cabin.* TESS *sidles up to* JOHN.]

TESS.    Was there much pretty
In the windows at Galena?

JOHN.    Your dress is the prettiest.

TESS.    Galena's not got much, I reckon.
I was to Springfield oncet.
They've got two dimestores
On the square.

JOHN.    Tessie, what do you know
About Jape?

TESS.                    Nothin.
I just don't pay him no mind.

JOHN.    I'm glad to hear you say so.

TESS.    I'm sorry I devilled ye
This mornin. I'm powerful
Sorry.

JOHN.                That's all right.
Now, here, dry your eyes.

TESS.    Ye are goin to dance with me?

JOHN.    Haven't I asked you
To leave me alone?

TESS.    But I'm wishful to be
Your taw!

JOHN.    Tessie, what is a taw?

TESS.    A dancin partner, one what's
Always a-waiting to dance with ye.
I ain't give up on ye yet!

[*Smiling again,* TESS *exits, right.* GAMP *enters from the cabin, and reaches to the cedar post which carries the rural electric line. He switches on the last strand of colored lights. From off stage left, comes the melody of a lone fiddle.*]

GAMP.    They's a-comin!

[*In a moment a bent old fiddler,* JESSE, *enters down left. He is followed by* BLIND OLD DAISY, *who holds on to his coat tail with*

*one hand and staffs her way along with the other. They are
followed by* EB *and* NELLIE TURNER; JAPE *and* GOOBER WHITTY;
MAYOLA HEMIE, *a single woman;* DODIE FAIRCHILD *and* TIBO
BASORE, *a courting couple, and the* GROUND HOG KIDS. *Guests at
the wedding supper wear their best. The women and girls wear
long dresses of print or plain cotton or challis, made with fitted
bodices and full skirts. They carry or wear knitted shawls or
cardigans. Their lisle stockings are black, or white, or tan, and
their shoes are leather and plain. Married women bind their
hair in tight knots; girls let their curls tumble about their
shoulders the better to show off. The men wear jackets, dark
or light shirts, trousers of similar or contrasting color or fabric.
No one has matched coat and trousers, since it is not the custom
to buy a whole suit at one time. They wear any kind of socks,
and heavy shoes. All sorts of hats, or none, are worn. One or
two men have pipes, or take snuff. As they arrive, the wedding
guests are clapping and singing.*]

WOMEN.   O Fiddler! Fiddler, play for me,
           For I'm as sad as sad can be.
           My true love's gone out o'er the sea—
           O Fiddler! Come and play for me!

MEN.      O Fiddler! Fiddler, fiddle away,
           Saw a pretty gal go by my way.
           Fiddle so sweet that she will stay—
           O Fiddler! Fiddler, fiddle away!

ALL.      O fiddle fiddle finny fiddle,
               Fiddle faddle fay!
           O fiddle faddle finny fiddle,
               Fiddle all day!

[GRANNY *enters from the cabin.* TESS *enters behind her, and lin-
gers near* JOHN, *while* GRANNY *heads for* GAMP. M.B. SI *enters
from down left.*]

M.B. SI.   Peace descend upon ye,
           Brethren! God are rewardin
           The righteous.

[M.B. SI *takes in the fancy clothes and decorations.*]
           Ain't this

                        The ding-bustinest,
                        Hog-killinist
                        Weddin supper
                        Ye ever did see?
ALL.                    Sure thing!

[GRANNY *picks up an empty tin plate, and with a wooden spoon, bangs on it and sings.*]

GRANNY.                 Vittles! Vittles! Get 'em here!
                        Corn-pone, hog-fat, turnip greens and beer!

                        Tessie! Come help me, child;
                        I need some one to off-bear.
                        Ye likewise, y'ol mule!
GAMP.                   Comin! Comin!
GRANNY.                 Goober Whitty, we could use
                        Another pair of hands.
GOOBER.                 Land sakes, M's Lankle,
                        I'm feelin so poorly
                        I'd just better set and rest up
                        Twill it's time to eat.
GRANNY.                 Vittles! Vittles! [*To* GAMP.] Get your thumb
                        Outer that sop-bowl! [*To* ALL.] Come folks, come!
M.B. SI.                Don't touch it!
                        Don't eat nary a bite as yet.
                        This food ain't sanctified.
GRANNY.                 Get to prayin over it, then, Si!

[M.B. SI *stands in a dignified attitude of prayer.* ALL *bow their heads for the blessing.* M.B. SI *puts out his hand to a plate of biscuits* TESS *is holding. They are too hot to handle, and he jerks his hand back. During the blessing he keeps touching the biscuits, and stops praying only when they are cool enough to eat.*]

M.B. SI.                Lord! Lord! Bless all this food:
                        Bless all the hog-fat bacon Big Duke brought,
                        And all the corn-pone Nellie Turner baked.
                        Bless the turnip greens Aunt Sadie sent
                        And give her comfort from her aches and pains

And miseries in the back, what kept her home.
Bless the pies that Grandma Lankle baked,
And give Gamp Lankle strength to cut more wood.
Bless the beer we all chipped in to buy,
And bless the Whittys, even though they come
And brought not one lil crumb for us to eat.

GOOBER.    You know we's poor folkses, Lord!

M.B. SI.   I said bless her and him, and lastly, bless
These fine big biscuits little Tessie made!
Amen!

ALL.       Amen!

[M.B. SI *snatches the biscuits and takes four or five before anyone else can get to them.* ALL *begin to eat. They scatter into
small groups.* JOHN *calls out to* GRANNY.]

JOHN.      Gravy! Gravy over here!
Granny, can I pass the gravy for you?

GRANNY.    Eh, boy, what?

JAPE.      It's sop the dang fool wants.
Foreign! Don't know the word for sop!

Ain't no room for foreigners
In these parts. Ye've heard me say
Get out before ye're druv.

JOHN.      You'd best come *with* me.

[M.B. SI *tries to snatch some more biscuits.*]

TESS.      Granny, don't let him!

GAMP.      Marryin-Buryin Si!
Ye old Bible-poundin,
Bone-headed,
Bare-knuckly finisher!
Put up your dukes
And fight!

M.B. SI.   Now, Gamp! Now, Gamp!
Ain't a lil funnin in order?
Now, Gamp!

[As he remonstrates with GAMP, M.B. SI *backs away.* GAMP *gandy-
dances around him, then swings at him wildly. Both are as-*

# GOOD-TIME CHARLEY

Jape

♩ = 92

O  I were knowed as  Good - Time Char-ley,

Love my  rye and I love my bar-ley, But corn lik-ker's beter n_

than that bar-ley, And good e-nough for_ Good-Time Charley!

*tonished when the blow is landed, and* M.B. SI *sits down suddenly.* GAMP *falls down from the shock.* ALL *roar applause, then sympathy.* JAPE, *his guitar cord slung around his neck, leans down to* M.B. SI.]

JAPE.  Preacher-man, are ye down there
Psalm-singin and prayin?

M.B. SI.  I allow as how a lil psalm-singin
Wouldn't hurt you, young man.

JAPE.  Roll offen me like water
Off a duck's back.

GRANNY.  My! As young-ones
Ye were cut-ups for sure.
It do sadden my heart
To see ye both
A-slowin down.

[GRANNY *pulls* GAMP *to his feet with one hand, and* M.B. SI *to his feet with her other. She dusts them off.* JAPE *strikes a chord.*]

GOOBER.  Go ahead and sing, son!

JAPE.  Gather round.

Oh! I were knowed as Good-time Charley,
Love my rye and I love my barley,
But corn-likker's better than that barley,
And good enough for Good-time Charley.

I offered a gal some good ol' brandy,
It were hot and moughty dandy,
Then I snuck up close and bussed her dandy—
And that were bettern than that brandy!

She said: "Your name be Good-time Charley,
Ye mought love me, but ye love that barley;
It's a man what don't drink up that barley
That I love, not Good-time Charley!

I were knowed as a devil with the brandy,
Though with the gals I be right handy,
I'm gonter stay a single dandy—
Ain't nothin bettern than that brandy!

[ALL *laugh and applaud* JAPE'S *song.* GRANNY *collars* GAMP *and leads him to the orange crate.*]

GRANNY.    Mount that box and call a set!

Give us a tune, Jesse.
Somethin to hearten us up
And set us on the move.

JESSE.    Gets cold 'long about this time.
All my joints is friz.

[*Silently* GRANNY *passes a whiskey jug under* GAMP'S *nose and across toward* JESSE, *but seeing* M.B. SI *with hands outstretched and eyes uplifted, she passes the jug across* JESSE *to* M.B. SI.]

M.B. SI.    Lo! The heart of the woman
Hath understandin!

[M.B. SI *drinks deep, then passes the jug to* GAMP.]

Lovin cup?

GAMP.    Sure thing!

[GAMP *passes the jug to* JESSE.]

JESSE.    Fire and vinegar!
He! he!

[JESSE *takes a drink, then rubs a little liquid corn on his bow before he passes the jug along to the other men.* JESSE *fiddles out the tune of "Fiddler, Fiddler."* GRANNY *settles herself at the melodeon,* JAPE *plays his guitar, and* MAYOLA *and* BLIND OLD

DAISY *seat themselves and blow into combs.* JOHN *stands by* GRANNY, *and after* GOOBER *has snared* BIG DUKE *for the first set,* LORNY *moves away to the fence.* M.B. SI *leads out* TESS, NELLIE *and* EB TURNER *and* DODIE *and* TIBO *make out the set.* GAMP *mounts the orange crate and calls the dance.*]

GAMP. Honor your partners, and the lady on the left!
    All join hands and circle to the left!

    Lady in the center with all hands round!
    Lady steps out and gent steps in,
    All join hands and circle again!

[*As the dancers continue to circle,* TESS *drops out and runs over to* JOHN. JAPE *puts down his guitar.*]

TESS. Be y' free, Mister Vincent?
JOHN. Granny's my partner, Tess,
    Even if she is too busy
    To dance with me.
TESS. But iffen she's playin,
    Ye're free!

[JAPE *laughs and leads* TESS *toward the dancers.*]

JAPE. Come along! He may
    Be free, but ye ain't.
TESS. Le' go my arm.
JAPE. Listen here to me,
    Why for ye want to make
    A fool of yourself?
TESS. He does like me,
    I just know he do.
JAPE. A no-account foreigner!
TESS. How many times o'er
    Must I tell ye?
    Ain't no one for me
    Long as bothen us
    Got air to breathe!
JAPE. Come along and dance.

[*The melody of the dance tune rises again.* GAMP *continues the call.*]

GAMP. Break your circle and make two lines!
Ladies doe, and gents you know!

Swing your partners!
Alamand left and a right and left six!
Balance six!

*[Again the melody softens but maintains its insistent rhythm, as the dancers continue to balance. They slow to half time. JOHN makes his way to LORNY.]*

LORNY. Ye've come to say good-bye,
H'ain't ye?

JOHN. I want you to go with me.

LORNY. Ye can't mean that! Not now.
I'm natured to these hills,
No other place. What would I do
Amongst town folk and foreigners?
All through this day
I've thought on your comin and goin.
This love between us must be set aside.

JOHN. You do love me?

LORNY. Ye know it well. But have
Ye given any thought to Big Duke?

JOHN. He wouldn't keep you here
When you don't love him.

LORNY. He needs me, I reckon.

JOHN. Is that his farm down there? The fields
And the house beyond the bend of the river?

LORNY. Yes. The house, the barn, the little shacks:
They's the henhouses. And there's
The grove where apple trees'll be
Set out some day.

JOHN. I'll go down there.

LORNY. Ye can't do that!

JOHN. I have to, Lorny.
When he brings you there,
And away from all these others,
I'll tell him.

LORNY.     I'm afeared for ye.

JOHN.      Don't be. You'll go,
           If I tell him?

LORNY.     Iffen he'll consent.

JOHN.      In all the Aprils to come
           When redbud, dogwood,
           Appleblossoms burn
           The winter-whitened eye
           With loveliness incredible,
           I'll lead you into the fires of spring
           And bind you close with wild grapevine,
           Choose for your delicate chains
           The pale tendrils
           Of my own enchantment.

LORNY.     Voice that moved me then and now,
           Voice that banishes my rest,
           Charm the bird from off the bough,
           Charm this heart from out my breast.

LORNY.  ⎫
JOHN.   ⎬  In all the Aprils to come
           When redbud, dogwood,
           Appleblossoms burn
           The winter-whitened eye
           With loveliness incredible,
           Ye'll lead me ⎫
           I'll lead you ⎬ into the fires of spring!

[LORNY *and* JOHN *embrace. The great tree shelters them from
the sight of the dancers.* BLIND OLD DAISY *begins to sing "Susie-
Sue." The dancers sway and clap their hands, and then dance
to its gentle music. This dance begins softly and slowly and
gradually works to a rowdy finish, with all the dancers shouting
the words as they dance and clap. While the music and dancing
is still soft,* JOHN *leaves* LORNY *by the tree and comes down left.*
TESS *again breaks from the dancers, and followed by* JAPE, *comes
to* JOHN.]

DAISY.     Susie-Sue, are ye gatherin greens?
           Turnip, dandelion, cress and beans—

Susie-Sue, are ye gatherin greens?

Susie-Sue, are ye gatherin wool?
Get to your chores whilst the mornin's cool.
Susie-Sue, don't gather no wool!

Susie-Sue, are ye gatherin twine
To string you up a washin line?
Susie-Sue, are ye gatherin twine?

Susie-Sue, are ye gatherin charms
To witch your true love into your arms?
Susie-Sue, don't gather no charms!

[*The dancers move away, but continue to hum and sing in the background.*]

TESS.    Oh, watch yourself! Nobody but me
Saw ye yonder with Lorny,
But what if they . . . ?

JOHN.    This doesn't concern you.

TESS.    Who pleaded for ye to stay?

JOHN.    I would have returned tonight,
No matter what.

[JOHN *turns to* JAPE, *insinuating.*]

You'd better get ready
To give them back,
Or pay them back!

JAPE.    Ye got no call to say nothin
To me. Y'ain't seen me
Do nothin. Y'ain't half
As concerned with all the families
As y'are with Big Duke's.

JOHN.    Where did you get all the chickens
You sold just outside of town
This afternoon? I saw you.

JAPE.    Raised 'em.

JOHN.    You never raised a chicken in your life.

I've been here long enough to know
You and your mother run a soft-drink stand
For tourists out on the highway.

JAPE.        Ye can't prove nothin.

JOHN.        Shall I stay till I can?

JAPE.        Y' damn high-and-moughty
From the outside!

[JAPE *reaches for his knife.*]

JOHN.        Draw your knife.
Let's see if you'll use it.

[JAPE *draws his knife suddenly. Silently* JOHN *grabs his wrist and forces* JAPE *to drop his knife.* JAPE *kneels to pick up his knife.*]

Tomorrow, Jape. Until tomorrow. . . .
Good-bye, Tess.

[TESS *raises her hands to him, pleadingly.* JOHN *touches her cheek gently and pityingly, then turns and exits down left.* JAPE *rises, puts away his knife and speaks with murderous quietness.*]

JAPE.        Go off somewheres. Leave me be,
But iffen I ever hear tell
Ye spoke a word o' this . . .

TESS.        It ain't a scene
I'd be proud to witness on,
Today!

[TESS *runs to the cabin steps and exits into the cabin.* JAPE *wipes his face with his hands, slicks back his hair. Over the rhythm of the dance music, comes* LORNY'S *voice.*]

LORNY.        O my mountains, O my mountains,
O my mountains, how can I leave f'om ye?

O my mountains, O my mountains,
O my mountains, my love asks me to leave ye.

O my mountains, O my mountains,
My high and wide blue mountains,
Fare ye well, God be wi' ye!

# SUSIE SUE

Su - sie Sue are ye gath - er - in' wool?

non pizzicato

Get to your chores whilst the morn - ins' cool

Su-sie Sue don' gather no wool.

pizzicato . . .

*All repetitions at the discretion of the director.

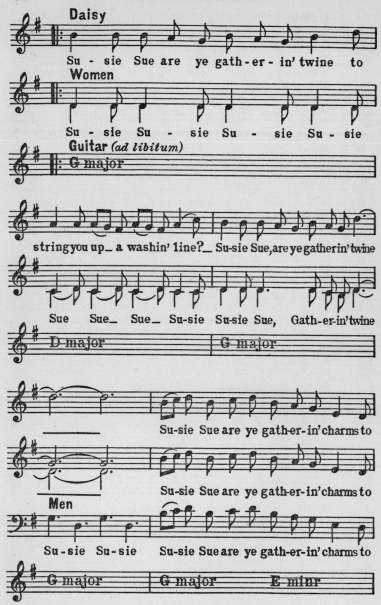

**Daisy**

Su - sie Sue are ye gath-er- in' twine to

**Women**

Su - sie Su - sie Su - sie Su - sie

**Guitar** (*ad libitum*)

G major

string you up_ a washin' line?_ Su-sie Sue, are ye gatherin' twine

Sue   Sue_   Sue_   Su-sie   Su-sie Sue,   Gath-er-in'twine

D major                    G major

Su-sie Sue are ye gath-er-in' charms to

Su-sie Sue are ye gath-er-in' charms to

**Men**

Su-sie   Su-sie     Su-sie Sue are ye gath-er-in' charms to

G major        G major        E minr

**Daisy**

witch your true love in-to your arms?

**Women**

witch your true love in-to your arms?

**Men**

witch your true love in-to your arms?

**Violin**

**Guitar**

D major

Su-sie Sue, don't gather no charms!

Su-sie Sue, don't gather no charms!

Su-sie Sue, don't gather no charms!

E minor          E minor

*(John exits D. L.)*

1. O    my mountains,  How  can  I  leave from
3. high and wide blue mountains,  Fare ye well God  be wi'

Su - sie  Oh _____  Su-sie Sue _____

Su - sie Sue  Su - sie

*First ending for verse 1*  |  *Second ending for verse 3*

ye! _____  ye! _____

Su-sie Sue. _____  Su-sie Sue. _____

Sue. _____  Sue. _____

*repeat pages 6-7 for verse 3*

love asks me to leave ye!

Oh!

Women     *cresc.*

Su-sie Sue   Sue   Su-sie Su-sie Sue   Sue   Su-sie

Men

Su - sie     Su - sie

Guitar
G major     D major

Melodeon and/or piano

*percussively*     *cresc.*

(Tess exits)

Gath-er-in' Gath-er-in' Gath-er-in' greens,—

Gath-er-in' wool,— gath-er-in' twine,

But—to make—my true love mine,—Gather-in' charms!

Gath-er-in' charms!

*(JAPE goes to LORNY. Music louder to the finish. Dancers clap and shout raucously as the dance progresses.)*

*(LORNY goes to GRANNY)*

Su - sie Sue are ye gath-er - in' twine to

*follow voices at the octave*

G major

string you up_ a wash - in' line?__

D major

[JAPE *goes to* LORNY *by the rail fence.*]

JAPE.  Tessie says Granny's
A-lookin for ye again.

LORNY.  Thank ye.

[LORNY *comes down from the rail fence. The music of "Susie-Sue" grows louder. Dancers begin to shout the words, clap and stamp. One of the dancers knocks over a chair. Another bumps against the table.* LORNY *goes to* GRANNY, *who now stands on the cabin steps with her pie plate and spoon. She bangs on the plate for attention.*]

GRANNY.  Quieten down, musikers!
Quieten down!

[*The music ceases and the dancers turn to* GRANNY.]

Peer's like we're running out of space.
Ladies, grab up them dishes, pots and pans.

GAMP.  Leave the jugs!

GRANNY.  And bring 'em around to the rear.
I could use your help on the kitchen chores.
Big Duke, you and Gamp move the table
Outen the way. Boys, get them chairs!
Marryin-Buryin Si, you and Jesse
Can break the seal on a fresh jug.
When ever'thing's redd up,
And iffen Jesse can still fiddle,
We'll have us another set.

GAMP.  Right work-brittle old woman!

[ALL *move to clear the table and do* GRANNY's *bidding. Quickly, all the women carry off the dishes. They exit both up right and down right.* GOOBER *re-enters from the cabin and flaps a dish towel at* GRANNY.]

GOOBER.  These be the ones we're to wipe with?

GRANNY.  They be. Come along, Lorny, ye can watch.
But don't ye dare to touch one single dish.

[GRANNY, GOOBER *and* LORNY *exit into the cabin.* BIG DUKE *and* EB TURNER *light their pipes. The other men gather around* M.B. SI *and the fresh jug.* JAPE *remains at the rail fence.*]

JESSE.  My! My! Ain't that a content o' likker!

[JESSE *pokes his finger in the jug, and again wets his bow. He begins to fiddle. The men pass the jug around to each other and take up the words to the tune* JESSE *plays.*]

| | |
|---|---|
| GAMP. | Now, boys! Let's not get muddle-headed. |
| | Just pass that lil jug to me. |
| | Someone's got to keep it safe. |
| M.B. SI. | I reckon it's as safe |
| | Warmin up my vitals as tis yorn! |
| GAMP. | Give't here, y'ol' booby! |
| JESSE. | He! He! |
| M.B. SI. | Big Duke? |
| BIG DUKE. | None for me. |
| MEN. | O my bottle of corn, O my bottle of corn, |
| | On a cold, cold night with my bottle of corn |
| | I'll be warm just as sure's ye're born. |
| GAMP. | Now my old woman may be layin in the bed, |
| | Covers all pulleyed up o'er her head, |
| | But she'll be cold before it's morn |
| | Like I won't be with my bottle of corn. |

[JAPE *comes down to the* MEN.]

| | |
|---|---|
| MEN. | O my bottle of corn, O my bottle of corn, |
| | On a cold, cold night with my bottle of corn, |
| | I'll be warm just as sure's ye're born. |
| JAPE. | Listen to me, d'ye still |
| | Want to catch that chicken-thief? |
| BIG DUKE. | Sure we do! |
| JAPE. | I see'd him a while ago. |
| M.B. SI. | What did ye see? |
| EB. | How come? |
| GAMP. | What d'ye mean? |
| JAPE. | I see'd somethin, a shadow most likely. |
| | Somebody was down past the ridge, |
| | Sorter movin creepy-like. |
| M.B. SI. | Ain't much to go on. |
| BIG DUKE. | How'd ye know it were the thief? |
| JAPE. | Seems most rightfully so: |
| | Who'd be out on them hills |

This time o' night? All's here
As belong here, ain't that so?

EB. Ain't much is right.

BIG DUKE. Bettern nothin.

JAPE. It makes sense, don't it?
Whole countryside knows
Ever'body's here tonight.
That gives him a clear field
To steal more. Ye got
Some new pullets, h'ain't ye,
Big Duke?

BIG DUKE. Gamp, I'm gonter put out these lights.

[BIG DUKE *steps up to the cedar post that carries the rural power line, and cuts off the shining of the colored lights. Suddenly, the rail fence and the mountains beyond stand out sharply in the moonlight.*]

Get your irons, boys.

[*All the* MEN *scatter. Some have parked their guns against the side of the porch.* GAMP *dashes up the cabin steps and exits into the cabin.* EB *gets* BIG DUKE'S *gun and his own, and follows* BIG DUKE *to the rail fence, where he stands with* JAPE, *who is pointing out over the ridge road.* GAMP *enters from the cabin. He is carrying an ancient gun.*]

GAMP. Thank the Lord all the women's
Gone down toward the spring.
I'm fit and ready to go!

BIG DUKE. No use to stalk him
No place else.
We'll bide right here.
I reckon iffen anything
Stirs near that farm o' mine,
We uns'll see it.

EB. This be a goose-chase?

BIG DUKE. Bettern not be.

EB. Iffen that iron o' yours speaks,
Twon't be.

JAPE. Ye got to be patient.

# BOTTLE OF CORN

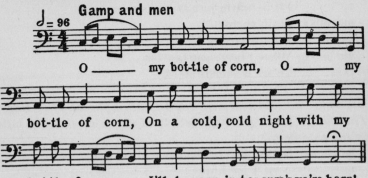

O ____ my bot-tle of corn, O ____ my bot-tle of corn, On a cold, cold night with my bot-tle of corn, ___ I'll be warm just as sure's ye're born!

[BIG DUKE *breaks his gun.*]

BIG DUKE.   I get edgy f'om waitin.
Just so Jape see'd what he see'd
And I catch a look o' the same.

JAPE.   It won't be far now,
It can't be long.

GAMP.   Cold night, for sure!

M.B. SI.   Plum fitten to freeze that jug
Iffen t'ain't drunk quick.

[GAMP *and* JESSE *settle not too close to the fence.* BIG DUKE *and* EB *stay by the fence and watch the land in the moonlight.* JESSE *pulls his fiddle from behind his back and begins to pluck the strings softly.* GAMP *leans back and scratches his back against a stump.* JAPE *moves from* BIG DUKE'S *side and grabs the jug from* GAMP. *The men hum and whistle the tune of "O My Bottle o' Corn."*]

JAPE.   Give't o'er!

M.B. SI.   Liquid courage!

GAMP.   Reckon Jape needs it right bad.

JAPE.   T'ain't my courage, it's my gullet
What needs warmin.

JESSE.   Peer's likely my gullet
Needs it likewise.

MEN.    O my bottle of corn, O my bottle of corn,
        On a cold, cold night with my bottle of corn
        I'll be warm just as sure's ye're born.

BIG DUKE.  Hush there!

GAMP.    What have ye?

BIG DUKE.  What I been watchin for.

JAPE.    Ye see'd somethin?

EB.      That so?

[BIG DUKE *motions the men down. They approach the ridge.
They flatten to the ground quietly, and watch out over the hills
in the pale light.*]

BIG DUKE.  See there? The shadow past the bed.

EB.      Now I see him!

JAPE.    Movin a pace, ain't he?

GAMP.    He's gettin near the barn.

JAPE.    He'll be headin for the hen-house!
        See? See? What did I tell ye, Big Duke?

BIG DUKE.  Ye weren't a-storyin, for oncet.

GAMP.    Three plugs of my best Peach-plug t'baccy
        Again your gun, he gets that one
        First lead.

EB.      Ain't bettin' on a sure thing.

[BIG DUKE *rises and braces his body against the fence rail for the
long shot he must make. He raises the gun, then stops to rub
his eyes. He spits on his thumb and touches it to the gun barrel.
The other men do not move.* BIG DUKE *takes aim, and the gun
follows its moving target for a moment.* BIG DUKE *fires. The men
jump up with shouts and cries, and over their voices* GAMP
*cries out.*]

GAMP.    Good for ye, Big Duke!
        Got him!
        Got him with the first lead,
        The very firstest one!

JAPE.    He done dropped like a stone!

BIG DUKE.  Well, I told ye, that lil old gun
        Of mine, she never did miss!

[BIG DUKE *hands his gun to* EB *and accepts the liquor jug from*

JAPE. *He tilts the jug across his arm and drinks deeply—as the lights slowly fade, to indicate the passing of the night.*]

*When the lights come up, it is nearly daylight, and the distant sky shows streaks of color.* NELLIE TURNER, MAYOLA HEMIE *and* DODIE FAIRCHILD, *their shawls tight about them, are huddled together on a bench on the cabin porch. Their backs are toward* GRANNY, *and they are humming softly the melody of the dirge.* GRANNY *sits on the porch steps. She is wide awake.* LORNY *is seated on a box nearby. Her head and arms rest on the fern stand. She appears to be sleeping.* M.B. SI *is sound asleep under the big tree. A blanket is tucked around his knees and a jug is overturned beside him.*

TESS. Goober Whitty's sound asleep
On the bed. Blind Old Daisy and
The least ones all are hunkered down
By what's left of last night's fire.
It's near daylight.

GRANNY. Sun'll be up inside an hour.
Set down, child.

TESS. Ain't the men
Come back as yet?

GRANNY. Not a sign of 'em.

TESS. What's goin on, Granny?
Where did all the men go?

GRANNY. Brother Silas!

M.B. SI. Huh?

GRANNY. Wake up, Si!

[M.B. SI *rouses himself, tries to get a last drop from the jug, then rises.*]

M.B. SI. I always did say
In life's great troubles:
What God's love can't cure,
Corn likker can.

[*At* M.B. SI'S *voice,* LORNY *stirs and wakes. She lifts her head and listens.*]

Are they comin up the road?

GRANNY. Reckon not. Tell Tessie

And Lorny what ye told me.

TESS.    Why'd they all
Go off like that?

M.B. SI.    To track down the chicken thief,
Or what's left of him.

[GOOBER *enters from the cabin. Her yawn vanishes at the words:
chicken thief.*]

GOOBER.    Where's my Jape-boy?

M.B. SI.    He's with the men. Jape claimed he seen
The chicken thief down on the ridge road.
We didn't take no count of it first,
But then, by goshen, Big Duke saw him
And shot him first lead.

GOOBER.    That Jape-boy!

M.B. SI.    So here I was all set to go,
And Gamp says they'd all be much obliged
Iffen I'd stay and watch o'er the women
Twill they got back, and so I said
Iffen ye think it's my Christian duty . . .
And they said . . .

GOOBER.    I'll jest go and tell the news
To Nellie and the others.

[GOOBER *moves upstage to the women.* LORNEY *rises and walks
to the fence.*]

M.B. SI.    And then they said . . .
Well, I'll be . . .

[M.B. SI's *tone is aggrieved. He walks back to the tree and sits
down again.* TESS *sets herself by* GRANNY.]

TESS.    Granny, I'm cold all over.
I'm scart.

[BLIND OLD DAISY *enters from the cabin. She brushes against*
JAPE's *guitar, which is hanging by its neck cord on a nail near
the door way. She touches the body of the guitar and then
strikes the strings.*]

DAISY.    There was three crow-birds sat on a tree,
They was as black as black could be.
One of them said to his mate:
"Where shall we our feedin take?

[TESS *rises.*]

> Down in yonder pasture lies
> A man what ne'er again will rise.
> His hounds they lie down at his feet,
> So well their lovin master keep.

NELLIE.
MAYOLA.
DODIE.
DAISY.

> His hawks they circle so eagerly
> There's no other bird dares to come nigh.
> But we will sit on his breast bone . . ."

TESS.　Don't sing that old song!

GOOBER.　Best not to whang on Jape's
New guitar, Daisy honey.
Best not . . .

[GOOBER'S *voice trails off, as she leads* BLIND OLD DAISY *to the other women.* M.B. SI *opens his eyes again.*]

M.B. SI.　Granny?

GRANNY.　Yes, Silas?

M.B. SI.　Ye got some sheets, extry?

GRANNY.　None to spare.

M.B. SI.　Need some for shroudin.

[BLIND OLD DAISY, GOOBER, MAYOLA, DODIE *and* NELLIE *begin a dirge.*]

WOMEN.　Wind him in his windin sheet,
Weep with the willow,
Wind him in his windin sheet,
And lay him low.

GRANNY.　Dodie! And ye, Mayola,
Go in to the table and fetch out
Two of Lorny's weddin sheets.

[DODIE *and* MAYOLA *exit into the cabin.* GOOBER, NELLIE *and* BLIND OLD DAISY *continue to sing.* TESS *speaks, over their voices.*]

TESS.　Granny, ask Brother Silas if John
Were with the men, or maybe,
Did they meet him on the way?
Oh, Granny, he went away again
After talkin to Jape and me.

## DIGE

Wind him in his wind-in sheet,

Make it clean and white as snow.

Wind him in his wind-in sheet,

Lay him where the wind does blow.

[DODIE *and* MAYOLA *enter from the cabin. They go upstage to* GOOBER, NELLIE *and* BLIND OLD DAISY. *The women continue to sing, as they tear the two sheets into ten inch width shrouding bands.*]

WOMEN.    Wind him in his windin sheet,
               Make it clean and white as snow.
               Wind him in his windin sheet,
               Lay him where the wind does blow.

TESS.    I want to know where John is.

GRANNY.    Ye love him truly, don't ye?

TESS.    Liken to none on this here earth.
               Liken to no other one.

GRANNY.    Poor, sorrowful gal-child,
               There ain't nothin nobody can do.

[*Voices and dragging footsteps of the men are heard.* EB *and* GAMP *enter down left.* TESS *runs back to* GRANNY.]

TESS.    There they be!

GRANNY.    'Bout high time it was, too.

[TIBO, JESSE *and* JAPE *enter from left. They carry* JOHN'S *body,*

*slung in a dark blanket. They lay* JOHN *at* GRANNY'S *feet.* BIG
DUKE *enters down left and stands before* GRANNY. *His head
hangs.* GAMP *has awakened* M.B. SI.]

TESS.            Granny! Granny! There's somethin
                 Terrible wrong. Jesse! Jape! Tibo!
                 What are it ye be totin? Big Duke,
                 Big Duke!

[GRANNY *rises. The women gather around her.* M.B. SI *and* GAMP
*approach.*]

BIG DUKE.        I done it, Granny.

[GRANNY *kneels beside the body. She plucks the blanket away
from* JOHN'S *face.* LORNY *comes to* GRANNY.]

GRANNY.          John! My poor John boy!
LORNY.           John!
GRANNY.          Part, you uns,
                 She mought best see.

[LORNY *drops to her knees beside* JOHN.]

BIG DUKE.        It were by no purpose. I know
                 He weren't no thief. But I see'd
                 Someone f'om the fence. He was
                 Over by my house. Granny, I . . .
ALL.             Wind him in his windin sheet,
                 Make it clean and white as snow.
                 Wind him in his windin sheet,
                 Lay him where the wind does blow.

                 Weep a-willow, weep a-woe,
                 Wind him in his windin sheet,
                 And lay him low, low, low.
                 Lay him down there low.

[*As the men and women join in singing the dirge,* TESS *breaks
through the crowd to* BIG DUKE.]

TESS.            Ye great fool!
                 Why'd ye have to shoot him for?
                 Was it a hen-snatcher
                 Ye were huntin?
                 Was it?

Why diden ye aim so's to hit
The right one?
Him!
By your side, Big Duke,
It were Jape ye were huntin!
Jape, he stol' your hens!

JAPE. Shut your trap, gal.

TESS. It were Jape! It's writ plain
All over him.
Aw, what am I sayin?
It don't make no matter, now.

[GAMP *holds* TESS *in his arms.* JAPE *is uneasy beneath the eyes of* BIG DUKE *and the men and women.* GOOBER *sidles over to* JAPE.]

JAPE. Y'ain't gonter believe that one,
Are ye, Big Duke? Are ye?

BIG DUKE. I don't rightly know what to believe.
John were such a fine one. God
Forgi' me! He were a friend o' mine.
I don't know what to believe.

LORNY. I loved him.
Ye can believe that.
Ye can fault me howe'er ye like
But I'm a-tellin ye straight out
I loved him.

BIG DUKE. I don't ever aim to
Fault ye, Lorny.
Not ever.

M.B. SI. I reckon we all loved him, gal.
Ain't one soul here
That wouldn't say the same.

[M.B. SI *folds his hands, and once again his hymn tune rises, this time with funeral words.*]

Lord Jesus took 'em high and low
To jine Him up in heaven.
He took 'em f'om the rich and poor
And all their states did leaven.

> For Jesus Lord did gather His sheep
> Into His spotless bosom,
> And there He will forever keep
> His flock, and He won't lose 'em.

GRANNY.　So don't ye cry and weep so sore
> For them what has been taken.
> They are in paradise with Him
> And have their humanness shaken!

ALL.　For every person has his'n turn.
> (Lord Jesus takes 'em high and low.)
> We uns are left here to mourn,
> But soon 'twill be our'n time to go.

[ALL *hum softly during the following speeches.*]

TESS.　He's dead, ain't he?

BIG DUKE.　God forgi' me!

GRANNY.　Don't take on so, boy,
> T'ain't fitten.

[GRANNY *goes to* BIG DUKE. JAPE *indicates* LORNY'S *grief.*]

JAPE.　See there!
> Chicken-thievin
> Ain't the worstest kind o' thievin!
> Ain't ye glad you kilt 'm now?
> Ain't ye?

GOOBER.　Chicken-thievin
> Ain't bad wrong thievin,
> No how. Besides,
> Ain't enough quick money in it.

[JAPE *and* GOOBER *cease.* GOOBER *gets out of the way.* BIG DUKE *turns on* JAPE *and throws him to the ground.* BIG DUKE *makes his way through the crowd of* WEDDING GUESTS *to the porch. He takes the blue shawl from the railing and puts it around* LORNY'S *shoulders. He draws her to her feet.* GRANNY *takes the box of hair pins from her pocket.*]

GRANNY.　Here's your pins.
> We'll await your hearth fire
> Next mornin.

[LORNY *takes the pins and follows* BIG DUKE *to the road. They exit down left.* GRANNY *and* TESS *kneel by* JOHN's *body. The voices rise in the final cadence of the hymn. Morning sunlight begins to burn away the mists.*]

ALL.      For Jesus Lord did gather His sheep
          Into His spotless bosom,
          And there He will forever keep
          His flock, and He won't lose 'em!


SLOW  CURTAIN

# SELECTED PLAYS OF THE YEAR

## AVAILABLE FOR PRODUCTION IN AMERICA

*(These lists include original American plays, adaptations, and dramatizations that have been published during the latter part of 1952 and 1953.)*

BERCOVICI, ERIC. HEART OF AGE. "New World Writing," 4th Mentor Selection. New American Library, New York.

In a small bar in New York, an assortment of characters are speaking out some of their pent-up emotions, which causes the Professor to explain, "In the heart of age, a child lay weeping."
*Drama. 9 men; 1 woman. Interior.*

CARLTON, JOSEPH. BAB BUYS A CAR. Baker, Boston.

Poor Bab was in a dither. It wasn't bad enough to have her mother accept a dinner invitation for her, but the out-of-town boy in the case bore the impossible name of "Algy." Bab would far rather go to night school and work in the auto mechanics class. Unbeknown to the family she bought a car, a dollar down and a dollar a week, and the very afternoon of the party she had taken it around the block to see whether it would run. It ran all right, down the street, right through a stop light, into the driveway of her home and up onto the side porch where it jammed between the posts. Then it stopped. The traffic officer was still pursuing her. That same afternoon her brother Jimsey rode his motorcycle down to the station to pick up Algy as a favor to his aunt. What happened thereafter added up to a $25.00 fine with one more member of the Preston family. Finally the situation clears and they are ready to start to the dinner. When Bab finds out Algy's friends call him "Butch" she's off for a delightful evening.
*Farce, 5 men; 4 women. Interior.*

EBERHART, RICHARD. THE VISIONARY FARMS. "New World Writing," 3rd Mentor Selection. New American Library, New York.

A verse play set on Everyman's farm in the Middle West in 1919, when things were booming and everybody expected that they always would do so.

*Satirical comedy. 17 men; 6 women. Open stage.*

ESTRADA, DORIS. THREE ON A BENCH. Row, Peterson, Evanston.

There's a bright green bench in a bright green park on this brightest of days in May. But it isn't a bright day at all for Betty, who's just out of high school, and Harry, an "older man"—two months older. She carries the lunch sack and wears a pout; he looks miserable as he tries to explain about the "other girl." Very quickly, their quarrel mounts to monumental, non-speaking proportions.

Then this Mrs. Moore trudges in, wedges her bulk comfortably between them, and begins to munch her egg sandwiches, scattering her crumbs of bread and wisdom with innocent abandon.

In no time at all, Betty and Harry see themselves and their love in a new light and are off, hand in hand, with new plans and happy hopes. . . . It's just as Officer Callahan (who's had a marryin' eye on Mrs. M. for some time now) puts it, "It's amazin' the way you can figure out human nature."

*Comedy. 2 men; 2 women. Exterior.*

KIMES, BRUCE. THE LOST CHRISTMAS. French, New York.

The play tells of the final and ultimate defeat of Miss Harriet Russell in her personal campaign against Christmas. Blinded, embittered and lonely, with her heart and home closed to the world, Harriet tries to force her unhappy, biased opinions upon the life and romance of her young niece, Laura. Then on the holiday eve, a strange little man bearing an even stranger gift—a gift from a ghost of Christmas past— invades the Russell mansion. In a warm and tender scene filled with mingled laughter and tears, Miss Harriet, at long last, comes to know the true meaning of The Lost Christmas.

*Drama. 4 men; 3 women.*

KOZLENKO, WILLIAM. JOURNEY OF PROMISE. Baker, Boston.

A drama about two refugees who are stowaways on a transocean liner. While hiding in the hold of the ship, they discover a time-bomb. Joseph's first reaction is to don a life preserver and make for escape through a porthole. But Zorana, his wife, feels duty bound to do what she can to save the lives of others on board. There is a struggle of conscience, then the captain and crew are summoned and Joseph displays outstanding heroism in trying to disconnect the bomb. Failing that, he throws the bomb out the porthole into the ocean. Because of his heroic action the light of freedom shines a welcoming greeting into a new land.

*Suspense drama. 7 men, and extras. 1 woman.*

MARSTON, JOHN. AND A SONG WAS BORN. French, New York.

The Narrator briefly tells how the composer was discovered and introduces us to the Austrian boy, Franz Xavier Gruber, and his peasant family of weavers, then the Narrator introduces the grown-up Franz and the young widow Elizabeth. Franz reveals his appointment as teacher, his love for Elizabeth and her two children. The Narrator introduces the two children, Kitty and Berta. Presents stacked in the sleigh, the family is ready to distribute its customary baskets to the poor, when Assistant Pastor Mohr arrives to announce: "I have brought a present. And I want Franz to do it up in holiday wrapping. It is for everyone who comes to midnight service tonight." Pastor Mohr reveals he has written a new Christmas song, and as his present Franz must write the music. Franz pleads there are only six hours until midnight and, besides, the organ is out of commission. Undeterred, Pastor Mohr persuades Franz to compose the music on his guitar. A few voices accompanied by guitar, swelling to full choir, sing "Silent Night" first in its original language, then in English.

*True Christmas story. 6 men; 4 women. Interior or drapes.*

NEUENBURG, EVELYN. STRANGE VICTORY. Baker, Boston.

During the siege of the town of Roncole, Italy, in 1813, Signora Verdi (mother of Giuseppe Verdi) takes refuge with her baby in the bell tower of the church. Here she is joined by her young servant girl, Carlotta, who, because of supernatural powers, is able to hear the music that constantly surrounds the Baby Giuseppe. When the soldiers discover their hiding place they begin to batter in the trap door but Carlotta, acting as a decoy, sacrifices her life that the mother and child might live.

*Drama; mystical. All women: 3 principals, extras, singer and accompanist. Interior.*

SPEARE, ELIZABETH GEORGE. THE ANCHOR. Baker, Boston.

The four Baxter girls have been separated for years. Each gets a letter from Faith asking her to make a return visit to the old home in Vermont. Individually they make the trip, each thinking she is the only one invited. Faith has been the envied one—she's had wealth, social position and travel all over the world. Too, she's had two wealthy husbands and is about to take on a college professor for the third. That's the reason for the gathering—to impress Malcolm with the stability of her New England background, to counteract her two previous failures in marriage. But things don't always work out as planned, and while admiration for Faith increases, envy turns to pity.

*Drama; family. 4 women. Interior.*

SPENCE, WALL. A MESSAGE FROM JOHN. Baker, Boston.

Laura and Connie, sisters, are left alone overnight in a rented cottage in the mountains. The former tenant has died but his spirit still remains, as his final message keeps the girls baffled. It baffles even a mysterious caller who proves to be a professional clairvoyant. To add to the mystery, disguises are found in a suitcase, news of stolen diamonds and escaped convicts sift in. Our mysterious caller becomes even more mysterious. Some quick thinking and a bit of subtlety on the part of Laura captures the culprit, bringing with it a $10,000 reward.

*Melodrama. 4 women. Interior.*

SPENCE, WALL. THE BRIDAL BOUQUET. Baker, Boston.

Grace Revere is out to get a husband and a rich one. She's very sure she's got what it takes, in her beauty, glamour and chic. After all, sister Annette caught a rich one with the same assets. When a $60.00 a week clerk invites her out she's definitely not interested but sees in him a prospect for Doris, poor cousin Doris, who is so dull and dowdy. While Grace goes stalking bigger game, she brings Frank and Doris together and they find compatability in their sense of values. They both dislike artificiality, and feel honesty, truth and love of beauty should come above all else. It is too late when Grace learns Frank is the boss's son and heir to millions, for he and Doris have plans for a future together.

*Comedy. 2 men; 2 women. Interior.*

TASHJIAN, VAHAN. THE EASTER STORY. Baker, Boston.

The Easter Story is not a new one but one which should be constantly refreshed in our minds. Through the character of the Interpreter, a homespun type, symbolic of Mr. Average Citizen in any town, we hear re-told the events leading up to the Resurrection. He tells the story in modern idiom and his approach is one of complete humbleness and sincerity. As he speaks, the characters of our play take their places on the stage and bring these same words to life in biblical form.

*Narrative drama. 10 men; 2 women. Open stage.*

WILDE, PERCIVAL. LEGEND. Baker, Boston.

The soul of Sister Ursula ascends on high, but finding that Heaven is the place where all wishes are granted, Sister Ursula wishes only to return to earth and continue her work for the good of mankind.

*Miracle play. 1 narrator; 9 mimes and extras.*

WILDE, PERCIVAL. SALT FOR SAVOR. Baker, Boston. (*Included in this volume.*)

# NEW COLLECTIONS OF SHORT PLAYS

## AVAILABLE FOR PRODUCTION IN AMERICA

*"Eternal Light,"* series of radio dramas, Jewish Theological Seminary, New York.

(*The weekly plays that have been broadcast over the National Broadcasting Company's network. Available gratis.*)

GROSS, EDWIN AND NATHALIE. TEEN THEATER. McGraw-Hill, New York.

(Includes six royalty-free one-act plays: *Belle, Date-Time, Dooley and the Amateur Hour, She Loves Him Yes, Marko goes a Courtin', A Party is Born,* together with notes on staging, and a glossary of theatre terms.)

PARKER, KEN. PARKER'S TELEVISION PLAYS. Northwestern Press, Minneapolis.

(A collection for stage and television. Includes *A Cup of Tea, Shall We Dance? Voice of the Machines, Star Minded, Within the Family, Cry on my Shoulder, Stand Up to Death, Double Identity.*)

*"Ways of Mankind,"* series of radio documentary dramas. Beacon Press, Boston.

(The series of radio dramas undertaken by the National Association of Educational Broadcasters under a grant of the Ford Foundation's Fund for Adult Education, one of which, *A Word in Your Ear,* is included in this volume. Available for rebroadcast from any commercial or educational radio station, through the Executive Director, National Association of Educational Broadcasters, 119 Gregory Hall, University of Illinois, Urbana, Illinois.)

## IMPORTANT DRAMA BOOKS

Bentley, Eric. FROM THE MODERN REPERTOIRE, Series 2. University of Denver Press, Col.
IN SEARCH OF THEATRE. Knopf, New York.

Engel, Edwin A. THE HAUNTED HEROES OF EUGENE O'NEILL. Harvard University Press, Cambridge, Mass.

Cole, Toby, and Helen Krich Chinoy. DIRECTING THE PLAY. Bobbs Merrill, Indianapolis.

*A Source Book of Stagecraft, by Antoine, Belasco, Craig, Shaw, Copeau, Hopkins, Jouvet, Guthrie, Logan, Stanislavsky, Reinhardt, Barrault, Brecht, Kazen, Clurman, and others.*

(All young play writers, and many not so young, should find this volume unexpectedly profitable reading.)

Conyn, Cornelius. THREE CENTURIES OF BALLET. Elsevier Press, Houston.

(A fascinating survey, as well as a book bargain. Extends from earliest beginnings to modern dance-drama and spoken dance. Contains 96 superb full-page photographs.)

Haar, Francis. JAPANESE THEATRE IN HIGHLIGHT, A Pictorial Commentary. Tuttle, Rutland, Vt.

(Includes illustrations from Japanese Noh plays, Bunraku, and Kabuki.)

Kronenberger, Louis. THE BEST PLAYS, 1952–1953. Dodd, Mead, New York.

LeGallienne, Eva. WITH A QUIET HEART. Viking, New York.

(More than a biography: a theatre philosophy.)

Livingston, Don. FILM AND THE DIRECTOR. Macmillan, New York.

(How to write, produce, or direct better films more economically.)

Mantle, Burns. THEATRE '53. Random House, New York.

Morris, Lloyd. CURTAIN TIME. Random House, New York.

(A spicy telling of our theatre history since 1820, from the perspective of some famous players and managements. Over 100 illustrations.)

*"Theatre Annual,"* published under auspices of the Theatre Library Association, Box 935, Grand Central, N.Y. 17.

Tooley, Howard. THE TELEVISION WORKSHOP. Northwestern Press, Minneapolis, Minn.

(A handbook for beginners, with illustrations and glossary of terms.)

*"World Theatre,"* a review published in French and English. Columbia University Press, New York.

# THE BEST ONE-ACT PLAYS
## OF 1937

| | |
|---|---|
| A Husband for Breakfast | Ronald Elwy Mitchell |
| Soldadera | Josephina Niggli |
| Devil Take a Whittler | Weldon Stone |
| The Foundling | Victor Mapes |
| If the Shoe Pinches | Babette Hughes |
| Twenty-five Cents | W. Eric Harris |
| The Maker of Laws | John Gainfort |
| Tobacco Alley | William M. Randall |
| This Earth Is Ours | William Kozlenko |
| Debt Takes a Holiday | Howard Buermann |
| The Fall of the City | Archibald MacLeish |
| Goodnight Please! | James L. Daggett |

# THE BEST ONE-ACT PLAYS
## OF 1938

| | |
|---|---|
| Mañana Bandits | Betty Smith and Chase Webb |
| Farewell to Love | Florence Ryerson and Colin Clements |
| The Feast of Ortolans | Maxwell Anderson |
| Hawk A-Flyin' | E. P. Conkle |
| Ballad of Youth | Alfred Kreymborg |
| Never No Third Degree | John Gainfort |
| Cloud Over Breakshin | Weldon Stone |
| Alma Mater | Paul Green |
| Dust | Edna Muldrow |
| Resurrection Ezra | Ronald Elwy Mitchell |
| This Is Villa | Josephina Niggli |
| Good Night, Caroline | Conrad Seiler |

# THE BEST ONE-ACT PLAYS
## OF 1939

| | |
|---|---|
| Air Raid | Archibald MacLeish |
| A World Elsewhere | Lynn Riggs |
| That's Hollywood | Florence Ryerson and Colin Clements |
| Gold Is Where You Don't Find It | E. P. Conkle |
| The Hungerers | William Saroyan |
| "The Captains and the Kings" | Channing Pollock |
| Hospital Scene | Lawrence Joseph Dugan |
| Haunted Water | Alfred Kreymborg |
| The Devil Is a Good Man | William Kozlenko |
| One-Car Wedding | Seyril Schochen |
| Of Time and the Blizzard | John Kirkpatrick |
| Day's End | William Rose Benét |


# THE BEST ONE-ACT PLAYS
## OF 1940

| | |
|---|---|
| Mr. F. | Percival Wilde |
| Moony's Kid Don't Cry | Tennessee Williams |
| Summer Comes to the Diamond O | Robert Finch and Betty Smith |
| Subway Circus | William Saroyan |
| Rainbows in Heaven | Weldon Stone |
| According to Law | Noel Houston |
| Farmer Brown's Pig | Stanley Young |
| Danbury Fair | Albert Carrière |
| Sleeping Dogs | John Kirkpatrick |
| Parting at Imsdorf | N. Richard Nusbaum |

# THE BEST ONE-ACT PLAYS
## OF 1941

| | |
|---|---|
| The States Talking | Archibald MacLeish |
| Until Charlot Comes Home | Rachel Reynolds |
| All-American Ape | William M. Kephart |
| Equinox | Arnold Sundgaard |
| The Lady of Larkspur Lotion | Tennessee Williams |
| The Miracle of the Danube | Maxwell Anderson |
| The Love of Annunziata | Pietro di Donato |
| The Doctor from Dunmore | Thomas Patrick Dillon and Nolan Leary |
| Hello out There | William Saroyan |
| It's Fun to Be Free | Ben Hecht and Charles Mac-Arthur |

# THE BEST ONE-ACT PLAYS
## OF 1942

| | |
|---|---|
| The Last of My Solid Gold Watches | Tennessee Williams |
| House Divided | Evelyn Neuenburg |
| The Courting of Marie Jenvrin | Gwen Pharis Ringwood |
| City Symphony | Barbara Elgin Jones |
| The Strangest Feeling | John Kirkpatrick |
| We Refuse to Die | Maxwell Shane |
| We Hold These Truths | Norman Corwin |
| Memo to Berchtesgaden | Arch Oboler |
| They Burned the Books | Stephen Vincent Benét |
| So Long, Son | Howard Vincent O'Brien |

# THE BEST ONE-ACT PLAYS
## OF 1943

| | |
|---|---|
| Letter to Jackie | Maxwell Anderson |
| God and Texas | Robert Ardrey |
| Quiet—Facing the Park | John Cecil Holm |
| A Tribute to Gallantry | Ben Hecht |
| Where E're We Go | Pfc. John B. O'Dea |
| Mid-Passage | Arnold Sundgaard |
| The Death of Aunt Aggie | Ranald MacDougall |
| Murder Is Fun! | Catherine Blankenship |
| They Asked for It | Del Smith |
| Journey for an Unknown Soldier | Doris Frankel |
| The Bridegroom Waits | Marrijane and Joseph Hayes |

# THE BEST ONE-ACT PLAYS
## OF 1944

| | |
|---|---|
| The Picnic | Arnold Sundgaard |
| It Ain't Brooklyn | David Dempsey, Staff Sgt. USMC |
| District of Columbia | Stanley Richards |
| That They May Win | Arthur Miller |
| Miracle on the Pullman | Ben Hecht |
| Concerning the Red Army | Norman Rosten |
| Slip Ahoy! | A. A. O'Keeffe, Y2C USNR |
| On the Way Home | Esther M. Hawley |
| Strange Rain | Sonia Brown |
| 27 Wagons Full of Cotton | Tennessee Williams |
| The Admiral | Archibald MacLeish |

# THE BEST ONE-ACT PLAYS
## OF 1945

| | |
|---|---|
| Atomic Bombs | Frank and Doris Hursley |
| On a Note of Triumph | Norman Corwin |
| The Face | Arthur Laurents |
| To the American People | Morton Wishengrad |
| A Bunyan Yarn | Stanley Young |
| Summer Fury | James Broughton |
| The Devil's Foot | Nicholas J. Biel |
| The Unsatisfactory Supper | Tennessee Williams |
| The Fisherman | Jonathan Tree |
| Silver Nails | Nicholas Bela |
| The Far-Distant Shore | Robert Finch and Betty Smith |

# THE BEST ONE-ACT PLAYS
## OF 1946–1947

| | |
|---|---|
| How They Knocked the Devil Out of Uncle Ezra | Morton Wishengrad |
| Freight | Kenneth White |
| Making the Bear | Theodore Apstein |
| Transition in India | Arnold Marquis |
| Skeletons | Nicholas Bela |
| Bride-Ship | Jack Jacobs |
| The Lord and Hawksaw Sadie (a play with music) | Elizabeth Wilson |
| Open Secret | Robert Adler, George Bellak, and Dr. Louis N. Ridenour |
| The Soldier Who Became a Great Dane | Joseph Shore and Richard Lincoln |
| The Eagle (a television script) | Ted Beebe |

# THE BEST ONE-ACT PLAYS
## OF 1947–1948

On This Green Bank — Sylvan Karchmer
The Sunny Side of the Atom — Carl Beier and Ruth Ashton
Suffer the Little Children — Nicholas Bela
Who Are the Weavers — Joseph Shore and Scott Graham Williamson

A Woman's Privilege — Marrijane and Joseph Hayes
Frankie and Albert (a play with music) — Elizabeth Wilson Hughes
Easter Eve — Anna F. Trevisan
Through a Glass, Darkly — Stanley Richards
The Meadow — Ray Bradbury
Before the Bullfight — Theodore Apstein


# THE BEST ONE-ACT PLAYS
## OF 1948–1949

For Each Man Kills — Gerty Agoston
Fortunata Writes a Letter — Theodore Apstein
A Bed with the Others — Scott Graham Williamson and Joseph Shore

Whistle, Daughter, Whistle — Ernest Kinoy
A Wake for Me and Thee — Ward Costello
Patrick Brontë and the Saint — Barbara Packer
Mind in the Shadow — Arnold Perl
O Distant Land — Stanley Richards
Wantin' Fever (a play with music) — Elizabeth Wilson Hughes

Impasse — Frederick A. Woodress

# THE BEST ONE-ACT PLAYS
## OF 1949–1950

| | |
|---|---|
| Doctor Faustus Lights the Lights | Gertrude Stein |
| The Camel and I | Morton Wishengrad |
| August Heat | Stanley Richards |
| Going Home | John Gainfort |
| The Beast | Gerty Agoston |
| Day Before Yesterday | Norman Holland |
| Exodus (A dance-drama) | Marvin W. Robinson |
| Period House | Walter Prichard Eaton |
| Fantasia on an Old Familiar Theme | Frank Lanzl |
| The Long Fall | Carroll V. Howe |


# THE BEST ONE-ACT PLAYS
## OF 1950–1951

| | |
|---|---|
| Turn Down an Empty Jug | Barbara Packer |
| Three Parsons | Gerty Agoston |
| Rise of Her Bloom (An Opera) | Elizabeth Wilson Hughes |
| Muletail Prime | E. P. Conkle |
| Valley of the Shadow | Anna F. Trevisan |
| Farewell Appearance | Norman Holland and Stanley Richards |
| Good-bye to the Clown (A Television script) | Ernest Kinoy |
| Gooseberry Tarts | Charles F. Lowe |
| Brothers | Edward Castro |
| The Matron of Ephesus | Georges Sion |

# THE BEST ONE-ACT PLAYS
## OF 1951–1952

The Least One — E. P. Conkle
Paradise Inn — Theodore Apstein
In Darkness — Howard Stein
Hugh of the Glen and His Clogs Are All One — Peter John Stephens
The Shadow of the Cathedral — Eric Kocher
Tour of Duty — Arthur Kelley
Glory Day — Goldie Lake
The Safecracker's Pride — Nicholas Bela
The Happy Housewife (A Television script) — Hedda Rosten
Sun Deck — Stanley Richards

# THE BEST SHORT PLAYS
## OF 1952–1953

Innermost I Land (a dramatic reading) — Vincent Ferrini
The Beams of Our House — Theodore Apstein
Dope — Maryat Lee
Tunnel of Love — Stanley Richards
A Trap Is a Small Place — Marjean Perry
Arbie, the Bug Boy — E. P. Conkle
The Youngest Shall Ask — David Shaber
Incident at a Grave — Goldie Lake
The Changeling — Peter John Stephens
The Imploring Flame — John Sheffield